PRACTICE PREVENTIVE CORPORATE LAW

American Law Institute
American Bar Association
Committee on Continuing Professional Education

ALI ABA

4025 Chestnut Street, Philadelphia, Pennsylvania 19104

PRACTICE PREVENTIVE CORPORATE LAW

RONALD L. JONES
of the Nebraska Bar

American Law Institute-
American Bar Association
Committee on Continuing
Professional Education

Library of Congress Catalog Number: 85-71419

Printed in the United States of America

ISBN: 0-8318-0477-7

James D. Maugans of the ALI-ABA staff
supervised the production of this book.

To Susan Ann

Foreword

Not too long ago, corporations employed outside counsel to handle most of their legal problems. Today, more and more corporations are forming or enlarging their own law departments and referring less and less of their legal affairs to law firms. *Practice Preventive Corporate Law* is addressed to lawyers who have to relate to corporate officers and personnel.

The technique is that of preventive problem solving—to anticipate and prevent legal problems from arising, and when they come about, to resolve them as quickly as possible. Mr. Jones teaches how a lawyer should approach a situation as a preventer and solver of legal problems, and his use of examples of actual troublesome situations and his suggestions for handling them should engrave the precepts of *Practice Preventive Corporate Law* upon the reader's mind.

The volume has value beyond the limits implied by its title. Its teachings may be applied to the practices of government counsel, lawyers in large and small firms, and solo practitioners. Thus this is a text that might well be studied by every attorney who begins to practice to learn the values of preventive law and read by every experienced lawyer as a reminder of those values. And, it goes without saying, it would be in the interest of corporate law offices to make this text required reading for every attorney they employ.

Ronald L. Jones presents a clear, highly readable exposition of an approach to the practice of the law that emphasizes prevention—the "stitch in time." This is a unique contribution that merits the profession's examination and appreciation.

PAUL A. WOLKIN
Executive Director
The American Law Institute-
American Bar Association Committee
on Continuing Professional Education

Preface

When a layman presents a problem, question, or idea, does he really want to know what the law says? Or does he want *a solution* to his problem? He may want both, but most of the time he wants a solution. He has a business purpose to accomplish, and he wants to know, from a legal standpoint, what is the best method to achieve that objective. He does not want a simple yes-or-no answer or a statement of compliance or noncompliance with the law—he wants a solution!

Too often, today's corporate attorney fails to go one step beyond a simple statement of the law and use his skills and knowledge as an attorney to find a solution. Perhaps justifiably. Finding a solution is not a subject taught in law schools, nor is it a type of law practice frequently found within the realm of the traditional "adversary" approach.

Nevertheless, practicing corporate law by finding solutions is a technique and method that can be defined, learned, and applied by the corporate counsel, to the great advantage of not only himself but also the corporation. Today, in-house corporate counsel is in a unique position within the law profession to take that one step beyond the traditional adversary practice of law.

This book is written for the corporate attorney. Its subject—practicing corporate law by finding solutions—is an essential component in today's corporate law practice and one that holds promise for the effectiveness and success of the law departments of the future.

I hope you will read it, think about it, and build upon it. You can then lead the destiny of the corporate law departments of tomorrow, which are sure to experience unparalleled growth and will need ever-increasing sophistication and capability.

RONALD L. JONES

Contents

Foreword ix
Preface xi
Introduction xix

PART A: LAY THE FOUNDATION FOR AN EFFECTIVE LAW PRACTICE

Introduction to Part A 1

Why Lay a Foundation? 1
The Starting Point 3

Step One: Learn the Business 7

Introduction 7
The More You Know, the Better 8
More Effective Communication 9
Pinpointing the Primary Legal Issue 11
Drafting Useable Documents 13
Understanding the Business Objectives 16
Learning About the Business 18
  Look at the Big Picture 18
  Learn the Terminology 19
  Examine Internal and Public Information 20
  Compare Industry and Competitor Information 21
  Ask Questions and Visit Operations 22
Case Study Number One: Acquisition of O'Foss, Inc. 24
  The Situation 24

The Question 25
What Actually Happened 25
Author's Comments 27

Step Two: Know the People 29

Introduction 29
A Good Client Relationship Is Crucial 29
Their Expertise Is a Valuable Resource 32
"Reading Between the Lines" 34
Who Is the Client? 37
Case Study Number Two: Letter from a Disgruntled Client 41
The Situation 41
The Question 42
What Actually Happened 42
Author's Comments 45

Step Three: Communicate with the Other Corporate Departments 47

Introduction 47
Learning About Potential Legal Problems 48
Checking the Impact of Legal Decisions 51
Knowing the Crossover Effect of Legal Decisions 55
Case Study Number Three: The Two-Day Licensing Agreement 59
The Situation 59
The Question 60
What Actually Happened 60
Author's Comments 62

Step Four: Understand the Law Department Function 65

Introduction 65
Why Have a Corporate Law Department? 66
Lack of Background in Law 69
Cost Justification 69
Explosion of Government Regulations 70

Immediate Access to Legal Advice Required 70
Remember the Traditional Functions 71
Focus on the Preventive Functions 72
Give Advice on Law/Business Issues 73
A Practical Case in Point 77
What Is Not the Function? 81
Case Study Number Four: The Fine Dividing Line 83
The Situation 83
The Question 84
What Actually Happened 85
Author's Comments 85

Step Five: Learn the Law in Your Industry 87

Introduction 87
Be Knowledgeable About All of It 88
Customs, Trade Usage, and Words of Art 89
Local, State, and Federal Statutes and Regulations 89
Court Decisions, Arbitration Awards, and Settlements 91
Focus Initially on the Most Relevant Laws 93
Become an Expert 97
How To Keep Current 100
Case Study Number Five: The Unorthodox Contract 104
The Situation 104
The Question 105
What Actually Happened 106
Author's Comments 107

PART B: PRACTICE PREVENTIVE LAW BY FINDING SOLUTIONS

Introduction to Part B 111

Introduction 111
What Is a Solution? 111
Why Look for Solutions? 112
How To Find a Solution 115

Key One: Set the Stage 117

Introduction 117
Be a Team Player 118
Attend Meetings, Go on Business Trips, and So Forth 120
  Attend Meetings 121
  Go on Business Trips 123
  Attend Corporate Social Functions 125
  Work with Other Department Attorneys 125
But Remain a Professional 127
Avoid Political Fights 131
  Avoid Working Too Much for One Executive or Group 133
  Avoid Doing Personal Legal Work 134
Case Study Number Six: Pinning Your Star to One Executive 136
  The Situation 136
  The Question 136
  What Actually Happened 136
  Author's Comments 137

Key Two: Find the Real Problem 139

Introduction 139
Being a Good Listener Is Crucial 140
  Be a Good Sounding Board 141
  Be Patient 143
Marshall the Facts 144
  Communicate 145
  Ask Questions 147
Distinguish Between Law and Business Issues 148
Do Not Forget Law/Business Issues 151
Weigh the Issues in a Business Context 154
Case Study Number Seven: Is the Dealer Going Under? 160
  The Situation 160
  The Question 161
  What Actually Happened 162
  Author's Comments 163

Key Three: Apply the Law 165

Introduction 165
Should One Shoot from the Hip? 166
Prepare Yourself 170
Should Partial Answers Be Given? 171
Know When To Say You Do Not Know 175
Case Study Number Eight: Right of First Refusal 180
  The Situation 180
  The Question 181
  What Actually Happened 181
  Author's Comments 182

Key Four: Know When To Go Outside 185

Introduction 185
Issues Beyond Counsel's Ability 185
  Beyond the Law Department's Scope 186
  Lack of Time or Other Resources 187
  Specialty of Law Beyond Counsel's Expertise 189
For a Second Opinion or Local Representation 191
Know When Not To Go Outside 195
Case Study Number Nine: The Mining Partnership 200
  The Situation 200
  The Question 201
  What Actually Happened 201
  Author's Comments 202

Key Five: Examine the Alternatives 203

Introduction 203
Ask How It Can Be Done 204
Search for All the Alternatives 208
  Use Imagination 209
  Use Issue Analysis as a Format 209
  Obtain a Second or Expert Opinion 210
A Complex and Practical Example 211
  The Facts in a Computer Company Case 212
  The Principal Issues 214
  The Alternatives 217
Which Alternative Is the Solution? 223

The Best Alternative in the Computer Company Case 223
From the Legal Standpoint 223
From the Business Standpoint 225
From the Law/Business Standpoint 225
The Solution in the Computer Company Case 227
General Principles To Implement 229
Use Judgment 229
Evaluate All Alternatives 229
Remember That Solutions Are Fluid 230
Make a Decision 230
Some Practical Pointers 231
Is There Another Business Purpose? 232
Is This the Simplest Alternative? 235
Can the Concept Be Quantified? 238
Is the Timing Correct? 241
Is Compromise an Alternative? 243
Reflection on Examining the Alternatives 244
Case Study Number Ten: The Unsatisfactory Project 246
The Situation 246
The Question 247
What Actually Happened 247
Author's Comments 249

Key Six: Issue Your Work Product 251

Introduction 251
What Did He Say? 252
So What's the Answer? 254
It's Probably Lost on His Desk! 257
Case Study Number Eleven: The Memorandum 261
The Situation 261
The Question 262
What Actually Happened 262
Author's Comments 263

Epilogue Story 265

Index of Subjects 269

Introduction

This book is designed as a blueprint upon which to build and refine the practice of corporate law. The principles contained in it are fundamental and practical and can be applied immediately. They are set forth in a logical and succinct fashion so that the Steps or Keys need not be read in order but may be studied individually.

Part A lays the foundation for finding solutions by examining five Steps that are fundamental to an effective practice of preventive corporate law. Part B examines what is perhaps the most specialized, though least discussed, technique of a preventive corporate law practice—finding a solution. Six succinct Keys are presented to point the way to the best alternative or answer to a legal problem—the solution.

The important point to focus upon is how to apply these principles in the practice of corporate law. They are not theories of law intended to be studied and memorized. They are, instead, techniques and methods to apply—to make maximum use of the knowledge of law and skills that a lawyer already possesses.

The purpose of this book is to concentrate upon the effective application of these Steps and Keys so that counsel's skills and knowledge can be fully used in the corporate environment. More than 60 examples and case studies based upon actual experiences are included in this book for that purpose. They are described and discussed in detail so that the mistakes, frustrations, and successes of others will provide a better understanding of the actual implementation and value of these principles in the practice of corporate law.

The examples and case studies should be read and thought about. They should be related to past and possible future experiences. Try to visualize how a situation could have been handled more effectively by integrating these principles into the practice of law. In that way both counsel and his corporation will receive the greatest benefits from this book.

The Steps and Keys presented in this book are fundamental to a successful practice of preventive law within a corporation. Naturally, the extent to which they will be used may vary depending upon the level of the position, the scope of your responsibilities, the make-up of the law department, the size of the corporation, and other circumstances. Nonetheless, these principles are designed to assist the corporate attorney at any stage in his career and in any corporation or location. In fact, most of these principles are of equal value in the private practice of law, with a governmental body, or in other segments of the law profession; but, unfortunately, the opportunities to use them in those areas are sometimes more limited because of the reduced amount of client contact, the tendency to pursue an adversary approach, or the different nature of legal issues commonly confronted.

This book is based upon my years of experience as corporate attorney, starting out at the lowest rung in the corporate law department and progressing through various stages to the position of general counsel. During this process I started a law department from scratch and worked as in-house counsel for several corporations in different industries and geographic locations. I think my experience has been sufficiently broad, diverse, and in-depth to make some useful comments; and I have attempted to do so here because I could never find a practical guide on practicing law in the corporation when I needed it most. If this book helps the reader to practice corporate law more effectively, then I will be more than satisfied.

Finally, do not take offense at any arbitrary use of masculine or feminine genders in this book, for no such offense is intended—rather the opposite—to make it easiest for the reader by avoiding repetitions, his/her references, and other awkward devices.

PART A

Lay the Foundation for an Effective Preventive Law Practice

PART A

LAY THE FOUNDATION FOR AN EFFECTIVE PREVENTIVE LAW PRACTICE

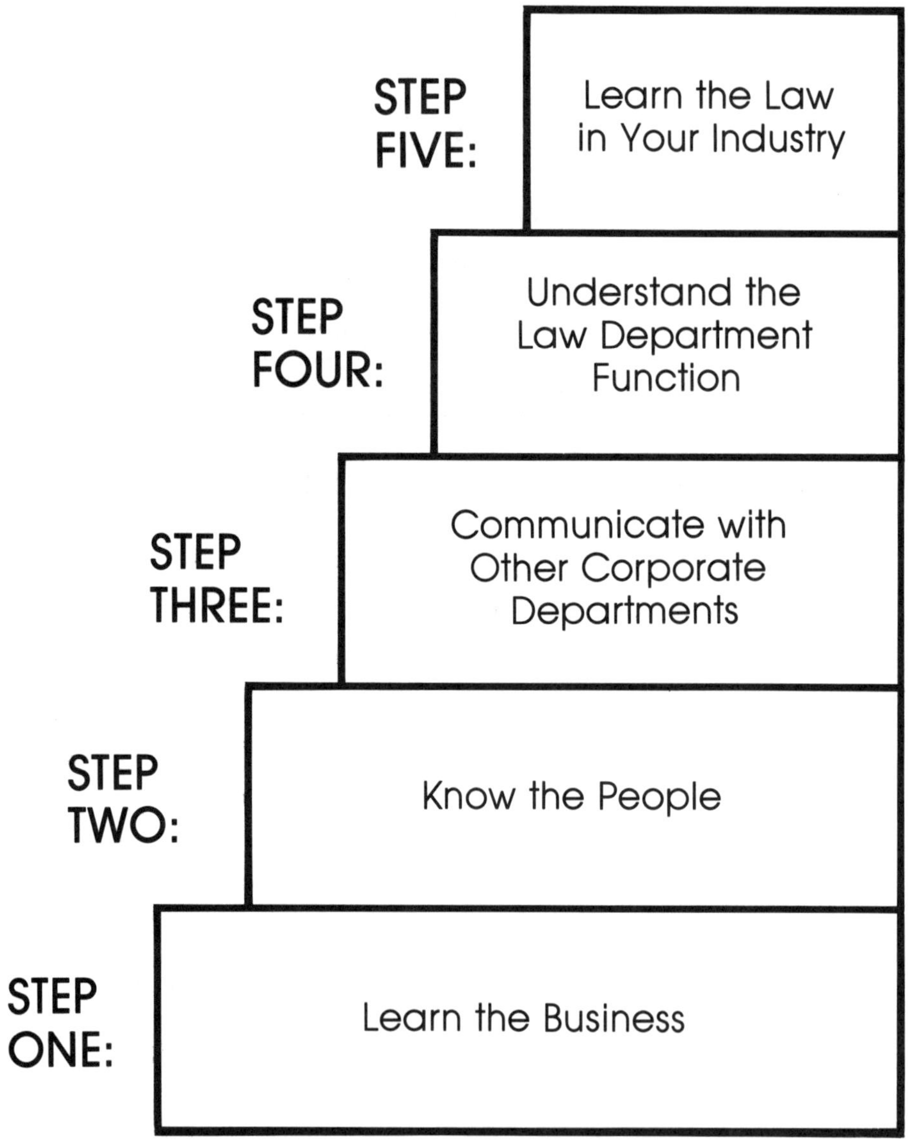

STEPS TO THE FOUNDATION (PART A)

Introduction to Part A

Why Lay a Foundation?

A foundation is necessary because without it it is impossible to build the more refined technique of finding a solution. First, the fundamentals of an effective preventive law practice in the corporation should be examined. A good foundation in practicing preventive law is necessary and essential if counsel is to find the best alternative or solution to the legal problems that will confront him.

Before looking at this foundation to be laid, the following questions should be asked: What is meant by the term *preventive corporate law?* And how does it differ from other types of law or law practice?

Preventive law can be visualized most easily by comparing the timing of its use and application with the more traditional "adversary" approach to practicing law. Often an attorney in private practice will not learn about the legal problem a client has until after the fact, that is, after the problem has already occurred and has become irresolvable (or so perceived) short of litigation. At that point under the traditional adversary approach, the job of the attorney is to assume the merits of his client's position and to prove the opponent is in the wrong.

On the other hand, the underlying purpose in a preventive law practice is to learn about and resolve (or even prevent the occurrence of) legal problems in their very early stages, before there is nothing left to do but initiate the litigation process.

Today the term *preventive law* as used in the corporate law department setting encompasses a variety of techniques and methods that are intended to prevent or diminish the probability of future legal problems occurring. For example, the periodic legal audit of corporate operations and departments can be very effective in spotting potential legal problems. The use of well-drafted standard corporate documents, such as contracts, purchase orders, release forms, and others, are also eminently useful in preventing later legal problems from arising. And there are many other good techniques of preventive law employed in corporate law departments today.

The Steps discussed in Part A to build a foundation for a preventive law practice do not focus on these more common and routine techniques for two reasons. First, those aspects of preventive law are more readily recognized and used by today's corporate attorney, and second, they are not the true foundation of an effective preventive law practice, but only the results or characteristics of one.

The true foundation upon which to build an effective preventive law practice is the one presented in Part A. The Steps discussed there are fundamental to an effective application of law in the corporation, after which, or because of which, the more routine (and perhaps innovative) techniques used to prevent the occurrance of legal problems are learned or become apparent.

For example, before knowing what kind of legal controls or standard documents are needed to help prevent legal problems from occurring in the corporation, it is necessary to know and understand the business or industry in which the corporation is engaged (STEP ONE: LEARN THE BUSINESS). How would counsel know to spot check or require documentation of hazardous waste disposal by his company if he is unaware that one of the by-products of the manufacturing process contains a chemical on the Environmental Protection Agency's (EPA) hazardous chemical list? And how would he know about the EPA hazardous chemical list in the first place if he were not knowledgeable about the laws and regulations that govern the industry (STEP FIVE: LEARN THE LAW IN YOUR INDUSTRY)?

The objective in Part A is to lay the true foundation for an effective practice of preventive law by discussing and learning to apply the fundamental principles contained in STEPS ONE through FIVE.

Part B will focus upon perhaps the most important, though least recognized and discussed, specialized technique of an effective preventive law practice—finding a solution.

The Starting Point

The starting point should be the corporate attorney. Whether he is just starting to practice law in a corporation, has been practicing for several years, or is just thinking about joining a corporate law department, he should sit back for a minute and ask himself a few questions. How good a foundation does he have for practicing corporate law—particularly, preventive corporate law? Does he know what to concentrate upon to build that foundation?

These questions are not asking whether counsel knows how to practice law as he was taught in law school or learned later as a practicing attorney. What is being asked is whether counsel has learned the most practical and effective way to apply his skills as an attorney and his knowledge of the law to the business environment; and whether counsel has taken advantage of the unique opportunities as corporate counsel to learn about his client (the corporation) in-depth: to learn about its business, its people, and its various departments, functions, and so on. This knowledge and understanding will make the difference between simply practicing law in the corporation, on the one hand, and, on the other, practicing truly effective preventive law, designed to find solutions to the legal problems confronting the client and to make the greatest and most significant contributions to the corporation.

Some may already have acquired a partial foundation, whether intentionally or not; others will not and must start from scratch.

The initial questions are What kind of corporation is corporate counsel working for? What kind of business is it in? Is it a manufacturing company? Does it make consumer products? Wholesale products?

Is the corporation in a service industry? Is its primary business to provide a service to consumers? To wholesalers? To dealers? Perhaps the corporation is a utility. Or perhaps a transportation company. It is important to know the kind of business activities in which the corporation engages. They will have an important effect upon the practice of law within the corporation. STEP ONE will address this topic.

It is also important to know the people (STEP TWO) in the corporation. Although the corporation is a statutory organization, it is always made up of people. Its typical organization is one of many people working at different tasks toward a common goal, usually to make a profit. The people make the corporation function, and they are important to the practice of corporate law.

Knowledge of the different departments found in the corporation is also valuable (STEP THREE). The objectives of a corporation are usually organized into separate functions by departments. These departments can be extremely important to the practice of law by providing information that otherwise might not be available about many activities taking place within the corporation.

Counsel should begin to consider the framework in which he is working as corporate attorney. He is in a corporation engaged in a certain kind or kinds of business. The objectives of that business are carried out by the people organized into various departments. Another important perspective to consider is counsel's function within that framework. What is the purpose of the corporate law department? What is the purpose of a corporate attorney within that department? These are some of the considerations discussed in STEP FOUR.

After considering the framework within which counsel will be working as a corporate attorney and his function or purpose within that framework, he will, of course, want to learn the law that is pervasive and unique within that industry (STEP FIVE). Then he will be ready to go to Part B and to start finding the solutions.

By now, one thought may have occurred to some of you: Aren't some of these steps in laying a good foundation for a preventive law practice partly nonlegal or really procedural in nature? The answer is yes, in some ways they are. Ironically enough, in order to work effectively in the business environment, an attorney must sometimes take off his legal hat a little bit and talk in the language of a layman (see STEP ONE). Although at first blush some of these steps may seem irrelevant to the practice of law, be assured that this is not the case. On the contrary, their use will significantly improve corporate counsel's effectiveness.

Step One: Learn the Business

Introduction

This is the first, and perhaps the most logical, step to employ when joining a corporate law department for the first time or in a different industry. This step is the most basic building block in the foundation upon which the practice of preventive law can later develop and flourish or, in the absence thereof, fail to be effective. There is simply no better method to produce as many tangible results as quickly in the practice of corporate law than learning the business in-depth. This step goes a long way toward insuring that counsel will not be practicing law in a vacuum, unaware of the real legal needs of his client, the corporation.

Logically, in order to prevent, or diminish the probability of, legal problems from occurring, one must first understand what it is about the character and nature of the corporate activities that have caused legal problems in the past and may do so in the future. One must understand the business before knowing what kinds of preventive law techniques can be applied with the most success. Finding the best alternative or solution to a legal problem or issue may also hinge upon understanding and consideration of the business objectives within the corporation.

How much should counsel know about the business? The more, the better! That knowledge will enable him to speak in the same sub-language and shorthand used by layman in the corporation and industry. It will point him toward the key legal issues, not simply inconsequential issues. Counsel will be able to draft better, more intelligible, useable documents. Significantly, it will minimize his frustration and increase his effectiveness because he will understand many of the business reasons behind corporate plans and decisions. These are some of the reasons to learn the business. Some examples will be examined in this section, before looking at some pointers about how one can actually go about learning the business in the corporation.

Learning the business is also one of the areas in which corporate counsel has greatest advantage over his fellow practitioners at the bar. Except for extremely large cases, attorneys in private practice frequently will not have the time, nor the ability to charge a fee for the time, necessary for them to learn the business of a particular client. Since corporate counsel, in contrast to the private practitioner, is working essentially for a single client entity, he has the unique opportunity to learn about the business of the corporation in-depth.

The More You Know, the Better

It is obvious that counsel should learn something about the business in which the corporation is engaged. No one would undertake to be chief counsel on a major medical malpractice suit without first learning something about medicine. But how much does counsel need to learn about the business of the corporation? As much as possible. Unfortunately, learning the business is an obvious but frequently overlooked step in corporate law. There are too many cases of attorneys in corporate practice who apparently became satisfied after gaining only a superficial familiarity with the business activities and going no further—to their detriment. The following is an example of such an instance:

> A senior attorney in a large corporation usually handled the drafting and negotiation of major contracts within a company. These negotiations often involved lengthy meetings with the customers during which the senior attorney and the operations vice president in charge of a division would sometimes jointly, and other times alternatively, argue the various points they wished to include in the contract.
>
> Because of a conflict one day, the senior attorney told the division vice president that another attorney

> in the law department, with whom this vice president had worked before, would take his place in a scheduled contract negotiation meeting. In expressing his reluctance to that arrangement, the division vice president simply stated about this attorney, "He doesn't know anything!"
>
> Upon further questioning, it became clear what the division vice president meant to say was not that this attorney was unknowledgeable about the law but that he did not know about the business in which the corporation was engaged. The vice president found it a continual hinderance during negotiation meetings, particularly in spot situations, to have to stop and explain the meaning of a business term or concept to his own attorney. More frequently, the vice president was forced to handle the negotiations alone, with the attorney not even being aware that he could have been of some assistance.

This was not simply a case of the division vice president's preferring the senior attorney with whom he was obviously more familiar and experienced, since the other attorney had been with the corporation for more than two years, which should have been enough time to learn about the business of a corporation. With an effort, an attorney can learn much within six months! This example is instead illustrative of the extent to which some attorneys practicing law within a corporation fail to become familiar with the business of the com pany. Either they rely on "osmosis" to learn about the business, or they simply feel that knowing the law is sufficient for them to perform their function as corporate counsel. Or maybe they really do not know how to go about learning the business of a corporation (see later in this section).

Whatever the case, the more counsel knows about the business of your corporation, the better. As in this example, the lack of such knowledge will show and directly affect the ability to practice law in the corporation.

More Effective Communication

Another reason to learn as much as possible about the business of the corporation is to communicate more effectively. Why? Because counsel will be able to speak the same language as others in this corporation. People communicate by the languge they speak. Attorneys are able to communicate much better about legal matters with other attorneys than with laymen. Notwithstanding their legal education, a great deal of that ease of communication is the result of understanding the legal terminology with which they speak.

In many industries there is also sublanguage, which, if learned, will make counsel a far better communicator. He will be able to speak in a kind of shorthand with far greater impact and meaning. For example, in the high technology industries of today, the unknowledgeable person is quickly distinguished because the meaning of many words and phrases are not commonly known to the outsider. Knowing an industry sublanguage is essential for any salesman, production manager, marketing, advertising personnel, and others in the corporation to learn. Why should it not be as essential for counsel? How can he effectively communicate with the people in his corporation and outside his corporation in the industry without becoming well-versed in this "sub-language"?

In contract negotiations involving projects in complex and rather technical areas, if counsel has the only a limited understanding of the applicable sublanguage, he is at a distinct disadvantage in being unable to effectively convey a point of argument he is trying to obtain.

> In a meeting to negotiate a contract for the engineering and construction of a large processing facility, the attorneys for one side are familiar with the terminology within the industry, and the attorneys for the other side are not.
>
> Because in a contract for a project of that magnitude, many issues and points of argument are expressed and turn on words of art, customs, and terminology unique to the engineering and construction industry, the attorneys familiar with them were often in a position of advantage. That side was able to obtain a number of good features in the contract simply because they were able to talk and understand the same language.

> The attorneys unfamliar with the industry terminology, however, suffered from the disadvantage of not speaking the same language as all the other negotiators. As a result, they frequently talked about something that was really not pertinent to the subject at hand or that had a meaning different from what some of them thought. This resulted in several exasperating moments for everyone, particularly the laymen who were well-versed in the engineering and construction industry language.

These negotiation meetings would have progressed much quicker and gone more smoothly if everyone had been well-versed in the industry sublanguage. This is only one example that illustrates the importance of taking the time and effort to learn the industry sublanguage (and business) of the company. Perhaps no other simple effort will produce such tangible, immediate, and beneficial results in the practice of corporate law than learning the sublanguage of the industry.

Pinpointing the Primary Legal Issue

Knowing the business will provide the proper perspective from which to analyze the facts and focus on the primary legal issue. Counsel will be able to go straight to the heart of the matter and will be less likely to be side-tracked on an inconsequential point of law or nonpersuasive factual argument. In the practice of preventive law the ability to spot legal issues based upon knowledge of the business without the necessity of having had experienced and researched a prior similar circumstance will be of particular value.

The following is an example in which an attorney's in-depth knowledge of the business enabled her to pinpoint the primary legal issue and effect an early and favorable settlement of litigation. She was corporate counsel for a contractor in a rather typical three-way argument between an owner, architect, and contractor. The problem regarded several lengthy cracks that appeared in the concrete floor of a warehouse a few months after completion and use of the facility.

> Several lengthy, large cracks appeared in the concrete floor slab laid on grade in a one hundred thou-

sand-square foot warehouse constructed for storage of large reels of cable by an electrical cable manufacturer. The owner-manufacturer contended the cracks were structural and wanted the slab removed and repoured. With the architect's advice and assistance, the owner filed suit against the contractor, alleging, among other things, that the cracks were the result of poor workmanship by the contractor. The contractor answered with a general denial of the allegations.

To support their case, the owner (architect) cited as examples of the poor workmanship the failure by the contractor to use the specified fill dirt, the inadequate compaction prior to pouring the concrete, failure to use a sufficient number of reinforcing steel rods to strengthen the concrete as specified, and failure to install the proper expansion joints throughout the slab.

In analyzing the facts and preparing the case for the contractor, the corporate counsel examined each of these allegations in great detail and at length. However, because of her in-depth knowledge of the industry, she also focused upon whether any of the specifications or design of the concrete and floor slab that were furnished by the architect were inadequate or in error.

During this investigation she learned of a fact that turned out to be crucial to their case. She learned that prior to commencing his design of the facility, the architect had been shown an existing warehouse in which the owner was storing similar large reels of electric cable. For some reason, the architect had failed to take into consideration the immense weight concentrated in a relatively small floor area by these large reels of electric cable, when stacked four and five reels high. At the existing facility the owner stacked the reels four high, but because of the increased roof height in the new warehouse, he was able to stack them five high. Because of this increased weight the architect should have specified 6-inch thickness of the concrete floor slab rather than the 4-inch thickness used at the existing warehouse.

Had the attorney for the contractor relied primarily upon defending the allegations of the owner (architect), she may not have prevailed. But because of her experience in the industry, this attorney was able to identify correctly at a very early stage in the dispute, that the primary legal issue was one of failure of the architect to design to a professional and adequate standard, rather than a failure of the contractor to use good workmanship. This early development of the primary legal issue was unquestionably the greatest factor contributing to an early settlement of the case, in the contractor's favor.

This example illustrates that an in-depth and thorough knowledge of the industry (the business) will greatly enhance counsel's ability to properly analyze the facts and find his way to the most important legal issue. Counsel's ability to pinpoint the primary legal issue will not only save time and frustration but also greatly increase his effectiveness in the practice of corporate law.

Drafting Useable Documents

If there is anything the law profession is well known for, it is the tendency to draft long and unintelligable documents—at least unintelligible to the average layman.

One reason for this is that many attorneys fail to learn and understand the business to which the agreement pertains. Then, in an overabundance of precaution, they will use any number of standard boilerplate phrases and paragraphs, intended to cover a circumstance or an occurrence that they know they may have missed or otherwise failed to know about the business activities. Likewise, if the standard form or document being used as a drafting guide has some language or boilerplate in it, they assume that it must be there for a purpose; and so they leave it in, even if they do not know why.

Using an excessive amount of boilerplate and unintelligible language (to the average laymen) sometimes results in the opposite of the excessive precaution intended. The best document or contract is often one that is filed away and never used again. It is never used because there is no need. It represents the intent of the parties, and they know its intent. Ideally, they helped write the document and thoroughly know the meaning of its provisions. It is a workable and useable document setting forth the relationship between the parties. Because it represents the meeting of the minds between the parties, they have no further need of it except to refresh their memories. There are no vague or unintelligible paragraphs that can be used later to start a dispute or argument.

As a practical matter, it is difficult to draft such a perfect document. Nevertheless, much of that difficulty can be avoided if counsel understands the business activities to which the agreement refers. Some legal jargon and boilerplate may remain necessary for legal purposes, but by knowing the business counsel will, more often than not, be able to correctly determine what is needed and what is simply excess baggage. He will also be able to rewrite it to make it more intelligible to, and useable by, the average layman.

For example, without knowing more, how would a force majeure clause from a supplier's standpoint in a "take-or-pay" contract be drafted? It would be advantageous to understand this type of requirements contract and how that relationship is usually expressed and conducted in the particular industry involved.

Generally, it describes an agreement in which the supplier is obligated to furnish a certain quantity or level of goods to a user, who is required to take that amount or pay a penalty. The following example is one way in which such a clause could be written, with a considerable amount of boilerplate.

> *Force majeure.* Notwithstanding anything to the contrary contained hereinbefore or hereinafter, or in any document incorporated or otherwise forming a part hereof, whether at the date hereof or subsequently by unauthorized modification, amendment or other acts of the parties hereto, the party of the first part shall not be obligated to perform to the party of the second part, and shall be excused from performance under the terms of this agreement or another agreement forming a part hereof when the performance thereof is made commercially unreasonable by a cir-

> cumstance caused in whole or in part by fire, hurricane, flood, act of God, act of public authority, whether local, state or federal, act of public carriers, an act of war, whether nuclear or conventional, an insurrection, acts of public enemies, mobs, or rioters, earthquake, explosion, sanctioned transportation embargos, or any other event beyond its reasonable control, regardless of whether an attempt or act to assert control, and whether reasonably attempted or otherwise, may have been instituted by the party of the first part.

Does that cover everything? It would seem to. Some boilerplate force majeure clauses, for example, those used in the finance and banking industries, are more comprehensive and longer than this one. Now examine the force majeure clause as rewritten.

> *Force majeure.* Notwithstanding anything to the contrary, the supplier shall be excused from performance under this agreement when the same is made commercially unreasonable by a circumstance caused, in whole or in part, by an act or event beyond its reasonable control, including, but not limited to, an act of God, fire, war, flooding, labor disruption, or domestic raw material shortgage.

What are the differences between these two clauses, and which would be more effective and useable by the parties? Besides the obvious elimination of needless legal jargon and unnecessary recitation of several miscellaneous events of force majeure, making the second clause more understandable and useable to the average layman (and to attorneys, as well), there is one crucial difference: In the second clause the drafter was aware that a not uncommon occurance and disputed circumstance encountered by parties under a requirements or take-or-pay contract is that of a raw material shortage. For that reason the drafter pin-pointed this issue by making "domestic raw material shortage" an event of force majeure. He knew the business and customs within the industry of his client, the supplier, and focused on the most likely event to occur and be disputed. He, in fact, practiced effective preventive law by knowing the business and providing for that contingency and that protection for his client.

On the other hand, the drafter of the first clause, probably because of his lack of knowledge about the supplier's business, resorted to the use of excessive boilerplate language in an attempt to cover contingencies unknown to him. His effort, although perhaps impressive to some, falls short of an effective and useable clause and even tends to weaken and obscure the paragraph as a whole.

If counsel learns the business, he will be able to draft practical and useful documents for his client. He will also find that it is much quicker and easier to draft these documents, since he will know what clauses to focus upon and which paragraphs are of lesser importance. With this knowledge he can eliminate a great deal of boilerplate and arrive at a document that may be less than half the length otherwise and yet be a more useful and legally effective agreement. He will have the confidence of knowing which clauses should be in the contract and which ones he can give up in a bargain-exchange for preferred language in other sections.

Understanding the Business Objectives

Is it necessary to know the business objectives of the company? The answer is yes! Although it is not necessary to know every aspect of the five- and ten-year business plans of the corporation or other technical details, some understanding of the strategies and objectives of the management of the corporation will go a long way toward minimizing frustration and increasing counsel's ability to perform legal work effectively. The following example from a service industry corporation is a good case in point.

> An attorney with several years experience negotiating agreements for a company was assigned to help negotiate the contract terms for a project with a client who was very important to the company. If this negotiation and project was successful, the company could expect a substantial number of future projects from this client and others in that industry.
>
> The corporate counsel reviewed the contract terms proposed by the prospective client and made his usual

legal objections to several paragraphs and phrases. Uncharacteristically, several managers of this company began to argue vehemently with him about a number of these legal objections.

Rather than simply remaining in a vaccum and saying, "That's what the law says, and that's my opinion (take it or leave it!)," he questioned the managers about why this proposed contract was different from others.

Upon learning the extreme importance of this project to the long-term business objectives of the company and the fact that they were willing to perform the contract at cost or even at a loss, the attorney reconsidered his objections.

Although he did not change his previous objections, he now balanced some of those risks with the new business objectives. As a result, he tempered his judgment to much of the objectionable language but actually increased his objections in a few instances. The end result was a more focused legal opinion, now balanced with the business objectives. Importantly, this did not require a compromise of high quality legal standards but did significantly eliminate much frustration on the part of all involved.

Because this attorney learned and understood the business objectives of the company, he was able to focus on the most crucial issues and legal objections. He was able to balance the legal risk with the business objectives of the company and know when to say no as well as yes. Too often, an attorney inexperienced or unknowledgeable about the business will tend to say no to everything and leave to the business managers the task of trying to evaluate the relative importance of the several legal objections.

It is not always easy for an attorney to balance the legal risks against the business objectives, but it is clearly a very difficult or impossible matter if he does not understand the business and business objectives of the corporation. This advice is not encouraging counsel to make business decisions or to compromise his professionalism, which will be considered in more detail in STEP FOUR: UNDERSTAND THE LAW DEPART-

MENT FUNCTION and Part B. Instead, counsel's efforts to understand the business objectives will not only enable him to practice more effective preventive law but also reduce his frustration and exasperation at the occasional, uncomprehending layman.

Since the effect of business objectives upon preventive law practice will be touched upon several times throughout the remainder of this book, the next step is to examine how to actually learn about the business in which the corporation is engaged.

Learning About The Business

How does counsel learn about the business of the corporation? There are many ways. Several methods will be suggested here.

Look at the Big Picture

First, look at the corporation and the industry from a overall standpoint. Try to grasp the big picture and practical information. For example, how many separate business activities is the company engaged in? Is it a small privately held company operating primarily in one line of business, or is it a large conglomerate participating in several different industries?

Is the industry considered mature and stable, cyclical, or new and emerging? Is it a service-oriented industry, a basic manufacturing one, a transportation or utility? Is it highly regulated by state or federal authorities? Are there many competitors, both domestic and foreign, or is it a small unpopulated specialty?

Does the company have regional offices or divisions? Subsidiaries? If so, how many, where, and what are the sales, earnings, and number of people at each? How many different manufacturing locations are there, and what is the contribution of each? What is the industry rank of the company in size, assets, market share, earnings, and number of employees?

Does the company mine, process, upgrade, buy, sell, or trade a natural resource or raw material? If so, how much or how many deposits exist domestically and internationally, verified and estimated, explored and unexplored? What chemicals, minerals, or other elements make up that raw material, and are combined in the processing and upgrading operations?

Does the corporation broker, wholesale, retail, or transport consumer goods? If so, what is the source of the goods, how much inventory does it carry, and what is the backlog in orders? If service-oriented, how labor intensive are the operations, and what percentage profit is obtained from material used or furnished? Where is the existing and potential customer base located, and how large is it?

If a high technology industry, what portion of earnings are used for research and product development, what companies or countries lead the technological development, and how fast is it changing? Is the technology theory-oriented, military- or government-employed, or consumer-oriented?

The answers to these questions will affect the practice of law in the corporation because these are some of the considerations the business manages use to operate, plan, forecast, and make decisions. To effectively apply the law within this framework and environment, counsel obviously needs to know something about it—and the more, the better.

Where are the answers to these questions and others found? It is not hard, but it does take some effort. In order to learn the business, counsel must first learn the terminology (referred to earlier), then examine the internal and public information about the corporation, its competitors, and the industry, and, perhaps most important, ask questions and visit the operation, plant, or retail sites.

Learn the Terminology

There are several sources to begin this learning process. Surprisingly to some, a good place to start in some industries, is at the public library—and do not forget the very basic encyclopedias and other reference books. At this point counsel is interested in simple, basic, and explanatory information.

A book store will sometimes have soft-bound paperback books that can be purchased inexpensively and can be useful. For example, bookstores today will have several books on the computer industry. Frequently, there is a glossary of terms in the back of such a book. Similarily, in the engineering and construction field it is easy to find books in the library or bookstore on how to design or build a house, an addition, patio, or deck. Often, these books are written for the do-it-yourselfer and will have a glossary of terms in the back. If counsel will be working for an insurance company, there are many books regarding the insurance policies available with detailed explanations of terminology. Likewise, in the banking industry, the farming and agricultural industries, oil and gas industry, and many other industries, there are books with glossaries available. It is also not unusual for a specialized law book within a particular industry to have an explanation or glossary of terms. Failing all else, or in addition to, counsel should check the many good publications by government agencies and trade associations. Many of these are excellent primers for the beginner in an industry.

Examine Internal and Public Information

The annual report, quarterly reports, the 10-K, and special news releases, sales brochures, corporate policy manuals, and similar documents can be extremely valuable to learn about the business of the corporation. With a document such as the 10-K, it may be necessary to read it several times to appreciate the significance of much of its content. This is particularly true in the financial sections and the many technical notes of a 10-K or annual report. To properly understand the business of a company, counsel will need to put many of the current figures, operating strategies, and objectives in perspective by comparing them with the performance in prior years, perhaps as much as five or even ten years ago. He will not always be able to obtain copies of 10-K's for that many years ago, but if he can, it is very useful. Also, if the company is privately held, as opposed to publicly held, it may not publish a report similar to the annual report or 10-K. This, of course, will make the job more difficult.

It is not essential to know the reason for, or significance of, every figure or total contained in the financial statements. It is helpful to know the difference between the basic statements, for example, between an income statement and the consolidated statement of operations. Similarly, it is important to know the annual and quarterly revenues of the company, the net income figures, the profit margins, the dividends paid, and the earnings per share. It is also useful to gain a perspective of the business activity of the corporation by knowing some of the common ratios employed to analyze a company, such as the price/earnings ratio (published in the *Wall Street Journal*), the debt to equity ratio, and others. Then as counsel becomes more accustomed to reading financial statements, he will begin to focus quickly upon the significance of any changes in these ratios or other items, such as total assets, total long-term debt, short-term debt, expenditures for research and development, selling and administrative expenses, and others.

The value of being aware of this type of financial information about the company is often significant even though counsel is functioning in the role of corporate attorney, and not a financial person. If the objective of your company is primarily to make a profit, then many decisions in the corporation will be based upon that objective. Some of those decisions will unavoidably have an impact upon the merits given to counsel's legal advice, opinion, and work product. Counsel must be aware of that impact so that he can deal with it, if appropriate. Also, knowing this type of financial information will make him seem less of a stranger and outsider to many of the laymen in the company. For example, if a manager says, "We can't extend that kind of warranty because it will cost too much and lower our profit margin below an acceptable standard", will counsel know enough not to be intimidated by the term "profit margin" and to ask, "But isn't it also important to maintain our market share and volume of sales by offering a warranty at least equal in value to the warranty offered by our competitors?"

Similiarily, how would an executive of the company counsel has just joined would view him if in a discussion counsel demonstrated his ignorance of a corporation's net income or profit margin? He might not view him as any less an attorney, but he might begin to wonder whether counsel practiced law within a vaccum and outside the real world of a corporation.

Compare Industry and Competitor Information

Examining the public information about competitors and the industry as a whole will provide a perspective on the company's activities and help counsel to understand the viewpoint from which many of the managers of the company look at its activities. One of the easiest ways to obtain this information is simply request to be put on the shareholder mailing list for the 10-K, 8 Q's, and other announcements. Several easily available reference books and other publications are also useful. Dun & Bradstreet's *Million Dollar Directory* series and Standard & Poor's *Register of Corporations, Directors and Executives* list summary information of many corporations. They also publish other references, such as *Moody's Industrial Manual* (Dun & Bradstreet) and *Corporations Records* series and the *Stock Reports* (Standard & Poors), that give a more extensive synopsis of a corporation's business and its financial performance. Publications such as *The Value Line Investment Survey* evaluate a industry as a whole and predict trends, in addition to giving detailed information about selected public companies.

Another valuable resource for learning about an industry are the various trade publications in that industry. There are many. If counsel can obtain them, a stock analyst's report about an industry or company within that industry, as well as consultant reports, often provide excellent information.

Ask Questions and Visit Operations

A most common and important method to learn about the company's business is to ask questions. Because a person may become annoyed with answering many questions, the time to do it is when counsel first arrives. Counsel should not be afraid to show that he does not know much about the industry. He is not expected to know much about the industry if he has not been in it before. Employees will be responsive to answering his questions and will be impressed by counsel's desire to learn. Counsel can learn a great deal from the long years of experience of many layman in the company. It is an excellent resource, and counsel should take advantage of it.

Try to find ways to visit the manufacturing plants, the retail locations, the regional offices, the research facilities, the mining or construction projects, or whatever else is associated with the business of your corporation. These visits will provide first-hand knowledge that is very difficult to learn in any other way. There is little more valuable when drafting a contract or trying to resolve a dispute than to have actually seen what counsel is writing about. The ability to understand what counsel is actually working on will sometimes eliminate extraneous or unrelated language or problems that counsel might have otherwise thought important and necessary.

Much has been covered in this STEP ONE: LEARN THE BUSINESS. That was intentional because this is a very basic and logical first step to use in the quest to successfully practice preventive corporate law. It, as much as any other step, points the way to learn how to effectively apply the skills and knowledge learned in law school to the business situation. It is a step in which to extend an effort and continue to work at throughout counsel's career.

Before going on to the next building block in the foundation for your practice of preventive law—STEP TWO: KNOW THE PEOPLE, a case study appears, which, although hypothetical, is based upon actual experience, as are all the case studies included at the end of the chapters in this book. It is intended to illustrate in a practical way many of the points discussed in this STEP ONE and situations not unlike those that counsel is apt to encounter during his career of practicing corporate law. Read the facts and description of the circumstances several times before trying to identify the practical issues in point. Then having found those issues, think about what you would imagine yourself doing in a similar situation as a corporate attorney. Then review what actually happened, and decide for yourself whether your actions or those that actually happened were more appropriate and a better example of the effective practice of preventive corporate law.

Case Study Number One: ACQUISITION OF O'FOSS, INC.

The Situation

A 500 million dollar (sales) manufacturer of heavy, industrial plant equipment had been experiencing a severe down-turn in its sales and backlog for orders because of the recessionary economy. As a result of several corporate strategic meetings, management determined that in order to minimize the impact on earnings during this and future downturns in the economy, they should diversify their operations by acquiring a service-oriented company, or at least one in a less capital-intensive, cyclical industry.

In furtherance of this objective, the corporate planning department with the assistance of an outside consultant determined that a company furnishing services to the oil and gas industry met these requirements and had an extremely favorable short-term outlook, as well as long-term growth potential (not entirely accurate, as we now know). After several months of investigation, they found a possible acquisition candidate located in a small port town in the state of Texas. The company's name was O'Foss, Inc., which stood for Offshore Fuel, Diesel Oil and Supply Service, Incorporated. Except for the current year, the company had experienced a very strong growth rate during the past five years of supplying fuel, diesel oil, and other supplies to tug boats, offshore oil rigs, and other vessels in the inland waterways and the Gulf of Mexico. The founder and driving force behind the company incurred a severe disability about a year ago, and as a result the company had recently been forced into Chapter 11 under the Bankruptcy Act by some slowly paid and unpaid creditor suppliers of the fuel and diesel oil sold by O'Foss.

The Vice President of Corporate Planning and the Vice President of Operations visited the O'Foss facilities and talked with the remaining management and the court-appointed bankruptcy trustee last week. They were favorably impressed and believed that the company was basically sound but lacked strong management and that a successful acquisition might be possible. Another trip is scheduled in two weeks, on which you will go as Corporate Counsel, along with the Vice President of Corporate Planning, the Vice President of Operations, the Vice President of Finance, and the Executive Vice President of your company. The purpose of the meeting is to find out more about the company and its financial condition, to investigate any legal problems, to talk with the attorney-trustee, and to determine whether agreeable terms of acquisition are possible.

The Question

As the corporate attorney representing the company on this trip, what would you do? Based upon what you have learned in this chapter, what steps would you take? What is the first thing you would do?

What Actually Happened

The first thing the attorney in this case did was to try to find out as much about the company O'Foss and its business as he could. He reviewed the documents the Vice President for Corporate Planning brought back with them from the previous meeting. They consisted of copies of two long-term fuel and oil supply contracts (not currently in effect), the annual report from the year before, and several advertising brochures.

Knowing this was insufficient information to learn about the company and its business, he arranged with the attorney acting as the trustee for bankruptcy court to express mail to him the last three (and five, if possible) annual reports, plus all documents filed in the bankruptcy court and copies of all previous and existing long-term purchase and supplies contracts of O'Foss. Additionally, he talked with the Operations Vice President and Vice President for Corporate Planning to learn as much about the practical aspects of the company's operations and the industry as possible.

As a result of this thorough examination of the documents and further information learned during the subsequent trip, the visit to the facilities, including discussions with the trustee attorney, the corporate attorney came to the following conclusions:

1. That an important key to the success of operating a business of the type of O'Foss was the ability to have a long-term purchase contract for diesel oil and fuel oil at

prices below market so that those supplies could, in turn, be sold for a profit.

2. That the past major suppliers of O'Foss were unwilling to extend them credit to purchase these supplies in view of the Chapter 11 proceedings but might do so with a guarantee of payment from your company.

3. That any arrangement negotiated by your company with O'Foss should first be sanctioned by the bankruptcy court and provide protection against existing creditors.

4. That the data compiled during the past year (just prior to Chapter 11 filing) was inadequate and inconclusive at best but appeared to confirm, along with the bankruptcy court filings, that liabilities significantly exceed assets and that O'Foss was still operating at a loss.

5. That in the event of some agreement, your company must provide strong on-site management to insure adequate legal and financial protection of your interest in O'Foss, both from existing creditors and from existing inadequate management and control.

Based upon these conclusions, he recommended to management of his company that should they wish to acquire O'Foss, it be structured as follows: (1) That they attempt to negotiate interim or joint venture agreement for a period of six months to a year, during which time they could learn more about soundness of the business and any pitfalls, and after which they would have an option to purchase the company at a previously negotiated price adjusted by the earnings during that period. (2) That any such arrangement would need the approval of the Bankruptcy creditors. (3) That any credit guaranteed by his company and all subsequent receivables, unless otherwise specifically agreed, would apply only against new purchases. (4) And that a strong operations manager should be placed at the job site during this interim period to monitor accounts and insure adequate controls are maintained.

An arrangement of this type was, in fact, developed and took place. The Corporate Counsel also had outside counsel experienced with the new bankruptcy regulations review the documentation he and others had developed. In this case after participating in the joint venture operations for six months, management of the company decided the earnings potential was not as great as they had thought, and they declined to exercise the option to purchase the O'Foss company.

Author's Comments

This case illustrates several points that we have discussed in STEP ONE: LEARN THE BUSINESS. The corporate attorney knew that he did not know much about the service or oil and gas industries, but he did try to learn as much as he could within the time available. Importantly, he obtained as many records and information (10-K's and other financial reports and long-term contracts) as possible and analyzed them.

From this investigation he was then able to talk halfway knowledgeably with (and in the language of) the existing O'Foss management and the trustee-attorney. He correctly concluded that below-market, long-term supply contracts were critical to successful operation of O'Foss and that the previous suppliers may be reluctant to do business.

Further, when it became apparent that an acquisition price would be difficult to agree upon, he came up with the excellent recommendation (as it turned out) to enter into an interim operating agreement, with an option to buy that included a fixed acquisition price adjusted by an interim earnings formula, all to be approved by the bankruptcy court and protected against creditors.

The result of these actions by this corporate counsel was development of a useable, practical, and workable operating and potential acquisition agreement, which, for the most part, was understood by all persons involved. Had he not made an effort to learn about the business of O'Foss, it is doubtful whether he would have first had the idea and then have been able to draft such an agreement. Additionally, he was able to develop several contingent or preventive paragraphs to protect his corporation in the event of unexpected legal and business problems occurring during the interim period.

Moreover, although he knew the risks associated with acquiring a company in Chapter 11, by balancing those risks against the business objectives of his company, that is, to diversify and enter into different industries, he was able to go forward objectively and provide the needed legal protection. He wisely consulted with an outside bankruptcy specialist (See Part B, KEY 4: KNOW WHEN TO GO OUTSIDE).

I have no doubt that you have other comments about this case, and I trust that many of them will be correct. The purpose of this case has been to try to stimulate your thinking and to show you in a practical way that learning a business is, in fact, an important step in your practice of preventive corporate law.

Step Two: Know the People

Introduction

Why should counsel get to know the people? Because it will help establish a good client relationship—something crucial to the effective practice of preventive law in the corporation. Counsel should also know where to go to draw upon the special expertise and skills possessed by many of the people in the corporation—an often valuable and time-saving resource. One may also need to "read between the lines" to uncover the complete story or truth. Finally, counsel should ask a question that is not as simple as it first appears: Who is the client?

Remember, because the people in the corporation actually cause it to exist and to operate either smoothly or inefficiently, counsel's knowledge of them and working relationship with them will play a critical role in the foundation for an effective practice of preventive law.

A Good Client Relationship Is Crucial

A good client relationship is crucial to an effective corporate practice of preventive law. One of the primary objectives in a preventive law practice is to find out about a potential legal problem before it occurs or in its very early stages. And in a corporation, counsel usually learns about legal problems in this early stage from the people, the employees and managers of the corporation. By the time he learns about a legal problem from a third party, another corporation, or another attorney representing his client, it is often too late to apply effective preventive measures.

The greater effort counsel makes to know the people in the corporation, the more this "client relationship" will encourage people to bring him potential legal problems. They should feel comfortable in bringing legal problems to counsel. If, on the other hand, counsel is perceived as being cynical, aloof, or superior, then a proper client relationship will not be established to give counsel the opportunity to practice effective preventive law. Since counsel is dealing with the people in the corporation on a daily, weekly, or, at least, monthly basis, he should get to know them. If counsel has not, then no doubt, he is at least partly at fault.

The very real and practical value of a good client relationship will be experienced time and again when practicing corporate law. In effect, one can set up an "early warning system" with a good client relationship. The people in the corporation will give counsel early warning of potential legal problems, often before they really know they have a problem or know what the law may be on a certain point. They are the people actually running the corporation and are usually closer to a potential legal problem than anyone else. Here is an example of a corporate counsel in the construction industry who had a good client relationship.

> A division manager with whom corporate counsel was well-acquainted, having worked with him on several occasions in the past, stopped by his office one day. Since the manager was based out of town, most of the conversation was just a friendly chat, but he eventually brought up one subject he had not intended to discuss. He didn't think he had a problem, but thought he might mention it anyway.
>
> One of the projects in his division was the ten-month construction project of a $20 million recreational facility to be used commercially. The facility was to be completed and ready for use by a certain month that coincided with the beginning of the tourist season. The contract price was lump sum, and liquidated damages were chargeable to the contractor (division manager) for each day of late completion.
>
> Because of the frequent design changes, the division manager had been regularly filing change orders

to adjust the lump-sum price to reflect the increased material and labor costs but not to extend the completion date, since he did not think time extensions would be allowed under the strict contract language. He was not sure whether he would be able to complete the facility on schedule without the use of several extra crews and double time during the last few months of the project.

After this brief discussion and review of the applicable contract language, the manager and counsel decided to look at all the change orders filed to date and try to evaluate the effect each had on the construction schedule. The manager assigned the assistant project manager to this task, and two weeks later he received an analysis based upon a critical path diagram that allocated the amount of hours and days delay that each change order had caused, including overall disruption to the schedule. The division manager was surprised with the results of this analysis.

They immediately filed for a change order requesting a time extension based upon this analysis, notwithstanding its questionable validity in view of the strict contract language. They also submitted similar change order (time extension) requests based on design changes during the remainder of the project.

The project was, in fact, completed 60 days late, with the resulting loss of use and revenue to the owner and a later assessment of liquidated damages against the contractor. The case entered litigation, and the architect became involved because of the many design changes. But because of the excellent documentation and timely filing of change orders for extensions (at least during the later stages of the project), the division manager was able to avoid most of the liquidated damages through a negotiated settlement (despite the unfavorable contract language).

This is an example of corporate counsel's having a good client relationship with a division manager, and because of that relationship he "happened to mention" a situation that, after discussion, they realized could escalate into a significant problem if preventative steps were not taken. Those steps were taken, and a substantial portion of the litigation process was thereby eliminated.

Although the division manager may have seen counsel or another member of the law department about this problem at some point in the future anyway, that is not the point. Having a good client relationship with people often makes a significant difference in how soon they will talk to counsel about a legal problem and how much they will tell him. The ability to practice effective preventive law hinges in large part upon knowing about an incident before it becomes a serious legal problem, particularly an irresolveable one.

The early warning system in a good client relationship, developed by counsel's effort to know the people, is of significant value in the practice of preventive law and to the corporation because in most cases he will learn about legal problems in the corporation either directly or indirectly through the people.

Their Expertise Is a Valuable Resource

Counsel has at his finger tips in the corporation a valuable resource of expertise and specialties in the people making up the corporation. Many laymen will have worked in the same field all of their careers and are far more expert in that area than counsel could ever hope to become. If one knows the people, he can save himself considerable time by drawing upon their experience and expertise to obtain answers otherwise not found.

Consider the following corporate counsel who made maximum use of the expertise available through the people within her corporation.

> A salesman in corporation that distributes and sells agricultural chemicals manufactured by another company brought a letter from a dissatisfied customer to the corporate counsel's office. In this letter the customer complained that the chemicals he had purchased from this salesman failed to control a particular disease, stunted the growth of his crops, and resulted in a greatly diminished yield at harvest, with

a substantial loss of profits to the customer. The salesman said that he did not tell the customer that this chemical would control the particular disease suffered by the crops and that the stunting of the plants was either the result of improper application of the chemical or poor cultivation of the crops.

Corporate counsel in this case knew where to begin her investigation. She first called a chemist and a plant biologist working in the research and development group of her company and reviewed the matter with them. At their suggestion she contacted the Farm Extension Agent in the county where this customer was located to find how prevalent this particular disease was in that area and to learn any facts about the cultivation practices of this particular farmer. The country agent had visited this farmer's field several months earlier and had some helpful information. He suggested checking with the Department of Agriculture's Relief Fund Program for prior years because he thought this farmer had applied for relief and such an application would show the yield on his cropland in those prior years.

The corporate chemist and biologist also suggested contacting an expert on this particular disease at a nearby university for whatever information hc might be able to provide, which they then proceeded to do.

Counsel also called the manager of the chemical division within her company and reviewed the case with him, who, in turn, called the chemical manufacturer to discuss the facts. Counsel also contacted the controller of her company to determine the current status of this customer's account and his past payment record. Then she called the manager in charge of sales in that region to obtain his opinion about whether this particular salesman might have extended unauthorized oral warranties to the customer.

After having gathered all the facts, analyses, and opinions from these individuals, counsel was able to make a preliminary determination that the farmer's case against her company was a weak one, that this particular disease was attacking almost all crops in the area, that the chemicals sold were not intended to protect against that particular disease, and that it was unlikely that their salesman had extended such a warranty.

As is readily seen in this example, counsel contacted five people with expertise in different specialties within her company. At their suggestions she and they contacted four other experts outside the company. In this case the investigation took a minimal amount of time and progressed rapidly. The attorney knew the people within her corporation and the various skills and expertise they possesed. She was able to make immediate contact with them and make maximum use of their services and talent. This clearly shows a case in which knowing the people and their special skills and expertise greatly enhanced this attorney's ability to handle this problem quickly and effectively.

This is only one example of the valuable resource counsel has available in the people of his corporation if he knows them. When preparing answers to complaints or interrogatories, one will often have need to draw upon the expertise of people in the corporation. When responding to an investigation by the Department of Justice, Federal Trade Commission, or other regulatory bodies, or during the preparation of Security and Exchange filings, counsel often has occasion to draw heavily upon the expertise of people in his corporation.

The people in the corporation are a resource counsel has that is not readily available to attorneys in private practice. It is a resource that is wise to uncover, learn about, and use to the maximum extent possible.

"Reading Between the Lines"

Does a corporate counsel really have to "read between the lines"? Sometimes. Recognize that dealing with people in a corporation is just like anywhere else—it's not always a perfect world. Not everybody is going to give the complete story or tell the whole truth. They may not intentionally tell an untruth—but they may neglect to give some important facts. If counsel does not know the person and his particular style of management, operation, or way of speaking about things, he may not be able to perceive whether they are giving the whole picture. Of course, a person can ask questions, but counsel may not know there is a reason to do so. Look at this example.

> A manager sticks his head in counsel's door and says, "Just wanted to let you know we have a small problem with so-and-so supplier company, but I just talked to the CEO (chief executive officer), and we got it covered." And counsel says, "O.K.! Thanks, Bob." Then she more or less forgets about it but may mention it to the CEO should she see him in the hallway. Right?
>
> Wrong! Counsel knows from experience that this particular manager does not like to get involved with the law department because he thinks they always cause problems. She has a pretty good guess that he was simply throwing her that information because the CEO had told him to inform counsel about the matter. In so doing, he could now tell the CEO, if he asked, that he had, in fact, told the law department. Knowing these facts counsel should have asked, "What problem?" And this should have been followed by many other questions.

This is a simplified but not uncommon instance of someone making a record of informing the law department about a problem but doing so in such a casual or incomplete fashion that the law department will not become involved. One might think that managers with this attitude will not last long in the corporation. This may be true, but these and other operating styles and attitudes exist to some degree in almost every corporation today, and if counsel is to successfully practice corporate law, he must be able to deal with them. The more one knows about a person and his particular style or mode of operation, the more one will enhance his ability to handle whatever problems may arise. With some people, counsel will have to read between the lines they give.

Although some people will try to hide something from counsel, others fail to tell the whole story simply because they are intimidated. Being in an attorney's office can be a frightening experience for some people; and if the attorney does not know the person well enough to know that he is intimidated or, perhaps knowing so, encourages that feeling, has not the attorney failed to read between the lines?

Ironically, other people will say too much. That is, too much from the point of view of the corporate counsel being a legitimate and valuable function within the corporation. This negative attitude by laymen toward attorneys is illustrated in the following example by a division vice president who liked to refer to the law department as the "negative sales department."

> An ambitious vice president in charge of a division within a service-oriented corporation wanted to increase the sales and size of his group as rapidly as possible. A standard contract written by the law department for use by this group contained several paragraphs limiting the corporation's liability for negligence, resulting damages, implied warranties, and so on.
>
> Although this language was commonplace within the industry, the vice president soon concluded that the sales of his group could be increased substantially if he could persuade the law department to subtantially modify or delete some of these clauses, which he failed to do. Perhaps because of an honest difference of opinion with the law department, the vice president began openly calling the law department "the negative sales department".
>
> Unfortunately, as one can imagine, the use of this nickname had the opposite effect intended by the vice president. The law department became even more attentive to changes in the contract language requested by people from his group. Naturally, the jobs of all concerned became more difficult and frustrating and did not change until the vice president, for other reasons, moved to a different position within the company.

Corporate counsel in many companies have similar stories to tell. Counsel should at least be alert to this type of attitude and, if there is no other solution, should simply grin and bear it, with the knowledge that many other attorneys have been confronted with identical problems. It is inherent in the position of corporate counsel that in working in such close and daily contact with business people, they sometimes consider themselves to be "dynamic and entreprenurial persons" and lawyers as "necessary evils".

In dealing with these less-than-perfect aspects of some laymen counsel, should be alert and know the people well enough to spot those situations that require him to "read between the lines." Whether to learn all the facts and the whole story or simply to handle a less than cooperative attitude on the part of a layman, knowing the people makes the job as a corporate counsel much easier and less frustrating and significantly enhances the effectiveness of the practice of law in the corporation.

Who is the Client?

To this point, some may have assumed that all of the people in the corporation are the clients of the corporate counsel. That assumption is correct as far as it goes. But one needs to go further. In contrast to the private practice of law in which the client is usually clearly represented by a single person or entity, in the corporate setting an attorney may deal with several different persons or groups of people at the same time, all with conflicting opinions and objectives on the same issue. In such a case are they all clients? Is one person or group more of a client than another? What about people who are not employees of the corporation, such as the shareholders (owners) of the corporation? Does counsel have legal duties and responsibilities to them, making them clients as well? Many would say yes. If so, then are shareholders "priority clients" over the officers of your corporation? What about the corporation as a whole, or as a separate entity? Is the investing public also a client in your practice of corporate law?

These questions are pertinent for all corporate counsel to examine. These persons, groups, and entities could be considered clients at some point and on some issues in the practice of corporate law. To that extent, it is of value to a counsel's practice to learn as much about them as he can. Which of these people or groups of people, if any, should be considered as a preferred or priority client is a difficult and largely unsettled question today. In theory, counsel would want to consider all clients or potential clients within the corporate universe as equal, to advise and counsel all with equanimity and impartiality. As a practical matter, counsel may encounter differing interests among these clients not unlike the traditional conflict of interest issues among clients found in private practice. The proper approach begins with impartiality to all, but beyond that counsel will have to use his own judgment as the facts and future issues in corporate law develop.

The equally important inquiry here is limited to identifying who among the number of different perons, groups of people, and entities in the corporate universe can be your clients and under what circumstances. The following example is based upon an actual occurrence not unlike one that may be encountered during a career of corporate law practice, as corporate acquisitions, mergers, and divestitures will undoubtedly continue to occur. Place yourself in the position of the general counsel and determine which of the parties in this example should be considered the client.

> The president of a multimillion-dollar, publicly held, manufacturing company called the general counsel into his office one morning. He said he had just received a telephone call from the president of another company in a related industry to inquire whether he would be willing to meet on a confidential basis to discuss a possible merger or acquisition of our company with (by) theirs. The president further told him that he had just finished talking with the chairman of the company who authorized meeting with them to listen to their proposal. The chairman, although inactive now in the daily business activities of the corporation, remains (with his immediate family members) a major shareholder. The president wanted counsel to attend the meeting with him, which he did the following week. The meeting lasted about two hours and was primarily for the purpose of establishing goodwill between the two companies and to

indicate that they, as the acquiring company, were not interested in a hostile takeover, but rather a friendly merger. Acquisition price was not discussed.

After the meeting your president polled the board members by telephone and because of an expression of interest primarily by the chairman of the board, another meeting was scheduled the following week, at which a preliminary acquisition price was discussed along with general principles about reorganization in the event of such a takeover or merger.

Soon thereafter at the next regular meeting of your board of directors, the proposed acquisition is discussed in detail. While five of the outside director who are related by family to the chairman were in favor of the proposed acquisition, two of the inside (employee) directors were not. The president, who is also a director but not family-related, holds a large block of option shares that would be purchased in the event of an acquisition and was therefore generally in favor of an acquisition—but felt some obligation to the inside directors and other managers of the corporation to protect the independent control of the corporation.

At this point several questions should occur to counsel. The primary issue is whether disclosure by the corporation of the acquisition negotiations is advisable or required under the applicable Security and Exchange rules. On the one hand, counsel knows that the chairman and family-related directors are concerned that a premature disclosure might result in a run-up of the price for the stock to a level that would effectively thwart the acquisition. On the other hand, counsel knows that the corporation has an obligation to its shareholders and the investing public to disclose significant information that they might find pertinent to their investing decisions. Furthermore, counsel knows that the nonfamily directors and officers of the corporation would prefer disclosure if that would help to discourage the acquisition and enable the corporation to remain independent. Counsel has obtained opposite opinions on this disclosure issue from two different attorneys specializing in security and exchange matters. Officially the position as general counsel reports to the board of directors of the corporation, and administratively to the president of the corporation.

To whom should counsel consider his legal obligations regarding disclosure to run? Who is the client? The board of directors? The shareholders? The president of your company to whom he reports administratively? The nonfamily directors and officers of the corporation? The managers and employees of the corporation? The corporation itself? The Securities & Exchange Commission? The applicable law or regulations, although ambiguous? The investing public? Himself as a professional? The Code of Legal Ethics? In this case the actual events progressed extremely rapidly making this question moot. Information about the negotiations was discovered by the media, and arbitrators quickly ran up the price of the stock, requiring its temporary suspension from trading and immediate public disclosure by both companies.

Nevertheless, this illustration demonstrates that sometimes corporate counsel deals with, and may be responsible to, several different groups of persons (some employees and others not) at the same time and on the same issue. The board of directors will look to counsel for legal advice, as will the officers of the corporation, and other employees. To the extent that their interest is the welfare of the corporation as opposed to a personal interest, they can be considered your clients. So, too, can other groups of people, such as the shareholders, at least insofar as counsel is representing the duties and obligations of the corporate entity that run to them. Therefore, these persons and groups of people represent clients or potential clients that counsel should try to learn about and know in order to lay the foundation for an effective preventive law practice.

Now, read the facts in the following case study and try to decide how you would handle the matter, keeping in mind the principles discussed in this Step Two.

Case Study Number Two: LETTER FROM A DISGRUNTLED SUBCONTRACTOR

The Situation

On Monday morning counsel is sitting in his office having his first cup of coffee, browsing through the incoming mail that arrived over the weekend and what was not done last Friday. He comes across a two-page handwritten letter with a note attached from the Chief Executive Officer that says in red ink, "You might want to check this." The letter is from a paving and dirt contractor located in a nearby state who was a major subcontractor for your company on a recently completed multimillion dollar manufacturing facility. In the rather poorly written letter addressed to the Chief Executive Officer of the company, the subcontractor complains that the company's project manager has "done him in." He says that he agreed to perform a considerable amount of extra work, including using double shifts and working at night, because the project manager promised to pay him well for the premium time. Now he says, "He won't pay the extra charges I sent him and won't talk to me anymore. You owe me more than $40,000."

The first thing to do is call the project manager (who now is on another construction project), tell him about the letter, and ask him what he knows about the situation. The project manager says that he knows all about that subcontractor and that he had all kinds of problems with him and that he practically had to threaten him with bodily harm just to get him to finish the paving work on schedule. At no time did he promise him any extra money or tell him to do any extra work that was not in the original contract. In addition, he says, "This subcontractor is an ex-alcoholic, has a criminal record, and is always chasing women—we don't owe him a red cent".

Counsel has not met this project manager but knows that he has a good reputation in the company for being a hard-driving, competent manager of projects. In addition, he knows that this particular project was brought in within the budget and on the time schedule, an achievement not always accomplished on projects of this scope and size. Counsel's thought is to write the subcontractor saying he has reviewed the matter and finds no justification for additional monies owed, to send a copy of that letter to the CEO, and to see what happens from that point. Then if the subcontractor responds, he can be asked to furnish more details and documents that will show he is owed the additional money.

The Question

Is that how you would handle the problem? What are other ways to handle it? What are the legal issues involved in this factual situation? At first impression the legal issues are the following: Was the extra work requested and performed, and if so, under what contractual terms. Assuming these legal issues, how would you proceed? What principles from the STEP Two would you apply?

What Actually Happened

The attorney in this case was about to follow the course of action outlined—of sending the subcontractor a simple denial letter. On second thought, he decided that since he really did not know the project manager very well—only by reputation—he should examine the facts one step further. Although the CEO had not told him to specifically investigate this matter, it would not look good if the facts turned out to be unfavorable and they received a lawsuit or other more serious complaints from the subcontractor.

So he decided to call the subcontractor to hear his side of the story. Upon so doing, he found the business telephone has been disconnected with no forwarding number. For the moment he decided he would have to look elsewhere for the other side of the story, if there was one. Knowing that the project had been completed, he wondered whether the files had been returned to the headquarters building. He called the director of purchasing with whom he had worked on several occasions and whom he knew well. He asked him whether he had files pertaining to this subcontractor and whether he knew anything about him. Although he did not know much, he said that the purchasing agent who was on that project was now in the headquarters building and that he would send him to his office with the files.

The purchasing agent brought this attorney the files and essentially confirmed the project manager's version of the facts, emphasizing that the project manager, not he, had handled the paperwork for that subcontractor. The purchasing agent appeared a little nervous and frequently answered questions, "I don't know." Counsel thought it unusual that he could not answer more questions because he believed that a purchasing agent on a project of this size was in a responsible and knowledgeable position.

Counsel looked through the subcontractor's file, and everything appeared to be in order. There were three properly written, executed contracts pertaining to work performed and twelve change order requests that seemed to be properly issued and signed, one of which was denied. Nonetheless, counsel knew that he did not have an in-depth knowledge about the purchasing practices and procedures in the company and that the purchasing agent did seem ill-at-ease, so he decided to try to draw upon another person's expertise.

He called the director of purchasing to whom he had already spoken and asked him if he could talk with him for five or ten minutes about this subcontractor and about some of the purchasing policies and procedures. He said "Of course."

The purchasing director reviewed the subcontractor's file with him and noted that many of the change orders had been signed by the project manager, rather than the purchasing agent as is usually done. In addition, he noted that some of the change orders were not signed by the subcontractor, which he found unusual. He called the purchasing agent into the office. The purchasing agent now provided a little more information. He said that although he knew it was unusual for a project manager to handle the paperwork on subcontracts himself, the project manager was, after all, the head man on the project, and he had to do what he was told. The director of purchasing did not like these statements. He told the purchasing agent that it remained his responsibility to approve all change orders, whether individually or jointly with a project manager, and that his line of reporting ran to him, not just the project manager.

After the purchasing agent left the office, the director of purchasing explained that although the handling of these change orders was unusual, he knew the project manager to be a competent individual and there was probably no problem in this case. Counsel discussed more about purchasing procedures with him and thanked him for his help.

Counsel went back to his office and was not completely satisfied. The purchasing agent had appeared nervous again. Although the director of purchasing had always been helpful and cooperative in the past, he also knew him to be a person who liked to "cover his tracks" and not have mistakes in his department discovered.

Counsel decided to check one more resource. He called one of the internal auditors with whom he had talked on many occasions regarding matters of litigation and claims. Counsel knew that he and his staff routinely post-audited selected projects completed by the company. He asked him if he would have a minute to look over this particular subcontractor's file. After looking at the files and noting that the approval signature was by the project manager rather than the purchasing agent, he stated that in his auditing experience this was the first time he can remember having seen this type of approval. He also noted that there were quite a few change orders and almost none of them had the normal backup documentation. Usually there was some sort of time records to back up a change order. He said he would have one of his staff cross-check the construction gate logs on this project to determine whether the subcontractor actually performed some of the night work detailed in one or two of the change orders. He said he would also try to find out why there were no payroll records of the subcontractor supporting the change orders requests.

A week later he and one of his staff asked if they could come to counsel's office. They told counsel that there was no duplicate documentation in any of the other project files supporting the work performed for these change orders. They thought it particularly unusual that the subcontractor was never logged through the construction gate, since he said he was running double shifts, one of them at night. They also found in a different project file maintained by the accounting department several change orders that had originally been drafted but were then canceled. Coincidentally, the amount of these canceled change orders equaled $40,000—the same amount the subcontractor says is owed him.

Events progress rapidly from this point forward. In attempting to do more checking of the facts, counsel found out the home telephone of the subcontractor, called him, and left a message for him to call. Instead, the following day the court-appointed trustee handling the recent Chapter 11 filing by the subcontractor (about which counsel knew nothing) called him, and repeated the contention that the subcontractor was owed $40,000 and requested to see the project files. Counsel said he was welcome to inspect the files but that his preliminary information showed there was improper documentation for almost all of the change orders and that the subcontractor may have been paid for improperly issued change orders. The trustee then tried to find some documentation in the subcontractor's files but could not because of poor recordkeeping. He then talked in-depth with the subcontractor and called this attorney a few days later. He said that the subcontractor had told him that there was a kick-back scheme involving the subcontractor and the project manager, in which change orders for nonexistent work would be issued and the money split between the two of them. The project manager did not pay him as they had agreed, however, and partially for revenge he was willing to "turn state's evidence" for immunity from prosecution.

Counsel quickly relayed this information to the CEO and subsequently called in the appropriate governmental authorities for further investigation. He additionally advised the CEO that because of the criminal nature of the alleged facts, the Board of Directors, as well as the owner of the project for whom their company had constructed the manufacturing facility, should be notified and kept apprised of the situation. The CEO agreed, this was done, and several months later the matter went to trial.

Author's Comments

There are several pertinent observations you should have made while reading this case study: (1) The attorney in this case knew that he did not have a good knowledge of the people involved, namely, the project manager and the subcontractor, and correctly decided to double-check the facts; (2) he lacked expertise in the policy and procedures of purchasing of his corporation and immediately drew upon that expertise by talking with the purchasing director with whom he had previously established a good client relationship; (3) he used another source to check the facts by requesting the expertise of the auditing department; (4) he "read between the lines" by wondering whether he was getting the complete picture from the purchasing agent and the director of purchasing; and (5) he correctly identified that his client in this case was the corporation and not the project manager, the director of purchasing, the purchasing agent, or the subcontractor. At some point had this been a public company, the attorney should have recognized that public disclosure of the allegations may have been desirable or necessary.

This example should have illustrated the value of knowing the people in the corporation. Although this example is unusual, it gives an idea of the complexity of some situations that may be encountered in your practice of corporate law. The ability to know the function and skills of people within the company so that their expertise can be drawn upon will be invaluable to the practice of preventive law. So, too, will be knowledge of various operating styles of managers and the ability not only to establish a good client relationship with them but also to read between the lines when necessary. Knowing the people in the corporation is an important part of the foundation of an effective and successful preventive law practice.

Step Three: Communicate with the Other Corporate Departments

Introduction

If a corporate counsel just sits in his office and waits for legal problems to come to him, and then, having received one, simply pulls out his hornbook, divines an answer, and issues a memorandum, he will not be practicing effective preventive law in the corporation. Counsel is not, or should not, be part of that separate and detached group on the sixth floor or in the far corner of the building who sometimes glorify themselves in imagined professionalism. That is not to say there is not a time, place and need to be a professional—but not at this point. If corporate counsel is trying to build a foundation to practice effective corporate law, he must communicate, communicate, and communicate!

A corporation is operated by people who are usually grouped by function or specialty into departments, divisions or other classifications. Regardless of whether a department is service-oriented (the law department) or a profit center (export division), they must function harmoniously and effectively together. This is especially true for the law department because of the pervasive and overlapping nature of its corporate functions. To accomplish that purpose and to practice effective preventive law within the corporation, corporate counsel must have good communication with all of the corporate departments and various operating groups.

Corporate counsel will often need specialized information and assistance from other corporate departments, for example, retrieval of purchase documentation (the purchasing department), copy of a signed credit application and disclosure statements (the credit department or accounting), or the last known address of former employees (the personnel department). When counsel does not know the specific individual to telephone to obtain the information needed, it is far easier if he can call a manager of a department and say, "I need this information; can you help me find it?" and receive an answer like "Let me see what I can do and I'll call you back"; rather than "I don't think we keep that kind of information, but you can come down and look for yourself if you want to." Although counsel can usually go through superiors and require such help and information, that type of assistance is usually not as useful and effective.

The various departments in the corporation also are vital sources for counsel to learn about potential legal matters and problems, often before they occur or become irresolvable. And by communicating with the other corporate departments, counsel can learn about the nonlegal considerations that may affect or be affected by his legal decisions. In short, they need counsel—but counsel needs them even more.

Learning About Potential Legal Problems

Other corporate departments will frequently know about a potential legal problem before corporate counsel will. Not uncommonly, a matter will be handled in their department before it reaches the corporate counsel. For example, a suit for collection of money owed is almost always preceded with final demand letters sent by the credit (or accounting) department. Similarly, a contract or purchase order dispute is often the subject of increasingly precipitous discussions and negotiations over a period of several weeks or months before finally reaching counsel. Also, the corporate planning/acquisition department could be well down the road toward purchasing another company before counsel is finally asked to put the details on paper.

If corporate counsel has established a good communicative working relationship with the other corporate departments, they will be more likely to casually mention or discuss with him a situation they are handling that they think may turn into a legal problem. If, on the other hand, they view counsel and the law department in a less than desirable way, it is unlikely that they will go out of their way to be cooperative. Counsel will, more often than not, be the "johnny come lately" on the scene and lose the opportunity to apply effective preventive law measures at an early stage.

It matters little to say that in a well-run company the professional managers should spot and bring potential legal problems to counsel at an early stage anyway. Or that a memo from the law department to all officers and managers requiring that all potential legal problems be brought to counsel's attention immediately will solve the problem. The simple fact in the real corporate world is that reliance upon the professional legal know-how of laymen or upon policy statements to bring counsel legal problems at an early stage is rarely as effective as an early warning system developed through counsel's cooperative and communicative working relationship with the other departments.

Innumerable examples can be cited in which another corporate department has been involved in a matter before it came to the attention of the law department (sometimes too late). The following case is an example of a good working relationship between the law department and tax department (separate departments in this corporation). Fortunately, in this instance, although the communication was only a brief "by the way" discussion in the hallway, it was sufficiently timely to allow the implementation of preventive law measures.

> The manager of a wholly-owned subsidiary of the parent corporation for which counsel worked wanted to engage in a new business venture. On a business trip in a nearby state, this manager met a jobber (independent contractor distributor) of diesel fuel supplying the interstate trucking market who was dissatisfied with his current situation. The jobber wanted to purchase diesel fuel supplies for resale from a more competitive refiner but lacked the capital and line of credit to do so.
>
> After discussion they developed a kind of joint venture arrangement in which the subsidiary manager would finance the diesel fuel purchases from the new

refiner for six months; the jobber would train a salesman working for the subsidiary manager in the basics of the business; they would split the profits (if any) at the end of the six-month period; and then they would decide whether to continue the venture and, if so, under what terms and conditions.

Because the jobber told the subsidiary manager that a federal tax identification number and special permit was required to sell diesel fuel intended for use in interstate transportation, the subsidiary manager contacted the tax department at the parent corporation and asked them to obtain the special permit and tax ID number.

Not long afterwards, the corporate tax manager saw counsel in the hallway and asked in a by-the-way manner whether she knew that this subsidiary manager had entered into an agreement with the jobber in a nearby state to sell diesel fuel. She said, "No, I hadn't heard," and started asking him some questions. She discovered that the permit and tax number had been applied for in the name of the subsidiary and that as far as the tax manager knew, they intended doing business in the name of the subsidiary rather than under the jobber's name.

Upon returning to her office, counsel looked in the corporate books of the subsidiary to determine whether they were authorized to do business in that nearby state and found they were not. She immediately called the subsidiary manager to confirm the facts of the business venture, whereupon she told him he would need to apply for a license for the subsidiary to do business in that state. He asked her to do so as soon as possible, since they had already started selling diesel fuel. Within three weeks counsel was able to obtain the appropriate license.

What potential legal problems were avoided by the action of counsel in this case? It is speculative to say, although it is highly questionable, whether the subsidiary could have used the court processes within that nearby state, and no doubt other legal problems would have resulted from not having the license.

Here, then, is a good example of how the other corporate departments in the company for which counsel works can alert him to potential legal problems. The attorney in this case had worked with the tax department manager on several previous occasions and had established good communications with him. Each had previously helped the other in his specialized area of knowledge. Even though the tax manager's comments were "by the way", having met the attorney in the hallway, that communication served as a sufficient early warning of a legal matter that needed attention.

Because other corporate departments are commonly involved with matters before they become serious legal problems, a good and communicative working relationship with them will greatly enhance a corporate counsel's ability to learn about and apply preventive measures to legal problems in the early stages.

Checking the Impact of Legal Decisions

Does this mean checking the legal impact of a corporate counsel's decision? No. Counsel knows what the legal impact of his decisions will be—usually one of achieving compliance with a regulation or law or of protecting against a potential risk. The impact discussed here is the nonlegal impact: The impact his legal decision will have upon the business activities of the corporation. Should that be of any concern to counsel? One can take the view, as some attorneys wrongly do, that counsel's only concern should be the legal impact—whether or not a legal decision achieves compliance with the law. If counsel adopts that perspective and attitude, then he will miss many challenging opportunities to practice truly effective preventive law.

Preventive corporate law simply cannot be practiced effectively in a vacuum without consideration given to the business activities, the people, and, as here, the other corporate departments. Most legal decisions will have a nonlegal impact upon the other corporate departments and their operations. For example, imagine the sweeping impact of a legal decision to require that all corporate expenditures in excess of $500 (or even $5000) be executed only on written contracts approved by the law department. Although counsel's primary concern must be and is correctly for the legal merits of his decision, when such a decision can be modified to diminish an undesirable nonlegal or business impact without lessening its legal merit, has not counsel practiced more effective law in the corporate environment?

Logically, counsel can find out about the nonlegal impact of his legal decisions by communicating with the other corporate departments *before* he issues his work product. Here is an example of an attorney who failed to do so, causing himself a significant amount of rework and wasted effort.

> The vice president in charge of the division responsible for purchasing and trading of industrial chemicals in a corporation (a large conglomerate) came to counsel's office one day with another person who was a recently retired executive of one of their competitors. Their plan was to form a new subsidiary and by utilizing the contacts this retired executive had developed over the years, to "make a killing" in the comparatively small and as yet unregulated marketplace of industrial chemical trading.
>
> They asked counsel to form the subsidiary. After ascertaining that management approval had been obtained, counsel commenced to form the subsidiary. Among the many questions he asked the vice president and the retired executive were in what state they wanted it to be incorporated, the exact nature of the business in which they intended to engage, the amount of capital available for start-up and to initially operate the business, and the persons who would be directors and officers of the subsidiary corporation.
>
> In part, they replied that the retired executive would contribute $20,000 of start-up capital while your company would contribute $80,000. They also said they might want to bring other industrial chemical traders into the venture as shareholders if they were successful. Therefore, counsel logically set-up the corporation with 5,000 common shares author-

ized, 200 to be issued to the retired executive and 800 to be issued to the parent corporation, in order to reflect the proportions of start-up capital contribution. Further, counsel choose to charter the new subsidiary in the state from which they intended to base its operations. He registered the corporate name, ordered a corporate seal, paid the state corporate filing and franchise fees, drafted and appropriately filed the stock subscription agreements, the articles of incorporation, the by-laws, and the first meeting of directors and shareholders.

Counsel made two copies of all the records and placed them in two separate minute books, one to be held at the subsidiary location and one to be held in his custody. He also made an extra copy for the files of the vice president and sent it to him with a note that he was now authorized to do business under the subsidiary company. The vice president then distributed some of these documents to the various departments within the corporation that would be concerned with the subsidiary operations. One such distribution was to the finance and accounting department.

Upon their receipt of these documents a minor crisis occurred. Unknown to counsel, the director of finance of the corporation (to whom the tax department reported) had previously determined that all future subsidiaries of the company should be structured so that they would not be deemed members of a controlled group (as is the case here, since 80 per cent or more of the stock is owned by the parent corporation) under the tax regulations that then require the more time-consuming and less desirable procedure of consolidating the parent's and subsidiary's tax returns. After examining the documents, the director of finance realized the tax returns would have to be consolidated.

The director of finance immediately went to counsel's office and, among other things, asked counsel in an unpleasant manner why he had not talked to him before forming the subsidiary. For some the con-

> versation would have quickly deteriorated from that point; however, this counsel instead tried to find out what was the real problem. Upon learning that the proportion of stock ownership in the subsidiary did not permit the desired form of tax reporting, counsel suggested that they call the vice president of purchasing and trading to see if it could be altered slightly.
>
> Receiving no objection because the relative amounts of start-up capital had just seen "ballpark numbers", counsel proceeded to draft (and refile) the subsidiary papers to increase the share ownership (and contributed capital) of the retired executive so that the parent corporation would own no more than 79 per cent (rather than 80 per cent) of the subsidiary.

Although this illustration had a happy ending, the road utilized to get there was not smooth. Extra work was required by counsel that could have been avoided had he checked with other corporate departments to determine the nonlegal or business impact of his legal decision before forming the subsidiary. He could have distributed the preliminary subsidiary documents before formally filing them. Or he could have telephoned or called a meeting with some of the department managers who would be concerned with the subsidiary and its operations. It makes little difference whether the attorney should have known the tax implications of the 80 per cent equity ownership or whether the finance director shold have previously announced his new policy. What counsel really failed to do was *communicate* with the other corporate departments.

Other corporate departments frequently consult the law department before handling certain business matters, why shouldn't the law department do the same? Why should counsel make a legal decision and implement it within the business framework without first checking with the other corporate departments that may be affected by that decision? The law and a legal decision are not so sacrosanct that they should not be fettered by laymen and business considerations. As a practical matter, since corporate counsel will not have the time nor the need to check with every corporate department about every decision he makes, he should be selective by knowing the crossover effect of his legal decisions.

Knowing the Crossover Effect of Legal Decisions

Most legal decisions made by corporate counsel will have an impact, whether large or small, on other corporate departments. Perhaps no other corporate department has such an across-the-board, pervasive effect on the operations of other corporate departments as does the law department. For that reason it will be of assistance to counsel in the practice of corporate law to know some typical areas and departments affected by his legal decisions.

The following chart depicts a typical organization of corporate departments and functions in a medium-sized industrial company. Try to determine what legal decisions a corporate counsel could make that would crossover and impact in their areas of responsibility. Then compare your results with the following table.

TYPICAL ORGANIZATION OF CORPORATE DEPARTMENTS

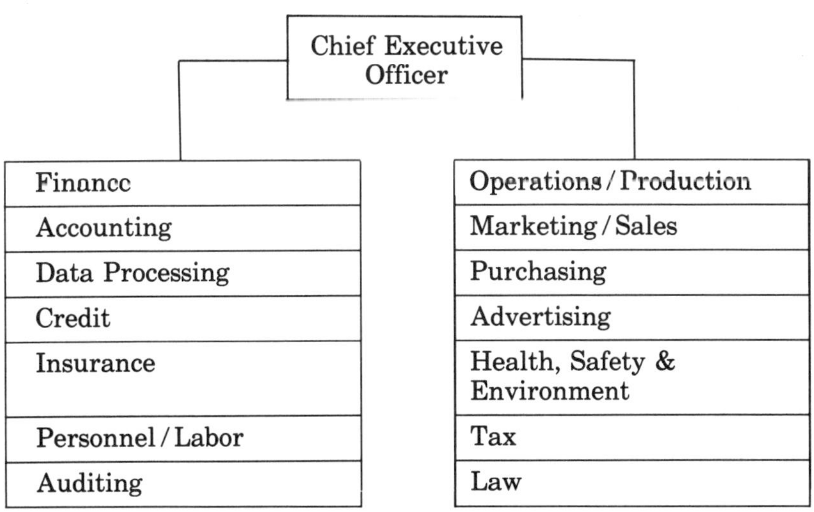

Corporate Department/ Function	Some Crossover Effects of a Legal Decision
Finance Department	
Handles investments, capital expenditures and other financing transactions for the corporation, records such transactions in the financial documents, such as the income statement and balance sheet.	Counsel's definition in contract language of an expenditure as an expense or long-term investment can determine whether the corporation will be able to expense or capitalize it, with the resulting different effects to the income statement.
	Counsel's judgment of the materiality of a lawsuit may effect whether it should be disclosed in the annual report (10K) of the corporation.
Accounting Department	
Records the financial transactions of the company, monitors accounts receivable and accounts payable	Counsel's judgment about whether a sale transaction has been completed may determine at what time the profit or loss can be recorded on the company books, thereby affecting the publicly reported earnings.
Tax Department	
Interprets tax regulations insures proper compliance and reporting in taxable transactions.	The method used to dissolve or liquidate a subsidiary can result in substantial tax benefits (or losses).
	Documentation of an acquisition or merger will substantially affect the resulting tax position.
Auditing Department	
Ascertains whether company operations are conducted and recorded in a generally acceptable manner.	Counsel's judgment whether an adverse decision in a lawsuit is remote, possible, or probable will affect whether an adequate reserve fund has een established and reported by the company.
Credit Department	
Establishes credit policies, monitors accounts receivable and collections.	Counsel's decision whether a claim should be settled, pursued, or defended.

Corporate Department / Function	Some Crossover Effects of a Legal Decision
Insurance Department	
Procures and manages insurance to protect against casualty and other risks.	Counsel's judgment of a lawsuit may affect the reserve balance set by insurance carrier. Counsel's acceptance of risk during contract negotiations.
Data Processing Department	
Processes data and information required to manage the corporation.	Counsel's decision regarding the length of time to retain certain records.
Personnel / Labor Department	
Handles administration of company employee matters and labor agreements or disputes.	Counsel's interpretation of Equal Opportunity regulations, ERISA regulations, and fair bargaining practices.
Purchasing Department	
Procures required materials and / or services required in the corporate operations.	Counsel's interpretation and implementation of Uniform Commercial Code provisions.
Advertising Department	
Promotes the company's product and / or services in various media.	Counsel's legal judgment of advertising copy and substantiation data.
Marketing / Sales Department	
Determines and implements product and / or service market penetration and activity.	Counsel's determination whether pricing policies violate antitrust regulations. Counsel's determination whether local business licenses are required.
Operations / Production Department	
Monitors and controls the production or service activities of the company.	Counsel's judgment of compliance with numerous federal and local regulations affecting operations.

CORPORATE DEPARTMENT/ FUNCTION	SOME CROSSOVER EFFECTS OF A LEGAL DECISION
Health, Safety and Environmental Departments. Establishes and monitors corporations compliance in designated areas.	Counsel's interpretation of the many pertinent federal and local regulations.

Did you know that your legal decisions could have such a pervasive crossover effect in the responsibilities and areas of the other corporate departments? This chart is not a comprehensive digest of the nonlegal ramifications of legal decisions—it is only a small sample of the actual crossover effects. It is presented here as a guide for counsel to begin thinking about and understanding some of the nonlegal ramifications of his decisions.

With that understanding, counsel can continue to build a sound foundation for an effective practice of preventive corporate law not only by establishing a good communicative working relationship with the other corporate departments but by asking about and weighing the nonlegal impact of one's decisions. Remember, the other corporate departments need counsel—but counsel also needs them.

Now read the following case study and decide how you would implement the principles discussed in this STEP THREE.

Case Study Number Three: THE TWO-DAY LICENSING AGREEMENT

The Situation

The executive vice president of the corporation and the president (owner) of a small research and development company come to counsel's office. The executive vice president says that he and this owner want to enter into a business arrangement.

The research and development company has developed and begun test-marketing prototype (catalytic substance) products produced through a unique manufacturing process (patent applied for) but lacks adequate capital to do the further product testing necessary to prove their effectiveness and set up a nationwide marketing campaign and distributor network. Because they believe another much larger company is about to develop a similar manufacturing process and products, he considers it imperative to penetrate the market quickly and effectively. The executive vice president of the corporation is also excited about the potential for these products and wants the corporation to participate in its future growth.

They have discussed an arrangement in which the corporation would obtain the exclusive rights to sell these products in the domestic United States, excluding (maybe) the territory now covered by eight small distributors. In exchange for these rights, the corporation would agree to furnish the necessary capital and personnel required to introduce, market, and distribute the products in a quickly staged nationwide program, limited only by the further product-testing that the corporation will also conduct. Further, they agreed that if the testing and marketing campaign is successful, then the corporation would have the option to obtain certain additional rights (such as manufacturing rights).

The president of the research company wants an agreement that during the next year the corporation will purchase a certain minimum monthly quantity of products at an agreed-upon fixed price to be determined by their cost of manufacturing and will give adequate notice of the corporation's projected monthly purchase requirements. The corporation may then resell the products at any price it can obtain—retaining the difference as profit. The sale and distribution of the products may be carried out under the corporation's name as long as the owner's (research company) trademark is clearly identified on all packages, products, and advertising literature.

The executive vice president wants to begin setting up a distributor organization, hiring people, and selling products on a limited basis within two weeks. They tell you they trust each other, have no problem working together, and have most of the details already settled. All they really need from you, they say, is a short agreement to get something down on paper. Moreover, the president (owner) is leaving town the day after tomorrow, and they want the agreement signed, sealed, and delivered prior to his departure.

The Question

Does that sound familiar to some of you? It seems as if everybody wants a very short agreement (yet everything covered) and they want it today.

What would you do? Tell them you need more time? Start looking in a contract law form book for a licensing or distributor agreement? Dictate or write the first sentence of an agreement off the top of your head when they left?

Although different lawyers would begin in different ways, they would arrive at similar and appropriate results. Probably the majority would have taken notes during the meeting and, after asking several questions, would already have some idea of the framework and type of agreement necessary to cover this projected business venture.

Within the context of this Step Three, what is the best way to proceed? How would the principles apply to these facts?

What Actually Happened

In this case the attorney had, in fact, taken notes and asked questions during the brief meeting and decided the basic type of agreement she would use would be an exclusive licensing agreement, with some provisions of distributor and joint venture agreements incorporated as well.

She subsequently determined that principal areas of discussion in the agreement should include the following: (1) A discussion of the rights, privileges, and territorial extent of the license to be conveyed; (2) a discussion of the obligations of the corporation with regard to the selling and distribution effort, as well as manufacturing should the corporation opt to do so; (3) definition of the minimum and maximum amount of each product the corporation would be required to purchase; (4) a delineation of a firm price list for each product to be purchased, arrived at by a precise formula of the manufacturer's fixed and variable costs; (5) a method to verify the costs used to compute the price list; (6) terms regarding the time schedules of inventory order and delivery and of billings and payment; (7) language regarding the rights and obligations of the parties in the event of unsuccessful product test results; (8) provisions regarding the obligations of the research and development company, including production guarantees, product quality, and warranty; and (9) a discussion regarding control and responsibility of existing distributors. (Can you think of other items that should be addressed? If so, they are probably appropriate.)

That evening and the following morning, this corporate counsel drafted a preliminary agreement incorporating these principal items. She then distributed the draft agreement to several corporate departments (and to the president (owner) and executive vice president), requesting their review and suggested changes at a meeting the following morning. (Which corporate departments would you have distributed it to?) She distributed the draft agreement to the following departments requesting they pay particular attention to the designated items.

Principal Item of Discussion	Department Recommendations Requested
1.	Marketing / Sales
2.	Marketing / Sales, and Operations / Production
3.	Purchasing
4.	Accounting and Finance
5.	Accounting and Auditing
6.	Purchasing and Credit
7.	Operations and Research & Development

8. Marketing / Sales and Purchasing
9. Marketing / Sales and Operations / Production.

At the meeting the following morning (most were prepared but not all), a lively discussion resulted in many useful comments and recommendations. For example, the accounting department stated they would have to meet with the controller of the research and development company for several days before they would be able to arrive at a precise formula for calculating the fixed and variable costs of manufacturing. The marketing / sales and operations departments said they wanted to meet with the eight existing small distributors before determining what responsibilities they would assume for their activities.

Many points were raised that had not been discussed by the owner and executive vice president. By the time the owner was due to leave town late that day, a good and comprehensive agreement was near-at-hand, but it needed substantial redrafting and revision as well as additional information to be forthcoming from the other departments. Everyone then realized that two days had been too short a time in which to put together an adequate agreement (which counsel already knew). The final document was prepared not long thereafter, slightly modified again, and signed.

Author's Comments

In this case it can be clearly seen how the attorney made maximum use of the expertise of the various corporate departments by asking for their changes and recommendations as soon as she drafted the preliminary agreement. She also anticipated the crossover effect and nonlegal impact of the many legal points and contract provisions and distributed it accordingly. For example, during the morning meeting she learned that the accounting department could not develop a precise formula of manufacturing costs without extensive on-site cost auditing and calculation, so she provided for that information to be added later by amendment in an appendix. She also learned about a potential legal problem: The market / sales department had received information about poor performance of some existing distributors—which accounted for their reluctance to assume responsibility for them. As a result, she included appropriate contingent language to protect the corporation.

Because corporate counsel here had good lines of communication with the other corporate departments and used them to the greatest extent possible, she was able to efficiently produce a comprehensive document that was practical, useful, and undoubtedly helpful in preventing future legal problems. This case demonstrates the value of communicating with other corporate departments when practicing effective preventive law in the corporation.

Step Four: Understand the Law Department Function

Introduction

The function of the law department in the corporation is obvious: to practice law. But there's more to it than just that.

Practicing law in the corporation can encompass a variety of styles, techniques, and approaches, in part resulting from the differently perceived functions of the law department. For example, one can point to the traditional styles of practicing law and perceive the law department's function as simply one of advising on legal issues (waiting for a client to ask a legal question) or of primarily engaging in adversary tactics (fighting legal battles with opponents).

In reality the typical law department's function in the corporation today includes those traditional functions as well as functions recently beginning to emerge and be recognized, such as practicing preventive law and advising on law-related (law / business) issues. These functions will be discussed with particular emphasis on giving advice in law-related areas, but, first, counsel should look at the corporate law department's function from an even broader perspective by asking the most basic question: "Why are law departments established in corporations in the first place?"

Answering that question gives corporate counsel a better perspective from which to practice preventive law. By grasping the law department's functions in the larger picture, one can then focus his own preventive law practice more effectively and successfully because a good foundation must include a solid understanding of all its parts. In the corporation, knowing not only the business, the people, and the other corporate departments but also the proper function of the law department is essential for any corporate counsel today.

Why Have a Corporate Law Department?

Ask the question of why have a corporate law department exists not from the viewpoint of a corporate counsel but from the viewpoint of a layman—the president or chief executive officer of the corporation. (Many CEO's have asked themselves that exact question, both derogatorily and otherwise.) It is useful for counsel to consider the corporate management's purpose behind a decision to establish (or expand) a corporate law department because in that way he will gain a necessary focus to guide his own practice of law in the corporation most effectively.

Some counsel assume that all large or rapidly growing corporations need lawyers in-house, just as they need other professionals like accountants, engineers, or data processing (computer) managers. They are wrong. Several of the largest, well-run companies in the United States today still operate exclusively with retained outside counsel or with a minimum in-house legal staff. And that is even more so in the case of medium and small corporations.

Nevertheless, one is correct if he observes a trend in recent years toward the establishment and expansion of in-house corporate law departments. The most popular reason given for this trend is that corporate law departments are more cost-effective. That could change in the years to come, however, as the private bar becomes more competitive and cost-conscious and as the costs to maintain a staff of corporate attorneys continue to increase. There are, however, many more less obvious reasons that the executive management of corporations hire lawyers in-house.

Place yourself in the position of the chief executive officer of a corporation in the following example and see how many reasons you can think of that would compel you to hire in-house counsel. Then ask yourself what relevance, if any, those reasons would have to your law practice had you been an in-house counsel for that corporation. In other words, what do those reasons tell you to focus upon when building your foundation for an effective preventive law practice?

Imagine you are the Chief Executive Officer (with a marketing background) for a small ($50 million sales) but rapidly growing company. You have three manufacturing facilities in geographically dispersed locations that upgrade a raw material into a product that your company then markets and distributes. Your company has always used outside counsel exclusively; however, the annual legal bill from the firm you have on retainer is now reaching an amount that prompts you to wonder whether the cost might justify in-house counsel. Your rapidly expanding manufacturing operations seem to draw the ever-increasing attention of numerous government regulations and rules.

An example is the regulations under the Occupational Safety and Health Act (OSHA). A facility at one of your locations was the subject of a random inspection by an OSHA agent about a month ago. That inspection resulted in a citation for two non-serious violations of the OSHA regulations. Since the violations were the first your company had received and the fines were minimal, you agreed to accept the citation without contesting its validity. Your outside law firm advised that you could contest the citations but that the expense to do so would be far in excess of the amount of the fines. They also correctly pointed out, however, that an accumulation of OSHA citations could lead to increased penalties for repeated violations.

One afternoon, you (the Chief Executive Officer) receive a telephone call from your plant manager at this same location. He tells you that the same OSHA inspector has returned and is sitting in his office. The OSHA inspector has received a complaint from one of the plant employees and wants to inspect the facility in order to investigate that complaint. The inspector says that you have the right to refuse to admit him to the premises, but if you do so, he can simply get a warrant for the inspeciton and return that same afternoon, at which time you would be required by law to admit him. The plant manager asks what he should do.

You say to the plant manager, "See if you can get the OSHA inspector to wait a few minutes while I check with our outside attorneys." You immediately call the law firm partner who handles the legal work for the corporation, but his secretary tells you that he is in court and won't be back except for a few minutes early tomorrow morning or until after the trial. You ask if there is any way he can be reached, and the secretary replies that it is very difficult to reach him while he is in trial. You ask whether the associate attorney who sometimes works with him is available, and she says he is also in court with the partner.

You impatiently say that you have an OSHA inspector wanting to look at your manufacturing facility, he is waiting in the plant manager's office, and you need to get back to them within ten or fifteen minutes. Is there any attorney I can talk to there who can answer some questions? She says, "Let me see, I think Mr. Young Attorney is in his office. Just a minute, please." You hold for four or five minutes, Mr. Young Attorney gets on the telephone line, and you quickly describe the situation to him and ask, "Do you think we should admit the OSHA inspector?" Mr. Young Attorney replies that he doesn't usually handle OSHA matters but can research the question and call you back. You say that the inspector is waiting in the office and that you need an answer very soon. He says he'll get right on it and try to get back to you as soon as possible.

After one hour the plant manager calls back and says to you, "The OSHA inspector decided we were trying to put him off, got mad, and just left to get a warrant, saying he would be back soon."

In the middle of the morning of the following day, Mr. Young Attorney calls to say that you are not required to admit the OSHA inspector, that you may refuse his admittance and require him to obtain a warrant. You say, "I know that. What I wanted to know was whether we should require him to get a warrant?" Mr. Young Attorney replies "Well, exactly what do you manufacture in this facility?" You say, "Never mind—the OSHA inspector already got a warrant and made his inspection early this morning . . . thanks, anyway" and hang up the phone.

Do some of you think this is an unusual example? It is not. An instance not unlike this one occurs frequently in today's business world and illustrates several reasons why there is a trend toward establishing a corporate law practice in-house.

Before going further, a qualification should be added to this example. This illustration is not intended to be critical of private law firms but is set forth rather as a commentary upon some of the problems involved when handling several clients simultaneously as opposed to one exclusively (as in the corporation). Indeed, many fine private firms have sufficient depth and expertise to prevent this type of problem from occurring, whereas the opposite is sometimes true in a corporate legal staff.

Having said that, what are some of the reasons that might prompt the Chief Executive Officer in this example to establish an in-house law department? Here are a few (taking them in the order of their appearance in this illustration):

Lack of Background in Law

The majority of chief executive officers and presidents do not have a background in law but rather in marketing, finance, production, or some other area. As a result, it is difficult for them to handle legal decisions even in a superficial manner, especially those requring on-the-spot judgments as in this OSHA incident. This difficulty becomes even more critical with the trend toward enforcement of government regulations by criminal sanction. Therefore, laymen management in the corporation feels the need to have legal expertise on their staff to complement their own background.

Cost Justification

As the company grows, so unavoidably does the annual billing for legal fees. In the example, one can safely assume the company would be billed for at least some of the time spent by Mr. Young Attorney researching the question, even though it turned out that the advice was neither timely nor on point. In order to achieve good corporate earnings, a chief executive officer must control expenditures as well as revenues.

Explosion of Government Regulations

Just consider the new regulations under the Environmental Protection Agency from 1956 to 1976:

1956—Water Pollution Control Act
1962—Hazaardous Substance Labeling Act
1967—Federal Hazardous Substance Act (FHSA)
1970—Consumer Product Safety Act (CPSA)
1970—Occupational Safety & Health Act (OSHA)
1970—Clean Air Act (CAA)
1972—Federal Water Pollution Control Act (FWPCA)
1974—Safe Drinking Water Act (SWDA)
1976—Resource Conservation and Recovery Act (RCRA)
1976—Toxic Substance Control Act

As a company grows and becomes larger, it often becomes overwhelmed with regulatory compliance problems not previously encountered, particularly if it has recently become publicly held. The in-house legal function is a logical place to centralize regulatory interpretation and compliance.

Immediate Access to Legal Advice Required

The corporate business world usually moves at a fast pace, especially in a rapidly growing company. An in-house legal staff not only increases access to legal advice but also the speed with which the advice can be received because the in-house attorney knows the business and the people and does not require lengthy explanations to routine questions before evaluating the facts. He is (or should be) an expert in the legal areas affecting the corporation most often.

Have you thought of some other reasons why this CEO would want to establish an in-house legal capability? If you did, they are probably correct. Now, what do these reasons tell a corporate counsel about his foundation for practicing corporate law? First, they demonstrate the importance of establishing a good, communicative client relationship so that immediate access to counsel's advice is available when needed. Second, it shows the value of knowing the business and of having a specialized knowledge of the laws and regulations affecting your industry (Step Five), all of which would have helped the outside attorney in this example. Also, this example should give counsel some insight about the intended functions of a law department—both the traditional functions and preventive ones. These functions will be discussed by carrying the OSHA illustration into the next several sections.

Remember the Traditional Functions

By reflecting upon the OSHA incident in the last section, one can easily see a traditional function of the corporate law department: to provide easy access for corporate management to legal advice from an attorney knowledgeable about the business and the laws and regulations affecting their industry.

This basic function can be called "advising on law issues" or, more simply, without intending to diminish its importance, "dispensing law." What should this function mean to the corporate attorney? For most, it should mean that one will not only want to build a broad foundation as a general practitioner of the corporate law but also become an expert in the pertinent industry laws. In most corporations, corporate counsel will be confronted with a wide variety of issues requiring knowledge in many different areas of the law. In short, counsel will feel as if he never knows enough law. That is all right, as long as he recognizes that fact and continues to build upon his foundation a greater knowledge of the law—time and experience will take care of much of that shortcoming. Specifically, in the OSHA illustration, the dispensing law function could have been performed by an in-house counsel, based on his knowledge of the OSHA regulations, by advising the CEO that they were not required to admit the OSHA inspector without a warrant and letting the CEO make the final decision whether to permit admission.

What else might the corporate counsel have advised the CEO? He could have performed another traditional function of the corporate law department by taking the "adversary approach." Counsel could have advised the CEO that he should refuse admittance to the inspector until he obtained a warrant so that they could later, in addition to contesting any resulting citations, challenge the validity of the warrant permitting the inspection. This is a valid approach to some legal issues that will confront corporate counsel and should be used when appropriate, for example, in the defense of unfounded claims or litigation.

Two traditional functions of the corporate law department then are "dispensing law" and the "adversary approach". Since these are well-recognized functions of a law practice, they will not be discussed further. Remember that both will have their place and be important in a counsel's practice of corporate law.

Now under the "preventive law functions" of the corporate law department, how would counsel advise the CEO in the OSHA example?

Focus on the Preventive Functions

In the OSHA incident the most obvious preventive law function that could have been used by a corporate counsel would have been to try to prevent the cause of the complaint resulting in the inspection in the first place. This might have been accomplished by spot or routine inspections conducted by the company itself (under the direction of the law department) or by other programs of training, monitoring, and control that promote compliance with pertinent law and regulations.

Another useful preventive law measure would have been to develop a company procedure to be followed in the event of such an incident. In-house counsel, in conjunction with the plant managers and other interested parties, could have predetermined the desired corporate response to a spot or routine OSHA inspection or perhaps a system of immediate notification to the law department and others, including appropriate back-up procedures if someone could not be reached.

Either of these "preventive law" measures could have eliminated the problems encountered by the CEO. They may have prevented a more serious legal problem from occurring by the mishandling of the incident or the inconsistent handling of such incidents on a company-wide basis, since OSHA violations accumulate regardless of plant location.

These approaches show the real and practical value to the corporation of the preventive function of the corporate law department. Preventive law measures are most frequently employed across the entire spectrum of corporate activities with the intent to achieve compliance or detect noncompliance with the law at an early stage—as opposed to the more traditional dispensing law and adversary functions, which tend to be responsive rather than preventive. Preventive law measures such as these are becoming increasingly recognized and sophisticated today not only by the corporate counsel but also by the lay corporate management, and a corporate counsel today is well advised to focus upon them.

Since these more routine preventive law measures are readily recognized and used by today's corporate counsel, however, they will not be discussed in detail. Instead the focus here is on a less recognized but equally valuable preventive law function of today's corporate law department. For lack of a better name, this function is called "giving advice on law/business issues".

Give Advice on Law/Business Issues

What exactly is the preventive law function of "giving advice on law/business issues?"

It is a recommendation made by corporate counsel to lay management on an issue that is somewhere between a pure legal question and a pure business decision. Some corporate counsel make decisions and recommendations like that every day. Many others, however, are afraid, feel restrained, or simply have not thought about departing from the pure legal question—by applying their skills as an attorney and knowledge of the law to the many issues in the business environment that need resolving.

Consider the OSHA incident again. Clearly, if corporate counsel advised the CEO that they were not required to admit the OSHA inspector without a warrant, he would be answering a legal issue. But if after receiving that legal answer, suppose the CEO said, "O.K. So what do you think we should do?" Would corporate counsel be correct in saying: "I don't know . . . that's a business decision?"

Many would say no and would consider counsel's recommendation of whether to admit the inspector to be a legitimate application of an attorney's skills and knowledge to the business environment. It is, in fact, giving advice on a law/business issue. It is somewhere between a pure legal decision and pure business one. Some counsel would no doubt disagree professionally and would be reluctant to give a definitive answer to the CEO's question. What about other responses the corporate counsel could make to the CEO's question?

Counsel could have responsded to the CEO by saying, "I recommend we ask the OSHA inspector what the exact purpose of his inspection is and, if we think it's reasonable, limit the scope of his inspection in writing to that purpose; and if he doesn't agree, require him to obtain a warrant." Is that a good recommendation? Does it not apply legal principles and legal judgment to find an answer? (Query: Is it not also a solution?) It should prevent the concern of legal problems (OSHA) arising because of an overbroad inspection. Granted, it is not as protective *on the surface* as the adversary approach of requiring a warrant. But the question here is Does that answer by counsel border upon making a business decision? Maybe, but this answer is better referred to as giving advice on a law/business issue. Does it make any difference what it is called? Yes. The function of the law department is not to make business decisions.

What if counsel simply responded, "I don't think we need to worry too much. Let's let him in." Or if he said, "No, let's give him as much trouble as we can—keep him out." Do these answers look more like counsel is making a nonlegal or business decision? Yes, because counsel is expressing a feeling or reaction rather than applying his skills and knowledge as an attorney. Oddly enough then, observe that the basis or rational used by counsel to arrive at an answer will sometimes change an otherwise legitimate answer to a law/business issue to one resembling purely a business decision.

At this point some may feel that there is a fine dividing line between what one could call a legal decision, a law/business decision, and a business decision. That is correct. No uncommonly in the business environment, legal and business issues go hand-in-hand and are inextricably intertwined. It is the gray area between the legal and business decisions that is referred to here as the law/business issues (or legal-related issues if you prefer). Notwithstanding the difficulty in sometimes defining and pinpointing them, addressing law/business issues is an important function in the effective practice of preventive corporate law. Why is giving advice on law/business issues such an important function of the corporate law practices and one upon which counsel will want to focus? There are several reasons.

First, it is an area in which counsel can make great contributions to the corporate operations. Confronting and searching for answers to law/business issues helps one find solutions to the corporate legal problems rather than just legal answers found within a vacuum with a result more akin to "dispensing law."

Second, this function represents one of the most effective applications of the skills and knowledge of an attorney to the business environment. It is often results in a more productive practice of preventive law within the corporate operations than the more familar, traditional approaches to practicing law, although both are needed.

Third, even though giving advice on law/business issues is one of the least recognized and discussed functions of the corporate law department, it holds the greatest promise for the successful evolution of future corporate law departments.

Fourth, corporate counsel are constantly confronted with law/business issues in their everyday law practice, but if they fail to recognize and act upon them, they will have neglected many unique opportunities to contribute to the corporation.

Fifth, because some law/business issues present difficult questions about the "fine dividing line" between the law and business issue, the more counsel focuses upon them, the more prepared he will be to handle them effectively.

Sixth, provided counsel has established a good foundation for practicing preventive corporate law, he is more qualified than most layment to decide law/business issues. He has the unique capability to apply his skills and knowledge as an attorney to arrive at a judgment that properly balances some of the business considerations with the legal considerations.

The following diagram depicts conceptually what has been discussed so far in this step. Note that because business considerations play a relatively small role in the traditional functions of the law department (dispensing law and the adversary approach), they are not as appropriate for answering the law/business issues as is the preventive law function. Also note that a layman with a legal background may be qualified to answer some law/business issues. And finally, some issues are decided by concurrence between the layman and law department.

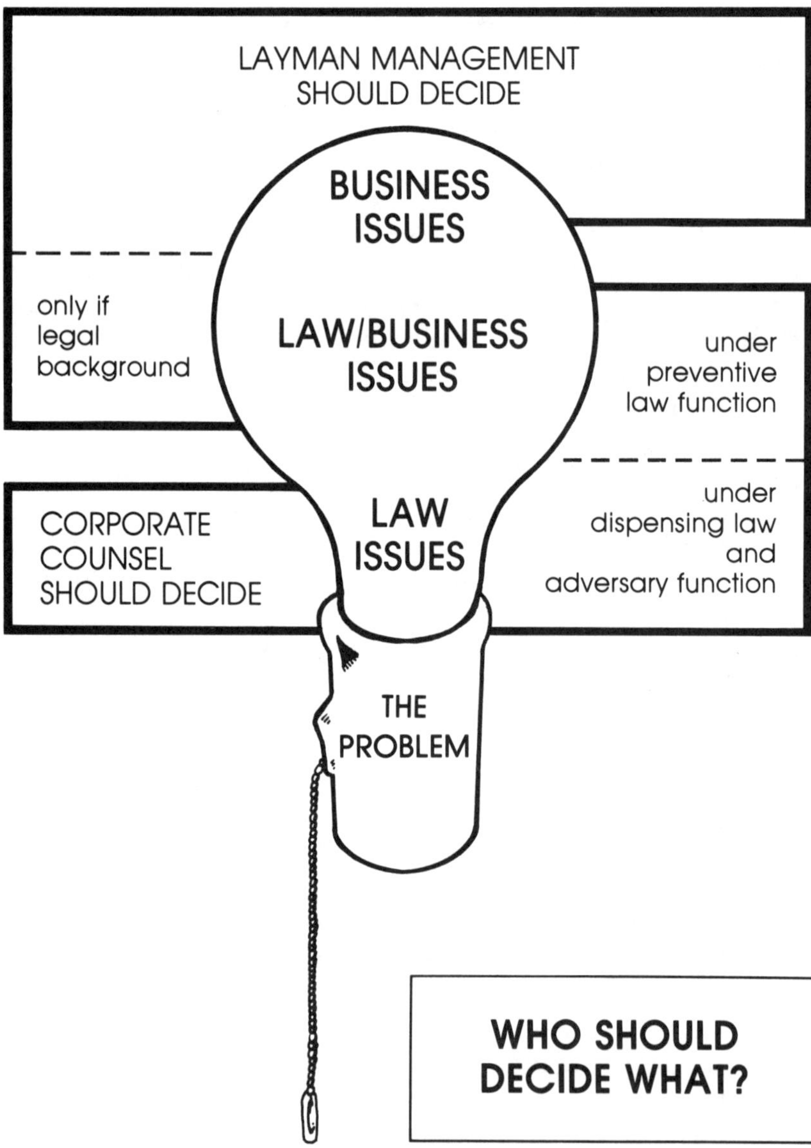

A Practical Case in Point

To this point, law/business has been described and its importance in the practice of preventive corporate law has been discussed. Turning to a practical case in point, note how the answers by counsel below progress from one of responding to the simple legal issue, to the law/business one, and finally to a business issue (decision).

Consider the common problem in corporate law of negligence. Assume that counsel is corporate counsel for a corporation engaged primarily in providing services and that there is no formal corporate (or law department) policy on the issue of accepting contractual liability for the company's negligence. Here are the facts followed by three different answers by corporate counsel.

<u>The Facts</u>

> A business manager in the corporation brings to the corporate counsel a contract form proposed by a potential client for whom he wants to perform a service for a fee. Counsel reads the contract and finds a paragraph stating that the corporation will be responsible for any cost, loss, or damage resulting from the company's negligence. The corporation's insurance carrier, as with most insurance companies, is very reluctant to give coverage for poor workmanship (negligence). So with respect to this paragraph, counsel is faced with an uninsurable risk, the cost of which cannot be competitively passed through in the price charged for the services performed. How should counsel advise the businss manager?
>
> Would he advise him as follows:

<u>Answer #1:</u>

> Counsel could point out the paragraph about liability for negligence to the business manager and advise him that by common law a person or company is resonsible for his negligence, that statutes court decisions and in a few states continue to apply this principle regardless of what a contract says, but that in the majority of jurisdictions corporations are free to agree upon and accept the extent to which each

will be liable for damages resulting from their negligence. Counsel further advises that this paragraph would make the company responsible for its negligence and, further, that this liability could include loss of profits and other consequential or indirect damages.

In response the business manager says, "I understand—what do you think we should do?"

Wisely keeping on his "legal hat", counsel says to the business manager, "Negligence is usually defined by the courts as a failure to exercise the due diligence as due care that would have been used by a reasonable man in a similar circumstance". He says, "What's that supposed to mean?" Counsel replies it means that if the employees performing this service use substantially poorer workmanship than would have been used by a majority of the corporation's competitors, then, depending upon the facts, a court might hold that the company failed to exercise due care and is therefore negligent and responsible for the resulting damages.

The manager says, "Well, we're not perfect—we make some mistakes—but I think we're as good as our competitors. But I don't have any extra money in the contract. If we had to redo some of our work, we would have to take a loss on the job, which I can't afford to do. How big a chance do you think we would be taking in accepting this negligence paragraph?"

The corporate counsel says, "I don't know. That's a business decision you will have to make."

Is that a correct answer by counsel? Clearly the advice about negligence and the meaning of the language in that paragraph constitutes giving advice on a legal issue (the dispensing law function). But what about on the issue of whether *to accept* the language in the paragraph? Would you call that a law/business issue? Or was this attorney correct in calling it a business decision? Some would say it it still a legal question because it is about negligence—a frequently appearing concept in the law. That, however, is not a well-reasoned conclusion unless the business managers in your corporation had first decided the negligence (or liability assumption) issue across-the-board, followed then by a law department policy, which councel was simply interpreting and applying. The question of whether to accept the paragraph is an example of a law/business issue because although the legal principles determine the meaning of the language, the business question of whether the company can afford financially to undertake the risk is equally pertinent. Consider this following second possible answer by corporate counsel.

Answer #2:

Counsel gives the same advise as in answer #1, but in response to the business manager's question about "how big a chance . . . would (we) be taking . . . would (we) be taking councel replies, "Based upon my knowledge of the problems you have had in past service contracts, it seems likely that you would be held negligent under this contract language for similar mistakes. The difference here is that you would have to pay for the rework and be responsible for other damages. If you have no extra money or contingency in your contract price, you should probably either delete this clause or arrive at some compromise—like setting a dollar amount limit on what you will be liable for in the event of your negligence."

Now stop and think a minute. Has this second answer by counsel entered into the realm of a business decision? Perhaps for some, but here it should be considered as a good and legitimate answer to a law/business issue. It constituted a considered judgment based, in part, upon this counsel's well-established preventive law foundation, that is, he knew the business, the people, and the industry law, which enabled him to appreciate the "problems . . . in past service contracts . . . ." and the potential results under this contract. With this background he was more qualified to make or strongly recommend the appropriate law/business decision than the business manager (assuming no legal background). It also demonstrates an effective application of his legal skills and knowledge to the business environment. The following is a third possible answer by counsel.

Answer #3:

What if counsel responded to the business manager's question about "how big a chance . . ." by saying "If I were you, I'd go ahead and take the risk. From what I understand you guys need the business, don't you?"

Now, does this answer constitute a business decision? Yes. Some might say this counsel's answer is really based upon his judgment that their risk of incurring liability (negligence) under this contract is minimal—but with the meager facts given, that is an unwarranted assumption. Instead, this attorney made a business decision, and did so in error, based upon his feelings and nonlegal opinion regarding a business matter (". . . you guys need the business, don't you?"), rather than using his legal judgment and skills to resolve the law/business issue, as counsel did in Answer #2. Making that type of decision is a pure business matter, not a part of the corporate law department function.

A fourth possible answer to the business manager's question has been deliberately omitted because it is really not an answer at all. Nevertheless, it used time and again by attorneys (sometimes unintentionally) to their great disadvantage and to the dissatisfaction of their client. As in the first answer, the attorney would begin by giving his advice to the legal issues on negligence and the meaning of the language. But in response to the question about whether to accept the language, rather than forthrightly saying that is a business decision (Answer #1) or offering his considered judgment to the law/business issue (Answer #2), the attorney would pretend to answer the question or at least sidestep the issue by dispensing more and more law, perhaps ad infinitum. Answering the question in that manner sometimes prompts the familar phrase used by layman after they leave an attorney's office of "What did he say?"

This case with its several different possible responses is only one illustration of many that will confront counsel today in the practice of corporate law. In fact, one can correctly say that the majority of problems confronting corporate counsel today are, or will be before they have finished working with them, involved with issues in law-related and law/business areas. For that reason, if none other, counsel is wise to recognize and be prepared to deal with law/business issues.

Confronting and resolving law/business issues, however, is also an emerging dimension and function in today's corporate law practice and is destined to become increasingly recognized and sophisticated. And because it is an excellent way for a attorney to apply his skills and knowledge of the law to the business setting in a practical and effective way, handling law/business issues will be addressed several times throughout the remainder of this book. Do not forget, however, the equally important traditional functions of the corporate law department. And also know what is not the function.

What Is Not the Function?

Occasionally attorneys become so involved with the business aspects of a problem that the result is to the detriment of their professionalism and of the law department. Although no one would want to impede the development of a corporate attorney into a business manager, should he and the corporation want that, a corporate attorney must always keep in mind that his function is in the law and law-related areas. Although counsel may often make decisions in the gray area between the business and legal issues, he should never be so presumptious to think he is "running the company" or making all the decisions for the business managers, as some counsel have. In most instances, that is simply not the case. There is usually much more to a business operation and decision than a corporate counsel will ever see or recognize when talking to a business manager. In other words, one should keep his legal hat on while applying his legal knowledge and skills to the business area (law/business issues) by always being careful to stay away from pure business decisions.

Some corporate officers and departments will resent corporate counsel's intrusion into their perceived area of business jurisdiction. Sometimes they are right. Counsel should learn to recognize these reactions, learn to deal with them, and continue to practice preventive law in the best way that he can—for the greatest benefit of the law department and the corporation.

Read the following case study, which provides a good illustration based upon an actual case involving the "Fine Dividing Line" between a corporate counsel's advice on legal issue and his subsequent advice when those legal issues turned into law/business issues or even pure business ones. You be the judge.

Case Study Number Four: THE FINE DIVIDING LINE.

The Situation

Counsel is an Assistant General Counsel in the law department of a corporation that manufactures and installs capital equipment and machinery used in the production and process lines of industrial plants. The company also performs limited engineering services necessary to adapt the machinery to a customer's particular specifications and needs. Such capital equipment for a single production line can involve millions of dollars worth of complex machinery housed within a facility larger than several auditoriums. For the past four years counsel has been involved with, or responsible for, the negotiation (from a legal standpoint) of nearly all major capital equipment contracts entered into by the company.

Counsel is presently in the final stages of drafting and negotiating with a customer a particularly long and complex contract for the manufacture and installation of machinery in two paper-mill production lines that includes a customer option for two additional production lines in a phased program. It is a multimillion dollar contract extending over several years and would be of obvious value to the earnings and reputation of your medium-sized company.

The division vice president in charge of this potential project is extremely eager, as are the other corporate officers of your company, to obtain the work because, among other reasons, the company has not previously dealt with this customer, who is one of the leaders in the domestic pulp wood and paper industry. The traditional posture during contract negotiations and the accepted function of the law department within the corporation is to advise on all legal issues and on legal-related (law/business) issues, when appropriate. Customarily, the business managers make the final decisions on whether to accept or reject specific contract language unless it is primarily legal.

To this point the negotiations have been unusually difficult for counsel because the division vice president has seemed to yield on nearly every point of dispute. The four key areas in most contract negotiations are (1) responsibility for errors in the design and specification of the capital equipment to be manufactured and installed by the company; (2) the language limiting the warranty for defective parts to one year and to two years in the case of a few integral parts; (3) indemnification and insurance provisions defining responsibility for negligence, and (4) the interpretation of, and payment for, any work required beyond the original scope.

Against counsel's advice, the division vice president has agreed that the capital equipment manufactured by the company will be "fit for the purpose intended by the customer" even though the customer is to furnish all design specifications. Further, he agreed to extend the warranty on all parts to two years, on the integral parts for five years, and to perform all required extra work at no cost unless "in the customer's opinion" the added work is "outside the intent of the original scope, and not caused by error of the company". The remaining key point to be settled is in the area of indemnification and insurance, and counsel has just learned the division vice president agreed to be responsible for any liability or damage resulting from the negligence of the company. (The company normally agrees to be responsible only for gross negligence and only then if adequate insurance coverage can be procured).

Counsel has learned further that the formal contract-signing event is to take place tomorrow afternoon and that counsel is to fly with them on the company plane and to be present at the meeting in case there are any last-minute changes or problems.

Counsel emphasized again to the division vice president the legal pitfalls and counsel's dissatisfaction with these contract provisions, but he said although he understood counsel's concerns, they could be overcome with good project management; and because this was such an extremely important project to the company, he was willing to take the risk involved with the work.

The Question

What would you do as this assistant general counsel? You strongly advised the division vice president about the legal and law/business issues raised by the key contract areas. The business manager listened to your advice but made a business decision to accept the risk and go forward. Should that be the end of the story? Is acceptance of each of these contract provisions a legal decision, a law/business one, or primarily a business decision? Or is it all three? Who should make those decisions? What about the decision to accept or reject the contract as a whole?

What Actually Happened

In this case the assistant general counsel "went over the head" of the division vice president. It was an extremely difficult decision for him to make, but he decided the circumstances were sufficiently unusual and potentially risky to the corporation to deserve a second opinion and second look. Therefore, after learning about the final agreement on the indemnification language and the impending contract-signing, the assistant general counsel reviewed the negotiations and contract provisions, with the general counsel of the corporation. He expressed his strong concern about the several contract provisions and said that although any one of them by itself may be acceptable, their cumulative effect constituted a risk substantially greater than the potential benefits of the project to the corporation. He said he knew he was entering into the business area of whether the contract as a whole should be accepted, but in this case he thought the potential risk demanded it.

The general counsel concurred with his judgment and immediately discussed the matter with the executive vice president of the corporation. The executive vice president became sufficiently concerned that he decided a last-minute meeting should be held with the customer. Early the following morning he, the general counsel, the assistant general counsel, and the division vice president flew to the customer's headquarters and worked well into the evening in an attempt to clarify and renegotiate several of the contract provisions before contract signing. In fact, a number of the provisions were modified, but the contract as finally signed represented greater risks than normally assumed by the company.

Author's Comments

In this case the assistant general counsel correctly identified the key contract provisions that raised significant legal and law/business issues. He further correctly distinguished that it was the business manager's responsibility to decide whether to accept those risks—at least with respect to the contract when taken as a whole.

Where he had difficulty was in the gray area confronted by many corporate attorneys, that is, the fine dividing line where a legal decision transforms into primarily a business decision or remains primarily a legal decision. Here, although each of the contract provisions taken individually could have been viewed correctly as legal or law/business issues appropriate for decision by the assistant general counsel rather than the division vice president, acceptance of the contract as a whole is traditionally the business decision. Nevertheless, in this case that business decision was sufficiently colored by significant law-related risk to justify intrusion by the law department.

As a practical matter, issues of this type are often resolved by joint decision and concurrence between both the legal and business counterparts in the corporation. But note especially that in this example the assistant general counsel did not limit himself to simply dispensing law by saying "Oh well, those are business decisions. I've given him my legal advice, and now it's his problem". Instead he confronted the problems and took action on issues that were somewhere between the pure legal matter and the pure business decision. He practiced effective preventive corporate law.

By way of collateral comment, you might speculate what the general counsel could have done had the executive vice president not scheduled the meeting to renegotiate the contract provisions. He might have then gone to the president of the corporation or to the board of directors had he felt it necessary—(law departments often report with a solid line to the board of directors to enable their independence of judgment and action). And then perhaps in a serious enough situation, he could have resigned. These are difficult decisions that you will encounter during your practice of corporate law, but ones that you will also find exciting and capable of giving you the feeling of accomplishment by having made significant contributions to the corporation.

Step Five: Learn the Law in Your Industry

Introduction

This is the last step in laying a solid foundation for an effective practice of preventive law in the corporation. Counsel should now be well-prepared about the corporate setting in which he will be practicing law. He should know the business of his corporation, he should know the people, he should be able to communicate with the other corporate departments, and he should understand the functions of the corporate law department.

Now, to round out that good foundation, he will need only to learn the law in his industry. Unfortunately, as will be seen, learning the law that is relevant to the industry will not, in some cases, be as easy as it sounds.

First, the kind of laws that are likely to affect the industry and some reasons why it will be necessary to become knowledgeable about them will be examined. Then an example showing why it is important to focus, at least initially, on those laws and regulations most relevant to the industry will be offered. Finally, an examination of why counsel must become an expert with many of those laws and some ways to keep current about new developments with them will be made.

The general principles and theories of law learned in law school, and perhaps later while practicing law, are excellent primers for practicing law in the corporation and ones that no attorney can do without. But they are not enough. Without becoming knowledgeable about the laws pertinent to his industry, counsel may end up practicing law from within a vacuum, not unlike trying to practice law without knowing the business of his corporation. Although an attorney can get by, as a few do, by relying on "osmosis" over a period of years to learn the industry laws, that is rarely, if ever, as effective as making a concentrated and deliberate effort to build the proper foundation. In order to spot a legal program, prevent a legal problem from occurring, or resolve a legal problem by finding a solution, counsel must first know the law applicable to that situation.

Corporate counsel is in the unique position of being able to devote a significant portion of his practice toward learning and working with the laws and regulations that frequently affect the industry(ies) of his corporation. It is an opportunity he will not want to pass up and one that will pay him many times over in the increased ease and effectiveness with which he will be able to practice corporate preventive law in his particular company.

Be Knowledgeable About All of It

Which body of law(s) should counsel become knowledgeable about? Not the type of laws he is likely to find succinctly summarized in a hornbook or textbook, although in a few industries he may be lucky enough to find such a partial listing. Nor just the traditional laws enacted by legislative bodies. In general, counsel should become knowledgeable about any law, regulation, rule, trade practice, or custom that affects the industry sufficiently that knowledge of it would help counsel detect, prevent, or resolve a legal problem in his corporation.

That is saying quite a bit. Counsel will not be able to learn all of those laws in six months, nor will he probably ever be able to become an expert in all of them. Remember, the law department must function in the entire gamut of corporate activities, and counsel will often feel as if he never knows enough. But unless he is assigned as, or has chosen to become, a specialist, counsel's first objective in practicing preventive law should be to establish a general practice in which he is knowledgeable about as many of these laws as possible. In so doing, he will then be prepared to detect and prevent the most frequently occurring legal problems in his company and industry.

In order to become knowledgeable about the laws affecting his industry, counsel may need to know more about how to identify them. The laws affecting most industries can be classified into three broad categories:

(1) Customs, trade usage, and words of art
(2) Local, state, and federal statutes and regulations, and
(3) Court decisions, arbitration awards, and settlements.

Attorneys who have already practiced corporate law for several years may prefer different classifications for the laws affecting their industries.

Customs, Trade Usage, and Words of Art

Some of the examples in STEP ONE: LEARN THE BUSINESS concerned words of art and customs in the industry, such as the "take-or-pay" contract. This first category of laws is an extremely important one to focus upon.

Words of art and unique customs are found within virtually every industry and are often accorded significant weight in court decisions. As seen earlier, they sometimes form a kind of sublanguage or shorthand communication between the parties. As such, they constitute a clear statement of intent and meeting of the minds and take on the color and force of law.

Counsel will be prudent in his practice of corporate law always to be alert for words, phrases, and concepts in his industry which are, or seem to be, based upon a custom, common practice, or some kind of trade usage. When he thinks he may have confronted terminology of this type, counsel should ask questions of laymen to try to determine their commonly understood meanings and ramnifications. He might consider that any words or phrases about which even one expert would testify to a commonly understood meaning worthy of his attention. This is a category of laws that counsel must learn and incorporate in his foundation for an effective preventive practice in the corporation and industry.

Local, State, and Federal Statutes and Regulations

The second broad category of laws, arbitrarily defined as local, state, and federal statutes and regulations, will be easier to identify and learn about, although they will be far more numerous. As can well be imagined, in today's society this is the category of laws a corporate attorney will probably be dealing with more than any other type. In fact, as discussed before, one of the reasons for the trend toward establishing in-house law departments is because of the enormous proliferation of regulations by the many governmental agencies, one example being the environmental regulations enacted during the recent twenty-year period.

Many federal and uniform state acts affect most industries across-the-board. A few examples are the Security and Exchange Commission regulations, Internal Revenue Service regulations, those issued by the Equal Employment Opportunity Commission, the Federal Trade Commission, and so on. Although corporate attorneys who have chosen or have been assigned to a specialty of law will often handle the more complex problems in one or more of these areas, it will be to counsel's distinct advantage to become as knowledgeable as possible about the many laws in this category.

The effectiveness of counsel's preventive practice of corporate law will hinge in large part upon his ability to detect a potential problem and to know where to go for the answer, if necessary. Legal issues and problems (and law/business issues) in the real world are rarely confined to a single subject of law but instead overlap and protrude into many law areas and specialties. A solid foundation for counsel's general practice of corporate law will, by necessity, include a general knowledge of all of the laws in this category that may potentially affect his industry and corporation.

Counsel will also not want to forget the local statutes and regulations in an area where his corporation may be operating. A good example of local regulation today is in the cable television industry. Local city governments usually issue the franchise or license to the cable television installers and operations. City councils then often issue ordinances or regulations drafted to regulate the operators in a manner deemed most suitable to their particular community's needs. Local statutes of this type would have an obvious impact on the practice of corporate counsel for a company in that industry. Although in some cases counsel would undoubtedly need to rely on the expertise (or political savy) of outside local counsel, his general knowledge of local regulations would be fundamental to the effective representation of his corporation's interests.

Court Decisions, Arbitration Awards, and Settlements

The third category of laws to become knowledgeable about is perhaps the most difficult to uncover, namely, court decisions, arbitration awards, and settlements. Many of the rules, dictum, decisions, awards, and compromises with the force of law in this category are simply not published or widely distributed. That makes the task of learning about them more difficult, but not less important. Somc ways to keep current in this category of laws will be addressed in the last section of this Step.

The primary point in this discussion about laws affecting counsel's corporation and industry is that he will want to search diligently and leave no categories or bodies of law uncovered. In many cases these laws will not be found conveniently set forth in a hornbook or textbook and will require significant effort to identify and learn about them. Notwithstanding this, knowledge of them is an essential building block in the foundation to an effective preventive law practice.

The following is an example of a corporate counsel who properly exerted an effort before the fact to become knowledgeable about a body of law, namely, the various state regulations affecting her corporation and, in so doing, prevented a potentially serious legal problem to the company and its subsidiary from arising.

> Not long after this attorney joined a manufacturing and distribution company in the agricultural industry as its first in-house counsel, she set about trying to build a good foundation for practicing preventive law in the corporation by, among other things, becoming knowledgeable about the laws affecting that industry. During this process she obtained and reviewed copies of the laws and regulations issued by the state departments of agriculture in the regions in which their company did business.
>
> As a result of this review, she learned that in most states before a product such as fertilizer or an agri-

> cultural chemical could be distributed and sold, a state permit or license approving the organic contents, container labeling, and other things must be obtained.
>
> Some time later while talking to a subsidiary dealer of their company on another matter, she learned that the subsidiary had recently begun providing a new service to the local farmers which appeared promising. It consisted basically of mixing a chemical pesticide product manufactured by another company with a liquid nitrogen fertilizer manufactured by their company at the subsidiary location and then transporting and applying the combination in bulk to the farmer's fields, thereby avoiding the expense of two separate applications.
>
> The corporate counsel asked the subsidiary manager if both products were properly licensed by the state authorities for sale and distribution. He replied yes. Nonetheless, the corporate counsel had an uncomfortable feeling after talking with the subsidiary manager.
>
> Later in the day she pulled out the copy of the laws and regulations that she had previously obtained from that state's agricultural department and reviewed it again, this time more closely. As she suspected, the regulations specifically required that the mixture of two or more agricultural products prior to sale required an additional permit of approval, even though each component product may have already been separately approved for sale and distribution. Counsel quickly suspended the mixing and sale activities at the dealer site while they applied for the state permit of approval of the product mixture.

Does this incident illustrate the value to a preventive law practice of becoming knowledgeable about the laws that affect the industry? In this case the attorney's efforts to learn about one body of law before a problem involving such laws occurred paid off multifold. She was able to apply effective preventive law because she had a feeling that there may have been a potential legal problem and prudently investigated the matter further. Counsel's efforts to become as knowledgeable as he can about the laws affecting his industry will be time similarly well spent.

Since the bodies (or categories) of law affecting an industry will tend to be large and voluminous, it will be useful to focus, at least initially, on those laws and regulations that are most pertinent and relevant to counsel's practice.

Focus Initially on the Most Relevant Laws

Although one of the objectives in building a good foundation is to become as knowledgeable as possible about all of the bodies of law that affect the industry, from a practical standpoint, it will be next to impossible to learn about all of them immediately or even in a short period of time. So it makes sense to focus, at least initially, on those laws and regulations that are most relevant to the practice of law in the company, namely, those that affect the industry and company most often and with which counsel will need to deal most.

Since that makes sense and is so obvious, why discuss it here? Because in more than one instance a corporate counsel's decision to learn about a certain body of law resulted in a misdirected effort, either intentionally or otherwise. He expended significant time and effort in an area of law according to his interest or whim rather than first examining which laws and regulations impact his company and industry most often and then directing his efforts toward learning those.

In many corporate law departments, counsel may not always have the luxury to choose which body or laws to concentrate upon. He will be so swamped with problems of one kind or another that the decision will, in effect, be made for him. And some may already be specialists by choice in one area of the law or another. Those circumstances notwithstanding, the majority of corporate counsel, at some point in their careers, will have an opportunity to choose to devote an effort toward learning one body of laws or another.

Should that opportunity arise (and even if it does not), then counsel should first conduct a deliberate and overall examination of the laws and regulations that affect his company and industry most frequently and significantly and then devote his efforts toward learning them. A good foundation for an effective preventive law practice must be focused at least initially toward those legal and law / business issues that are more relevant to the primary activities of his corporation. It makes the difference between becoming well-equipped and prepared before the fact to handle the legal problems most likely to occur in the corporation and industry and not being so equipped. And being prepared before the fact is one hallmark of an effective practice of preventive law in the corporation.

Read the following example of a misdirected effort by a very fine corporate attorney. Whether his decision to learn the particular body of law that he did was intentional or not, the attorney provided the corporation with little as a result except, perhaps, the residual benefits accompanying his justified sense of accomplishment.

> An attorney worked in a corporation engaged primarily in the lease, sale, and finance of mobile equipment typically used by factories and industrial plants in their maintenance and renovation programs and in some operations. The law department was a small one in which the individual members handled whatever legal issues happened to come before them or with which they had informally agreed among themselves to have an inclination toward or time for. (Incidentally, that is not an uncommon way for smaller law departments to be organized.)
>
> One day the manager of the corporate division in charge of the lease and sale of small hand tools (items priced at $1,500 or less) came to corporate counsel's office with one of his foreman. He said that for the past several months they had been working on a modification to a standard small hand tool which they thought was innovative and very marketable. They said that the corporate management was not interested in pursuing development of this modified hand tool for several reasons, not the least of which was that the corporation did not want to enter a manufacturing business. Nevertheless, they said

they wanted to proceed with its development and either convince management that they were in error or produce it themselves. They asked the corporate counsel whether he thought their hand tool, as modified, was patentable.

The attorney, having a civil engineering degree, became intensely interested in the project. (We will not discuss whether he should have declined to talk with them further.) He told them he would investigate the matter and get back to them. For several weeks thereafter, he spent a significant amount of time researching the possibility of obtaining a patent—a subject with which he had not previously dealt. He attempted to draft preliminary documents for a patent and several months later, after working with an outside patent attorney, determined that the modification was not sufficiently unique to qualify for a patent, and the project was disbanded.

Notwithstanding this, the attorney's interest in patent law had been piqued. To his credit, during the next few years he spent a significant amount of time (both in the office and on his own time) learning about patent and intellectual property law, including attending several seminars (afforded attorneys in that law department) on the subject of patent law, and subsequently became a member of the patent law bar.

Although most attorneys would commend this achievement, the situation looks different when examined from the corporation's point of view. Over a period of years this attorney focused a significant amount of his time upon a body of law that was not relevant to the primary business of the company for which he worked. After becoming a member of the patent bar, this misdirected focus continued. Apparently because of his newly gained expertise, he was inclined to address issues that did not exist.

For example, many of the corporation's customers preferred to use their own purchase order forms when leasing equipment. These forms usually contained standard paragraphs dealing with the confidentiality of proprietary information about their manufacturing processes. Since his company operated as a service organization without any manufacturing operations or proprietary plans, this type of language on confidential information was usually considered to be of little consequence. Nonetheless, this attorney now began to focus his expertise in intellectual and property law on those paragraphs during purchase order and contract negotiations. Sometimes this focus resulted in a stumbling block because the attorneys for the customers were naturally vitally concerned with the confidentiality of their manufacturing processes. In effect, the misdirected focus on irrelevant laws by this corporate counsel worked not only to his disadvantage but also to the detriment of the corporation.

Although this example is an unusually vivid case of misdirected focus by a corporate counsel, it serves to illustrate the principle, that is, when there is the opportunity to learn a body of law, assuming there is a choice, be sure it is one that is relevant (preferably the most relevant) to the existing practice of preventive law and to the primary activities of the corporation. In that way not only will counsel be building a good foundation for an effective preventive law practice, but he will also be refining his skills and knowledge for the greatest benefit of the corporation. Should those particular bodies of relevant law not interest him, then he might consider trying to become a limited specialist in an area of law that does, or perhaps he might move to another industry or think about a career change. Whatever the case, remember that he cannot learn all of the laws immediately, so his efforts and attention should be focused wisely.

To build a good foundation for an effective practice of preventive law in his corporation, counsel will want to become knowledgeable about all the laws and regulations that affect his company and industry, while at the same time, or at least initially, he focuses his efforts toward those bodies of law that are more relevant in terms of frequency and significance of impact. The counsel must go one step further: He must become an expert, if he is not already, with those laws having the most impact.

Become an Expert

In addition to building a good foundation as a general practitioner by becoming knowledgeable about the laws that affect his industry and company, counsel should endeavor to become an expert with those laws and regulations that he has pinpointed previously as being more relevant, namely, the bodies of law that affect his company most frequently and significantly.

Although this means going substantially beyond the stage of simply being knowledgeable about a body of laws, it does not mean that counsel must become one of the most renowned authorities in the world on the correct statement of, or interpretation of, a body of laws. In fact, that comprehensive knowledge, without more, is not the kind of expertise that will usually enable counsel to practice the most effective preventive law in the corporation. On the contrary, the term *expert* means an in-depth knowledge about a body of laws as well as enough experience and perspective in working with a particular body of laws, so that counsel can go beyond the simple statement of the law and actually use his expertise to find the correct and best solution or answer to the issue or problem confronting him. In other words, in addition to being authority on a particular body of law, he must be able to use and apply that knowledge correctly in the real world involving the business activities of his corporation.

Remember, the premise of this book is not to study and memorize (as might have been done in law school) but to search for principles that can be used to apply the knowledge and skills of an attorney. Although it is first necessary to learn (study) the laws in the industry, that is for the primary purpose of being able to apply them effectively in the practice of preventive law. So in striving to become an "expert" in those laws affecting his industry most often, counsel should remember to visualize their direct application in his practice and try to use them effectively whenever he confronts problems to which they are pertinent.

Becoming this kind of expert with a body of laws will require a substantial and sustained effort over an extended period of time, but it is an effort that will be repaid many times over during a career of practicing corporate law. There is a distinct difference between a corporate counsel who is simply knowledgeable about a body of law and the attorney who is an expert with it. The expert is able to understand the reasons or causes that shaped a particular body of laws. This perspective enables him to use and apply the law in business situations that may be unique, as yet undecided by legal precedent, or otherwise not exactly falling within the traditional and routine circumstances addressed by a body of laws.

Counsel's objective in building a good foundation to practice preventive corporate law and later in finding solutions to the problems confronting him will be well-served and dramatically enhanced by possessing expertise with the laws affecting his industry. Counsel should constantly improve his level of expertise with a body of law(s) throughout his career as corporate counsel.

The following example demonstates that the "expertise" of counsel extended not only to an in-depth knowledge of the applicable body of law but also to the use and application of its legal principles in a very real business situation and problem. Counsel's expertise here unquestionably prevented substantial legal problems to the corporation from occurring.

> The construction industry in the United States has traditionally been divided into two competitive groups, one consisting of companies that exclusively use unionized labor and the other group that uses nonunion or "open shop" labor. There has been discord between these two groups, particularly in areas of the country where one or the other group seems to dominate.
>
> Corporate counsel for an "open shop" contractor recognizes these facts and considers the issues and law surrounding union and nonunion disputes to have great impact on his industry and company. As a result, and over a period of years, he has become an "expert" in the body of laws and their application that deal with labor matters involving construction projects. He has also always tried to keep current about problems in this area experienced by other contractors in his industry.

Part of his expertise extends to legislation and court decisions concerning secondary boycotts. Greatly simplified, this body of law states that it is an "illegal secondary boycott" for unionized labor to picket in a manner that prevents nonunion labor from entering a construction project through a gate which has been reserved exclusively for their use. Counsel also knows that it is not uncommon for union labor to picket all gates at a construction project in an attempt to shut down the job to compel the exclusive use of union labor. Counsel has read and knows about cases in which other contractors have been able to obtain an injunction preventing the union from engaging in such "illegal secondary boycotts."

Therefore, when counsel's company obtains a bid to build a facility using an open-shop labor posture in an area of the country where almost all previous construction projects have been built by union labor, he goes to work. He first tries to negotiate as many favorable contract provisions for the corporation as possible that would apply in the event of disruption of labor. Second, he and the construction project managers and the customer insure that the proper number of project gates will be constructed at a sufficient distance from each other and with ingress and egress restrictions clearly displayed, so that the provisions of secondary boycott rules will apply. He also takes several more important preventive law measures prior to the inception of the project. He drafts a motion for preliminary injunction that could be filed in the event of an illegal secondary boycott by the union. He retains a local attorney, briefs him, and requests that he be prepared to file the injunction on a moment's notice, should it be necessary. If possible, he meets with the local police and sheriff departments to be sure they are informed about the construction gates, the applicable secondary boycott law, and his company's plans for the project and requests their assistance in the event of any problems. Also, if possible, he asks the local attorney to brief the judicial

> authorities who would receive and act upon the injunction. During this process he is careful that all action remains within the bounds of good ethical conduct.
>
> By these means he applied effective preventive law based upon his expertise. He focused his attention upon a legal problem having great impact in his industry, and he knew it prudent to take as many precautionary steps as possible prior to inception of the project. These steps were, in fact, taken by him and his corporate management on this project and on several later projects with favorable results, although not always without problems.

The corporate counsel in this example was able to use his expertise in secondary boycott law to the great advantage of the corporation. His expertise enabled the proper application of several preventive measures based upon the principles in that body of law. It is a good illustration of the significant value that expertise in the laws having substantial impact in the industry can have in the ability to practice truly effective preventive law in the corporation. This is a building block in the foundation that is necessary to establish and keep current during a career as corporate counsel.

How To Keep Current

One of the best ways to identify and keep current on legal issues affecting your company and industry is by using one of the techniques used by counsel to learn the business. That technique is subscribing to trade publications, magazines, and newsletters, joining trade associations and attending their conventions, participating with certain lobby groups, and attending seminars made up of, and organized for the benefit of, members of the industry. In other words, simply being aware of what is going on in the industry.

Several of these publications and conventions will be directly primarily at the layman in the industry, which does not mean that they are of no benefit to lawyers. Often, some of the subjects in these publications and meetings are directly or indirectly related to legal problems. That may be because law is an area in which the layman has the least training and the most difficulty. Whatever the reason, they will alert counsel to legal areas with which he should be concerned. Although counsel will probably need to investigate and learn more of the substantive law on a particular point from other sources, the identification of the legal issues and the learning of facts surrounding the experiences of others with those issues can be invaluable to him.

A great deal can also be learned during trade association meetings and conventions by simply talking with contemporaries from the corporate law departments of other companies within your industry. Sometimes trade associations will have subcommittees composed of those corporate attorneys. If that is the case, it is vital for counsel to participate. Not only will he learn about many substantive legal issues and the different ways that they are handled by his contemporaries, but he will also acquire a better perspective of the issues. By comparison with the experiences of his contemporaries, counsel can often see that legal problems existing within his company are not so unique or unusual as he may have thought or perhaps vice-versa. Also, if counsel is acquainted with a colleague from talking with him at meetings and knows that he has dealt previously with a legal problem similar to the one confronting counsel, a great deal of time and effort can be saved if counsel can call him and discuss it. In most cases fellow attorneys will be most helpful, if not overly so. It is as though lawyers share a sort of camraderie through dealing with a particular body of law affecting their industry. By all means, try to cultivate and utilize this valuable source of legal information and expertise as much possible.

Another valuable resource for keeping current with the laws in the industry is the various bar association meetings. Some of the largest state bar associations sponsor excellent educational conventions, seminars, and meetings often dealing with new developments in regulatory areas and presented by actual participants in those developments or court proceedings. In addition, the subcommittees and publications of the American Bar Association are excellent forums within which to learn about new developments in the law and to share and gain the insights of your contemporaries. There are, of course, seminars organized by private enterprise on innumerable subjects of law, some of which are excellent and comprehensive. To assist in his practice and keep current about new developments, counsel should participate in these events to the extent that he is able to do so.

An excellent source for information on industry laws are the many books, manuals, and multivolume legal reporting services published by national law publishing houses. Counsel is probably familiar with several of these already. They cover many regulatory areas of law affecting the corporation, such as SEC, ERISA, IRS, OSHA, EPA, Government contracting, FTC, FCC, labor, and many others. They are frequently published and organized so that a brief summary of the new developments in an area can be read and a particular point can be studied in more depth should you wish. These publications will become essential in counsel's efforts to become and remain an expert in a particular body of law. He is well-advised, while laying his foundation for an effective practice of preventive law, to become familiar with the many fine publications of this type, if he is not already, and regularly during his career to find the time necessary to peruse their updating services so that he can keep abreast of the new developments in the bodies of law that affect his industry. There are other ways to learn about, and keep current in, the law affecting your industry. For example, many good continuing legal education (CLE) programs are now offered by several law schools and local bar associations. The important thing is to do it and keep at it!

The principle that should be kept in mind about this step in building a foundation to practice corporate law effectively is exactly as recited in the title: Learn the law in your industry. Only by becoming knowledgeable about the laws and regulations that affect the industry and becoming an expert with those that affect his company most frequently and significantly will counsel be able to fully apply his knowledge as an attorney to find the best alternatives or preventive measures to the legal and law/business issues that he will confront. His continual efforts to learn the law in his industry during his career will be repaid many times over.

This following is a case study of an attorney who became an expert in a certain body of law affecting the corporation for which she worked and, as a result, was able to negotiate and draft a contract that although unorthodox in character and concept, provided both a mechanism for the accomplishment of the business objectives of the corporation (namely, successful award and then completion of the project at a profit) and legal protection for the company.

Case Study Number Five: THE UNORTHODOX CONTRACT

The Situation

For the past eight years, counsel has worked as an in-house counsel in the engineering and construction industry. Because the responsibilities in her present position (and for the past three years) involve a significant amount of negotiation and drafting of the contracts under which her company engineers and constructs projects for its customers, she has worked assiduously to become an expert with the laws, practices, and customs most frequently affecting the contractual relationship between engineer/contractors and their customers.

She has studied the few books available on the subject; has attended pertinent seminars; has become a member of the American Bar Association Forum Committee on the Construction Industry; has studied in great detail the recommended contract standard forms issued by the trade associations for architects, for engineers, and for contractors as well as the contract forms used by the federal government in public contracting; and has examined copies of several contracts used by competitors in the industry. She has discussed issues and problems in engineering/construction contracting with colleagues in other companies and has tried to keep current about new developments by subscribing to industry periodicals and newsletters and by obtaining opinions of relevant court decisions that she has learned about. During this period of time she has also sought to apply her skills and knowledge in this area of law by devising detailed checklists for use during negotiations, by continually updating the contracting forms used by her company, and by always questioning and trying to understand the underlying reasons for, and relationships between, the language and concepts typically used in engineering/construction contracts in the industry. In short, she became an expert.

During the past three months she has been involved in a complex contract negotiation involving the engineering and construction of a $200 million manufacturing facility for a customer. The negotiations started out with the company's standard cost-reimbursable form, customarily used on this type of project but have progressed to a point at which many of the contract provisions are barely recognizable and several additional concepts and sections have been added. The foremost reason for these changes is attributable to the differing ideas and philosophies of the customer company with whom she is negotiating. Although the manufacturing facility will be located in the United States, the customer is incorporated and headquartered in the United Kingdom and is accustomed to contracting for engineering and construction under the most common approach there of a fixed-price contract or lump sum.

As a result, the contract, now in its final stages, resembles neither a pure cost-plus contract nor a lump-sum one but an unusual hybrid of both. For example, although the total estimated price quoted by the company to do the engineering and construction of the facility remains unfixed in concept, and therefore reimbursable (for the most part) to the extent of actual costs incurred (plus a fee), many of its components, such as the furnishing of small hand tools required on the project, have either become fixed and reimbursable only in a stated lump-sum amount or, although still reimbursed on an actual cost incurred basis, have a stipulated maximum limitation on that reimbursement (guaranteed maximum concept). In addition, some other important provisions in standard cost-plus industry contracts, such as the replacement of defective work section and the change order clause, have been similarly modified or turned around.

The Question

As the contract negotiations draw to a conclusion, some of the company managers become concerned with the unorthodox character of the resulting contract document(s). To some it appears to be primarily a lump-sum contract, while others think it is more like a guaranteed maximum or cost-plus type of contract.

They want to know what counsel thinks. They wonder whether a higher fee should be quoted to cover the unknown cost contingencies, as customarily done in lump-sum contracts. They also wonder whether this contract is a losing proposition and one that they would be better off declining. They ask counsel whether the company is legally protected.

As corporate counsel, how would you advise the management of the corporation on these issues and questions? Remember, you are an expert in this area.

What Actually Happened

In this case the in-house counsel, because of her expertise, was able to confidently advise corporate management that from a legal standpoint she did not see a significant problem. Although it was true that some of the provisions were lump sum and others were more like the guaranteed maximum or cost-plus concepts, when she drafted the document, she was careful to insure that each section was definitely set forth and segregated from the others. Further, inconsistencies between these contracting methods and concepts were adequately provided for or eliminated by this careful analysis and drafting.

Corporate counsel pointed out, for example, that although the contract provides that "all necessary small hand tools" used by workmen on the project will be provided "for the lump-sum amount of $100,000," she added to that provision the standard change-order language found in lump-sum contracts, so that if there was a significant modification or increase in the scope of work, a mechanism was provided to increase the lump-sum amount. Then, by way of comparison, she pointed out to the corporate managers that when negotiating and drafting the section regarding the project site preparation, all parties agreed that the test borings of the soil were inadequate to determine whether unexpected subsurface rock formations might be encountered. Therefore, the language provided that site preparatory work would be reimbursed on an actual cost incurred basis, consistent with the conditions discovered during the progress of the work. Also for that reason, she pointed out, the detailed lump-sum type of change-order language provided for in the small tool section was both unnecessary and inappropriate in this section. She also noted that the standard replacement of work clause had been modified to fit particular sections of the contract, depending upon the contracts contained in it.

She gave more examples to management showing how some of the contract provisions varied from either the traditional concept of lump sum, guaranteed maximum, or cost-plus contracting but pointed out again that in her opinion the contract was sufficiently detailed and segregated, with inconsistencies eliminated, so that from a legal standpoint it was acceptable, although admittedly unorthodox.

She was also quick to point out that because of the unusual nature of this contract, they should consider from a business standpoint whether or not it was feasible to operate under as a practical matter. She suggested that the managers of the project team assigned to engineer and construct the project get together with her and others to discuss the various contract provisions and determine whether they could, in fact, be implemented in a proper fashion. She suggested that some of the cost accounting features of the project would need to be detailed, segregated, and closely monitored, that certain area superintendents would need to have a good grasp of various contract provisions, and that close attention throughout the project would be required to properly execute the project. She stated generally that the contract was one-third lump sum and two-thirds cost-plus, so that from a business standpoint, they might want to consider increasing the fee.

Several meetings were held prior to the contract signing, and it was determined that although this was an unusual and different method of contracting for the company (as well as in the industry), with adequate preparation and control corporate management felt it should be a successful project. Perhaps because of this increased attention the project became one of the most successful performed by the company that year.

Author's Comments

Although this example lacked a great many details about the various contract provisions, the reader should have been able to grasp the basic essentials of this illustration. Because of this attorney's efforts to become an expert in engineering and construction contracting, she was able to extend her understanding and knowledge beyond the simple written words contained in the company's standard contracts. She was well-versed with the different contracting concepts utilized in the industry and the underlying reason for them.

As a result, in this case of negotiating with a foreign company accustomed to doing business in a different manner, she was able to suggest and draft contractual provisions that represented a compromise between the parties and that, although admittedly unorthodox, ultimately satisfied the objectives of both parties. Importantly, she was able to apply her expertise with a body of laws to a difficult situation facing not only her as an attorney but the corporation and to find a workable and appropriate solution, which otherwise probably would not have been developed or adequately addressed. Also note that her expertise enabled her to judiciously address and advise upon the law/business issues. (For example, should a higher fee be quoted.)

This case is a good practical illustration of the great benefits that counsel's efforts to become an expert in the laws affecting his industry will have in his practice of corporate law and to the corporation.

Although this case may seem to be one of unique circumstances, it is not. Whenever two sets or groups of people are negotiating to arrive at their own objectives, there will be differences of opinion between respective concepts and language. In those situations, expertise in the law affecting the industry will enhance counsel's ability to know when to extend a compromise or refrain from doing so and to know how to arrive at a workable solution to the differing objectives. Counsel will be able to do so because his expertise supplies the basic understanding to grasp the practical, as well as the technical points of law with which he will be dealing.

PART B

Practice Preventive Law by Finding Solutions

PART B
PRACTICE PREVENTIVE LAW BY FINDING SOLUTIONS

KEYS TO THE SOLUTION (PART B)

Introduction to Part B

Introduction

Now it is time to build on the solid foundation for practicing preventive law established in Part A one of the most specialized and effective techniques for practicing law in the corporation: practicing preventive corporate law by finding solutions.

As will be seen, the foundation that has been laid will be invaluable to successfully implement the techniques for finding solutions to the legal problems that will confront corporate counsel. The one goes before the other, but both are interrelated, so counsel should continue to reflect and build upon the principles of his foundation as counsel's career progresses and his abilities to practice effective corporate law become more sophisticated.

The first step in searching for solutions is to ask: "What is a solution?"

What Is a Solution?

The dictionaries define a solution as an answer to a problem. What does that mean in the context of practicing law in the corporation?

That depends in part upon the type of problem. If the problem consists of a pure legal issue or perhaps a law-related problem but with a significant, overriding legal consideration, such as illegality, then the solution will be the answer found by application of the correct rules of law and nothing more (although that is easier said than done).

On the other hand, if the problem consists of a combination of law and business issues, as is most often the case in a corporate law practice, then the task of finding an answer will not be so simply accomplished. In addition to applying the correct rules of law, the business objectives must be weighed because the answer that represents the best alternative from both the legal and business standpoint is the solution.

Put another way, the solution to most problems confronting corporate counsel is those alternative courses of action or decisions that accomplish the business objectives of the corporation to the extent possible while still maintaining high quality legal practices within determined levels of legal risk, exposure, and cost to the corporation. That is the definition of a solution in the context of practicing corporate law.

From a practical standpoint the solution to a problem will simply be counsel's best legal judgment after consideration of the business objectives. A better picture of a solution will emerge after looking at the several examples and cases in this Part B. The important principle here is not to fail to weigh the business considerations, as some corporate counsel do, when searching for solutions. The next section will explain why counsel will always want to look for solutions in his practice of corporate law.

Why Look for Solutions?

Counsel should look for solutions because by finding them, he will be making his greatest contribution to the corporation. This is how counsel can be more effective than his fellow attorneys who do not employ the techniques of practicing preventive law by finding solutions. Practicing preventive law by finding solutions, which is the fullest adaptation of one's knowledge of the law and skills as an attorney to the business environment, requires counsel to go one step beyond the traditional adversary notion of law practice. He should not be content with simply determining compliance or noncompliance with a body of law but should take the problem one step further and achieve an end result.

The question that laymen seem to most frequently ask corporate attorneys is "Can we do this?" A business manager who wants to distribute a new product manufactured by another company shows counsel a copy of the other company's proposed distributor agreement and asks, "Can we accept this contract?" After reviewing the agreement, counsel says no. By saying no, and perhaps even by saying yes, counsel has not practiced effective preventive law. He has probably not found a solution, or at least not the best one; he has simply issued a legal decision based upon his opinion about the language in the agreement.

In order to find a solution, counsel must go one step further and paraphrase the business manager's question into "How can we *best* do it?" Then, he must try to answer that question by looking for the best alternative course of action. For example, he would tell the layman how the proposed distributor contract could be revised or modified to make it acceptable from a legal standpoint (if that is possible) while still maintaining its basic business scheme and purpose. Although many lawyers would have revised the contract as a matter of routine, this example nevertheless serves to illustrate the value of practicing preventive law by finding solutions.

A correct and valid statement of the law solves little in the real world unless it is used to point the way toward a certain purpose. In the corporate environment that purpose is usually a business objective. Although the traditional functions of a law department, like determining compliance with law, are mandatory and fundamental to an effective practice of law in the corporation, in this context they frequently constitute only a first step. The ultimate objective is to find the best course of action that will accomplish, to the extent possible, the business purposes of the corporation while still maintaining high quality legal practices and compliance within determined levels of minimum legal risk, exposure, and cost. In other words, put bluntly and unceremoniously, the practice of law in a corporation should not be an end in itself but rather a tool by which management can achieve the business objectives of the corporation. By adopting this perspective, counsel will have taken a big step toward being able to practice his most effective and productive law in the corporation. For that reason alone, he should always look for solutions.

But there is another good reason to practice preventive law by finding solutions. It will help decrease the likelihood of a subsequent legal problem arising. That is because a problem or a question that is "answered" without a "solution" is not answered at all. It is an unfinished set of facts, which, by its nature, will often cause a problem to arise again, only with a different face and look about it. An even worse result is that failing to look for a solution may prompt a layman (your client) to go his own way without your advice, with even more risk to the corporation. More than one business manager has gone ahead with a business venture under a verbal agreement or some other kind of arrangement, after having received what he considered (perhaps correctly) to be an inadequate answer or effort from corporate counsel.

Most questions or problems have several alternative answers or possible courses of action. The attorney's knowledge of law and skills provide the unique capability to ferret out those alternatives that are most acceptable under a particular body of law while at the same time achieving the business objectives and purpose. That is the capability to be developed in this Part B—to refine the practice of preventive law developed in Part A into one that will maximize the ability to find solutions to problems that will confront corporate counsel so that he can practice law in the corporation most effectively and successfully.

Increasingly today, the corporate attorney is faced with problems and issues that demand a solution rather than simple pronouncement of legal theory. This is due, in part, to the ever-increasing practice of preventive law and the resulting confrontation of legal problems in their very early stages. Finding solutions is an aspect of the corporate law practice that is unique and emerging and that holds the promise and future for the corporate law departments of tomorrow.

It has particular merit today because of the dramatically increased opportunities for corporate counsel to practice this type of law. Rarely before have attorneys been so closely associated with, and had such in-depth knowledge of, their clients, both prerequisites to an effective preventive law practice. By applying the principles in Part B in the practice of corporate law, counsel will lead the destiny of future corporate law departments.

How To Find a Solution

How to practice preventive corporate law by finding solutions is the topic of the remainder of this book. There is a kind of process or methodology that can be used to maximize the ability to find solutions. It will involve a series of techniques or keys through which counsel can not only position himself in the corporation to be receptive and responsive to legal problems but also can properly analyze the facts and the circumstances confronting him and search for all of the alternatives available for a solution.

This approach is not just a matter of counsel's saying to himself, "I'm going to find a solution," and then having one magically appear. It is usually not that easy. Instead it is prudent to start at the very beginning with basic fundamentals, for example, with counsel, his posture in the corporation, and the stage he sets (or fails to set) to be receptive to, and perceptive about, legal problems (KEY ONE). Then after implementing that fundamental principle in his practice, counsel can move on to the next logical step of discovering the real problem (KEY TWO), namely, whether there really is a problem, and if there is, whether it is a legal problem, a business problem, or some combination thereof. Then counsel can apply the law (KEY THREE) in the most effective way, and if he lacks the resources availale in-house to determine the law on a particular issue, go outside to a private law firm (KEY FOUR).

Is that all counsel must do to find the solution? No. He usually needs to take another important step. He needs to search for all the possible alternative answers in order to then determine which one is best and represents the solution (KEY FIVE). Evaluating all possible alternative ways to handle a problem is an area in which counsel can excel and greatly benefit his corporation. Finally, after counsel has found the solution or the best alternatives, he issues his work product (KEY SIX) in a simple, understandable, and productive way.

This is the blueprint and methodology for developing the ability to find solutions to the problems encountered in the practice of preventive corporate law. It is one upon which counsel can continue to build throughout his career. The keys and principles in this methodology are not set forth as theories of law to be studied and memorized. They are set forth as tools to be used to apply to the business environment and corporate setting the skills and knowledge an attorney already possesses. They are illustrated with examples and case studies based upon actual occurrences in the practice of corporate law for that purpose. Although a few principles may appear nonlegal or procedural in nature, and therefore irrelevant to the practice of law in the corporation, that is not the case, as will be seen.

Now, before going to KEY ONE, the question may arise whether implementation of each of these six keys is always necessary to find a solution may arise. Not always. A solution to a problem may be immediately apparent to counsel because he knows the business (STEP ONE) and law in his industry (STEP THREE) and can easily and correctly conclude that a proposed business activity is illegal, unethical, or whatever. That proper foundation laid in Part A may point the way to a solution without the necessity of deliberately following each of these keys in sequence. Or in a few cases the correct solution to a problem may be found by using a more traditional approach to practicing law, like dispensing law or taking an adversary posture. And the level and responsibility of counsel's position and the legal assignments given to him may determine the character and complexity of problems confronting him and his resulting opportunity to fully implement all six keys in this approach.

Nevertheless, the majority of legal problems encountered by corporate counsel will be most easily and effectively resolved by application of most, if not all, of the principles set forth in the keys in this section. Too often, the best solution to a problem is overlooked because of failure to apply one or more these fundamental keys and principles.

Key One: Set the Stage

Introduction

From the sound of it, this key appears to be the most nonlegal, and therefore the least important, principle in the process of finding a solution. Perhaps that is the reason this key is the one that tends to be most overlooked or neglected by some corporate counsel. More than one very fine attorney has been unable to function effectively within the corporate environment because he, either intentionally or otherwise, failed to set and maintain a proper stage, conduct, posture of law, or demeanor in his practice of law in the corporation.

Setting the stage means the style, tone, and professionalism of counsel's personal practice of law in the corporation. Although primarily nonlegal in character, these attributes have a profound effect upon his opportunity and capability to practice effective corporate law. For example, the stage set for the practice of law in the corporation will either help establish a good client relationship, or destroy one, which, in turn, will affect when and to what extent, if at all, counsel learns about a potential legal problem.

The principle and the value of being a "team player" will be discussed first, and an example of an attorney who did not function as part of the corporate team, to the detriment of his practice, will be examined. Equally important to setting the stage for your practice of law is the necessity for counsel to divorce himself from the "corporate team" at times and maintain his professional demeanor, posture, and judgment. Counsel should also stand apart from "corporate political" fights and avoid working too much for one executive or group (if he has a choice).

The first key is to establish (or refine) the stage for the practice of law in the corporation, so counsel will be able to apply the skills and knowledge he already possesses as an attorney most effectively within the corporate environment. By concentrating upon this key, counsel will then be most prepared to later find the real problem (Key Two) and then proceed on toward finding the proper and best solutions. Without implementation of this key, counsel may very well limit his ability when handling a legal problem to, at best, the more traditional adversary or "dispensing law" functions or, at worst, to not learning about the problem in the first place or until it has become irresolveable.

Be a Team Player

Being a team player means simply adopting the attitude and perspective that corporate counsel is working for the corporation, not just himself or the law department. Some attorneys seem to have difficulty accepting this demeanor or posture, particularly if they are recent graduates from law school, who are still flush with their accomplishment, or experienced counsel who have lost their interest and enthusiasm for the law profession.

A corporation is a distinct entity consisting of people focused toward certain common goals and objectives. Often, if not always, a corporation will have a certain, although sometimes illusive and undefinable, identity and character. The personnel and managers who make up a corporation usually consider themselves to be a part of this corporate identity and, in fact, contributors to it. Why not counsel? This participation in the corporate identity and, in some degree, in the goals and objectives of the corporation is part of what is meant by being a "team player." To some that concept may appear derrogatory or demeaning, but it should not be. Being able to function as an effective corporate counsel, as part of the corporate team and corporate identity (while still maintaining your professionalism), is an accomplishment to be proud of and one that will enable counsel to practice far more effective preventive law.

One reason is that being a part of the corporate team is one of the best ways to help build a good client relationship.

Counsel will not be able to practice corporate law effectively if he has failed to establish a good client relationship. Counsel in not entirely correct in thinking that, in contrast to private practice, in a corporation he has a ready-made clientel which does not require an effort on his part to keep and retain. No matter how many directives are issued by the general counsel or chief executive officer of the corporation or how many rubber stamps stating "Approved by Law Department" are required on corporate documents, some people within the corporation will be less willing than others to use counsel's services. Not uncommonly, the people who are least willing to use his services need them most. One way to reach clients, particularly reluctant ones, is to make an effort to be a part of the corporation—setting the stage. If the stage counsel has set is one of aloofness, superiority, or disdain, his clientel will know it, and his ability to practice preventive law will suffer as a result. Consider the following unfortunate example.

> A very fine and bright, young attorney worked in the law department of a corporation immediately after graduation for about two years, before joining a firm in private practice. From the start she appeared eager and excited to perform her work. It did not take her long, however, to display an attitude of cynicism toward several of the business managers and officers in the corporation. Although some of these laymen were not perceptive about legal issues, that was no reason to criticize them, since that was not their job.
>
> As time went by and as this attitude of the attorney seemed to magnify, the number of people in the corporation wanting to use her services seemed to decrease proportionately. It got to the point that except for a few managers in the corporation who delighted and shared in her cynical views, much of the work this attorney performed was spillover work given to her by other attorneys in the department.

If having the attitude of being a part of the corporate team is distasteful or repuguant to one, then counsel be more suited to, and more productive in, a different type of environment. The wisest course is to recognize that and move on—or accept the fact that a corporation has its own particular demands and style of operating and make an effort to function within it as effectively as possible.

Another reason to be a part of the corporate team is to learn the correct perspective from which to weigh business considerations. In the previous example how would the attorney have viewed the business considerations involved in legal problems she handled? If she bothered to give any weight at all to the business aspect of a problem, it probably would have been from a limited or theoretical legal point of view, that is, from an "ill-conceived" perspective. Finding a solution must, by definition, include balancing the business aspects of a problem or set of circumstances. How else will counsel be able to find the alternative course of action that satisfies the business objectives of the corporation to the extent possible and still maintains high legal compliance and minimum legal risk? It is impossible—unless counsel functions as a member of the corporation and acquires the proper perspective of the business issues. Just as trying to practice law in a corporation without knowing the business is like practicing law from within a vacuum, so here, too, the best solutions to problems will not be found from an ill-conceived perspective.

Besides adopting the proper attitude and perspective, what are some other ways to implement the principle of being a team player into the stage for practicing effective corporate law by finding solutions?

Attend Meetings, Go on Business Trips, and So Forth

Attending as many meetings in the corporation as possible, going on business trips whenever possible, attending corporate social functions, and working with the other law department attorneys are among some of the simplest, yet the best, ways to set a good stage for the practice of preventive law by finding solutions. By so doing, counsel is not only functioning as a team player but also gaining valuable insight and perspective about the corporation, its business strategies, and the thinking of its managers about particular issues, including potential or unrecognized legal problems.

Attend Meetings

Attending meetings in a corporation is worthwhile because business decisions are commonly discussed and made in them. The inherent structure of corporations seems to lend itself to that type of operating style. A corporation is usually divided into different departments, each with its own speciality. Any business activity or transaction of significance usually requires information from several different departments. Often the easiest and most expeditious way to obtain information and discuss different viewpoints upon a subject or problem will be by having a meeting of the people concerned. Many people feel that it is simpler to have a meeting then take the time and make the effort to write a memo or proposal for distribution.

Counsel's attendance at meetings in a corporation can serve at least a two-fold purpose. First, it is an excellent way to alert himself to potential legal problems in their early stages; and, second, he will gain a better perspective of the business considerations surrounding a problem. It will enable him to grasp the flavor and tenor of issues he may confront then or later. Many things are said in meetings that are not put on paper in a document summarizing the meeting. A meeting provides an opportunity to investigate some of the comments that are not put on paper, to ask questions, and to go directly to the real problem, if there is one. Moreover, an attorney who must deal with the complexity of the law will often find it easier to make himself understood when he is speaking directly to other people in a meeting. He will be able to read their faces, see their reactions, know whether they understand or not and whether they have questions. Although counsel may be able to write very fine and impressive-looking memos, their complexity will deter many people from reading them.

The following is an exaggerated but actual example of the importance of meetings in some corporations.

> In lengthy negotiations about a proposed business transaction with a large corporation that manufactured and marketed consumer products, counsel and his associates noticed frequent "silent" communications between the persons in the other corporation

> seated at the table. They would often nod at each other or look at each other when a question arose. Sometimes they left the room or huddled in a far corner of the room to discuss an issue. After several hours of this type of communication, they eventually became more open and actually began to take a poll or informal vote about how each felt on a particular point of dispute in the business transaction. Although this behavior was unusual, it was not necessarily disturbing to the negotiations.
>
> During a break, counsel asked some questions about their apparent style of operating by taking a vote on everything. He learned that this concensus style of operation and management was characteristic throughout their corporation. In fact, several had attended training seminars to learn and develop that style of operation. Most decisions by the corporation were made "democratically" by a majority of the members of one committee or another. The style of management by the corporation was by committee rather than individual action.

Although this extreme may be an unusual style of operating, it points out how meetings can be of obvious importance to business activity. Input was received and decisions made in meetings by the consensus action of the group or committee members. An attorney working in a corporation with this style of management would by necessity attend all such meetings.

Some attorneys may say that if they attended all the meetings they were invited to in the corporation, they would have no time left to do anything else. In these circumstances it may be helpful to attend the part of the meeting pertinent to law, rather than not attend it at all. Although it is not a good practice for a corporate attorney always to go late to meetings, it is perfectly proper for him to graciously excuse himself when he thinks the legal issues with which he should be concerned have been discussed. Some meetings will seem like a waste of time; however, the majority of them will help set the stage for the practice of preventive law.

Go on Business Trips

In addition to attending meetings, going on many business trips with the layman management in the corporation will help set a good stage for the practice of preventive law by finding solutions. If the trip involves meeting with some of the competitors in the industry or companies for whom counsel will be performing a service, he may gain an insight about how they view his corporation, about how others in the industry operate, and about how they are handling problems or issues which he may later encounter. This perspective will help him to be more objective about circumstances and problems he may confront than if he had simply relied upon the exuberant opinions and judgment of some of the managers in the company. In addition, visiting the company facilities or operations during the trip can be extremely valuable in learning about the business.

Beyond gaining the perspective about the corporation and industry as viewed by third parties, going on business trips can be helpful to learn the viewpoints of the people in the corporation with whom counsel is traveling. For some reason, it seems that some people will more readily express their opinions and judgments upon issues and about the corporation when they are on a business trip than they will in their offices in the headquarters building. Listen to this vivid experience of an experienced corporate counsel who had recently joined a new corporation.

> Only a few weeks after joining a new company, this experienced corporate counsel was asked by a senior vice president to go on a two-day trip with him. Not having worked on, or being aware of, any problems in this vice president's area of responsibility and being extremely busy since joining the corporation, the corporate counsel wondered what the purpose of the trip was. The senior vice president stated a number of small reasons, none of which seemed very important. Nevertheless, following the principles being discussed here, he agreed to go with him.
>
> In addition to visiting some of the company facilities, which he found enlightening at this early stage, the real purpose of the trip soon became apparent.

> There were two political factions within the management of this company, and this senior vice president was testing the counsel to see if he would side with one faction or the other and, if so, wanted to be sure that he would be on their side. The senior vice president apparently felt these issues were too involved and sensitive to be discussed in the headquarter offices and instead chose a business trip to make them known.

What was the value of the trip to his practice of preventive law? Certainly not that this senior vice president made some derrogatory remarks or "gossip" about the other political faction in the corporation. What did help was that he learned there were two different groups and philosophies of management within the corporation. He was therefore alerted to a situation, however good or bad, that existed and with which he knew he would have to deal. From then on, he attempted to work objectively and equally with both groups without prejudice to either and without being manipulated by either.

In sum, this corporate counsel tried to set a stage that would be responsive to both groups, for the good of the corporation as a whole, while remaining a professional toward both. Had he not gone on this particular business trip, he might have unknowingly associated himself with one political faction or the other to the detriment of his ability to practice preventive law. Although he would have undoubtably learned the same thing at some point, the important observation to make is that some people need to get away from the office in order to give you their real opinion about the people, the corporation, and the business activities in which they are all engaged. Thus business trips, even though time-consuming, as is the case with meetings, should be viewed as an important method to gain not only the perspective and viewpoint of others (third parties) but also those of the managers within the corporation. It is another practical method of implementing the principles of this key so that counsel will not be practicing law from within a vacuum or from an ill-conceived perspective.

Attend Corporate Social Functions

There is little about this subject—not because it is not important but because it falls more within the realm of personal preferences. An attorney can practice corporate law and never attend a social function sponsored by the corporation or a department within it, but such a course of action is not recommended because in some corporations social functions are viewed as an important part of the company activities and its esprit de corps. They give the employees and managers alike an opportunity to meet and talk with each other, and in some cases their families, on a different level and in different circumstances from those found in the corporate offices.

If counsel is to function effectively within the corporation as a member of the corporate team, then it is probably advisable to participate in these corporate functions. In fact, counsel will probably find them enjoyable. In any event, he should be aware of them, for they will probably confront him during his career. He should not feel slighted, however, if he is not invited to a function that is sponsored by a group of laymen, even though he has performed a considerable amount of work for that group during the past year. Especially in larger companies, operating personnel do not always feel it appropriate to socialize with the staff personnel in the headquarters group, such as accounting, law, purchasing, and others.

Work with Other Department Attorneys

Working with other attorneys will not be a problem for most of you, but occasionally the opposite is true, either intentionally or otherwise. Functioning as a member of the "corporate law department team" can be as important to the stage set for practicing corporate law as is functioning as a part of the overall corporate team, if not more so.

No matter how many times counsel has handled a problem in a certain legal area before, it is often helpful to run a complex problem by another attorney in the department to get his opinion on the matter. Sometimes counsel will be overloaded with work, and another attorney can take some of counsel's work load in exchange for aiding him at a later time. By knowing what some of the other attorneys are doing and how they are solving legal problems, counsel will prepare himself for those legal problems should he encounter them. For these and other reasons, counsel would be well-advised to establish and maintain a good working relationship with the other attorneys in the law department. Just as in his relationship with clients, the corporate laymen, it is to counsel's advantage within the corporate law department not to be isolated or remote from the department as a whole, as in the following example.

> A hard-working, bright young attorney found herself within a disorganized and havoc-ridden law department. The attorneys seemed to be mostly jumping from one crisis to the next, or in corporate law department legal jargon, "putting out fires".
>
> In an effort to insulate herself from these daily commotions and to make her efforts more productive, she took to keeping the door of her office closed most of the time. After a while the other attorneys in the department got the idea that she did not care what else was going on, what other legal problems were surfacing, and how they were being resolved but was instead simply interested in the particular matters she might be working on at the time.
>
> Note that the other attorneys "got the idea." That perception was not entirely correct. This attorney was, in fact, interested in other legal problems occurring within the corporation and did, on occasion and particularly in staff meetings, wholly participate in discussions about them. Nonetheless, however unintended, the result was much the same. In many cases this attorney was not aware about what was being handled by other members in the law department. She did not share a close working relationship with them, to her disadvantage and to the disadvantage of her practice of law in the corporation.

In developing the stage for the practice of effective preventive law in the corporation, counsel should not neglect the value of his contemporaries in his own law department (as well as in the law departments at competitive companies).

But Remain a Professional

The discussion of how to set the stage for practice of corporate law by finding solutions has emphasized the value of becoming a part of the corporate team by having the proper attitude and demeanor toward the corporation and the people composing it and by implementing this principle in practical ways, such as attending meetings, going on business trips, and so on. But this raises a potentially serious question: Does being a team player affect an attorney's ability to remain a professional? The effect should be negligible, provided counsel remembers that he is a professional. The two principles are separate and distinct. Although counsel should know and understand his client, and to some extent "be one of the boys" in order to effectively practice preventive law within the corporation, this need not (and obviously should not) involve a change in professional judgment, ethics, or conduct. When it comes to evaluating the legal issue or exercising legal judgment, counsel must be objective and stand apart from the rest of the corporation should the need arise. Although legal judgment may be tempered by business considerations, counsel's professionalism to detach himself and remain objective should never be tempered.

This is particularly true for corporate attorneys because of the environment in which they usually work. Often the corporate attorney is in a small law department without the confidence of support from several associates and peers, as he might have in a private law firm, for example. So, too, in the practice of corporate law he will be dealing with many of the same managers and people on a weekly, if not daily, basis. This frequent and recurring contact with the same client year in and year out naturally results in a growing familiarity. This can work to counsel's advantage in setting the stage for an effective practice of preventive law, but it can also work to his disadvantage should he let it influence his legal judgment.

Counsel will also want to always remain objective when exercising his legal judgment and to stand apart from the corporation, if necessary, because he frequently will learn about potential legal problems at a very early stage. In those instances he may need to adopt the posture of a judge or arbiter. In contrast to private practice, in which problems are commonly confronted after they have reached a more mature and unresolvable stage, at which point little remains but to be an advocate of the client's viewpoint, the uniqueness of a corporate practice lies in the ability to avoid a potential legal problem altogether by adopting a proper perspective at the inception of the problem. At times this may require counsel to be a judge against his own company's case and for the merits of a customer's argument. Obviously, he will not be able to do so unless he remains a professional in his legal judgment. In other words, he may need to resist being swept along with the tide of opinion in his corporation, even if that opinion comes from the top management level and in spite of the fact that a clearly defined legal issue has not as yet been formed.

Place yourself in the office of the following corporate counsel, and ask whether you would have remained as professional in your legal judgment as she did.

> One day counsel gets a phone call from the irate vice president of marketing in the corporation. He says that one of the dealers he set up a few years ago to market the company's products is selling out to a competitor. The marketing vice president says, "He can't do that—let's take him to court!" While counsel is talking to him trying to obtain more facts, the chief executive officer and the executive vice president of the corporation walk into her office and interrupt the telephone call with the same exhortion after having just learned about the circumstances a few minutes before. Counsel puts the marketing vice president on her telephone conference speaker and lets everyone rant and rave while she gets the dealers name and phone number and asks the marketing vice president to have the pertinent contracts and documents sent over to her office, promising to do everything she can. The last words she hears from all concerned are "Let's take him to court tomorrow — if not today."
>
> Later that afternoon after receiving the pertinent documents from the marketing vice president, coun-

sel learns that the contractural arrangement between the company and the dealer is really one of a commissioned agency, which is terminable at will by either party without notice. This arrangement had been set forth (without counsel's knowledge) on an outdated contract form that had been used by the company many years ago. Although the company had originally helped this dealer (commissioned agent) expand his pre-existing business by selling him certain service equipment at substantially discounted rates so that he could market the corporation's products effectively, there were no provisions in the relationship that would prevent the immediate termination (without penalty) by either party or the sale or change of his business arrangements to that of a competitor.

Counsel advised the officers of the company of these facts and also of her legal opinion that there was no appropriate cause of action against the dealer or the competitor company. She further advised them that the corporation would not be required to supply any further inventory to the dealer and that they could set up a separate dealership at a nearby location to compete with him.

They were not satisfied and still wanted to take him to court. The corporate executives said they would not have sold the service equipment to him at such reduced prices if they known that he was going to sell-out to a competitor two years later. Having looked at the documents of sale for the equipment, counsel stated that although the company retained a security lien on the equipment, the dealer had properly tendered the remaining unpaid purchase price on the equipment by way of a certified check, and pursuant to the documents of sale the lien was therefore effectively extinguished.

Counsel did say further, however, that she could call the attorney representing the dealer and try to settle with him by saying that the company would refuse to release the security lien, send the certified check back to them, and claim ownership of the

> equipment unless they agreed to negotiate a fair market value purchase price for the equipment. Of course, the corporate executives all said, "Do it!" But counsel cautioned them it was not a good enough case to go to court on. After talking with the attorney representing the dealer, it was clear to counsel that this tactic would not work and that the best position was to accept final payment on the equipment before even that was retracted. Nobody liked these facts and legal opinions that counsel expressed, but because they respected her legal judgment and professionalism, the corporate executives relented.

Did counsel handle this matter correctly? Especially in view of the adamant desires of the chief executive officer, the executive vice president, and the vice president of marketing to go to court? Perhaps she could have thought of a nonfrivolous cause of action worth pursuing. Under the adversary approach she might have recommended filing suit based upon several allegations and causes of actions and then later tried to determine the merits of the case and settlement potential through the discovery process. She also could have contacted a local attorney in the area to investigate the facts and applicable law further (sometimes a second opinion is needed).

But would any of those approaches been of real value to the corporation? Probably not. Although it might have been easier for counsel to go along with the tide of opinion and pursue those approaches or another, this case illustrates an occasion on which counsel remained a professional in her legal evaluation and judgment and stood apart from "corporate team" opinion and desires. Even though some corporate officers may leave counsel's office muttering under their breath, "Damn attorneys," they will respect counsel and her professional opinion far more than if she simply capitulates and goes along with their desires.

The distinction between being a "team player" and "remaining a professional" should be clear. They are two different principles, each important in the stage set for an effective corporate law practice, and each not to be confused with the other.

Avoid Political Fights

Along with remaining a professional, it is axiomatic that counsel will want to avoid becoming involved in or drawn into political fights among the laymen in the corporation. A professional's job is to support the truth and reality of an issue, not the particular views, persuasions, or ambitions of one political faction or another within the corporation.

A corporation, however large, is a small world. Should it be perceived that counsel is favoring one political faction or another without adequate legal justification, this fact will become known, and some will hold it against him. Obviously counsel cannot practice effective preventive law when he is perceived as engaging in the world of corporate politics. And counsel need not become involved in corporate politics to have a successful career as a corporate counsel. One reason the law department in many corporations reports directly to the office of the president or to the chairman or Board of Directors is to insulate the law department from political pressures within the corporation. It is recognized that corporate counsel must be professionally objective and not subject to the undue influence or retribution from one particular executive or group.

The majority of lawyers will not intentionally engage in corporate politics, but because they are sometimes subtle in nature, counsel will want to be alert and not become unknowingly involved. He should not allow himself or his legal judgment to be manipulated by one political group or another. One way to avoid being manipulated is to get all the facts on an issue or problem, not just the facts one person or group may provide.

The following example is an incident of an attempted manipulation of a corporate attorney that almost worked. It has a few political overtones to note.

> The policy of a group executive was that his division managers should submit proposals only for construction projects which were "cost-plus". He considered "lump-sum" construction work to be too risky. One of his division managers disagreed with this policy and continually tried to persuade the group executive to let him bid "lump-sum" work. The group

> executive also had told his managers that a certain attorney in the law department must approve all contracts in his division before they could be bid upon or signed.
>
> One day the division manager who wanted to bid "lump-sum" work enthusiastically rushed a "lump-sum" bid proposal contract to this attorney, asking him to approve it as soon as possible. He said it was for a tremendous construction project that they really wanted. Perhaps because of the division manager's excitement, the attorney assumed that he had received prior clearance from the group executive to bid on this "lump-sum" contract, provided the language was acceptable. Therefore, the attorney reviewed the documents and replied to the division manager, "As far as lump-sum contracts go, this one is not particularly bad," and proceeded to give him a few exceptions to be taken to the contract language when submitting the bid.
>
> About a week later the group executive stormed into the attorney's office asking him why he approved that lump-sum contract. The attorney said, "What do you mean?" The group executive replied that he had just found out that this division manager had bid on a lump-sum contract and that when he called him to ask why he did so against his policy, the division manager replied that he thought it had been cleared and approved, because the attorney had approved the contract language.
>
> The attorney replied, "I approved the contract language as far as a lump-sum contract goes, but I did not tell him he could bid it! That's a business decision between you and him. He knows that's all I approved. He never asked me whether I had cleared it with you or not."

Do you see how this division manager attempted to use the law department and this attorney to accomplish his own objective? Some people will try to use the law department to their advantage and for their purposes. As long as counsel recognizes that fact, especially when it has political overtones, and stands apart from it and remains professionally objective, always seeking the truth and reality of an issue, then he will have set a stage from which to practice corporate law effectively.

Avoid Working Too Much for One Executive or Group

Closely allied to the principles of avoiding corporate political arguments is that of avoiding working too much for one executive or group of people (department) within the corporation.

Counsel may not have a choice. If he has been assigned to handle the legal work arising out of one division or group within the corporation, he may find that by necessity he will work primarily with one or two managers in that division. But assuming that is not the case, he should try to allocate his work efforts across the board in the corporation. Some areas will need his services more than others, and, naturally, he will need to concentrate on them. But some groups and individuals will want to use his services too much and others, not enough. It is prudent for counsel to recognize that fact and allocate his workload and efforts accordingly, again assuming there is a choice.

Remember who the client is—essentially, the whole corporation and all the people working in it. Counsel's position is not like the salesman or the engineer who is concerned with a single marketing region or project within his division; counsel, and the law department, is responsible for the entire gamut of activities within the corporation.

Another result of working excessively with one group of people within the corporation or one executive is that counsel may become known as "so-and-so's attorney." Read the case study at the end of this key for a good example of just that. Counsel would be unwise to "pin his star" to one executive, thinking that he may enhance his career opportunities. A corporate attorney does not need to do that in order to succeed in a corporation, and in many cases, it will have the opposite effect. An attorney should always remain a professional not only in his legal judgment but also in the judicious allocation of work effort across the board within the corporation, circumstances permitting. In this way, the most receptive and responsive stage for an effective preventive law practice will be set.

Avoid Doing Personal Legal Work

Here is one last "avoid" subject. Counsel should not do personal legal work for any of the people within the corporation if he can avoid it. In some law departments there will be a policy against it, and that makes it simple. In others it will be more difficult. Naturally, there are some individuals whom counsel would like to help for one reason or another. Counsel should try to resist.

If counsel starts giving legal advice to corporate employees on their personal legal problems, the word will get around. The friend counsel briefly advised on a certain legal point will have another friend or someone in his department to whom he will suggest dropping in. Furthermore, everyone seems to think the advice should be free. If counsel starts dispensing personal legal advice, he will find that it will not be long before it mushrooms and becomes time-consuming.

Remember, counsel is being paid a salary to perform legal work for the corporation. Unless part of a corporate fringe benefit program, that does not include advising corporate employees on their personal legal problems. A particularly difficult problem occurs when the chief executive officer or some other high-level officer in the corporation casually asks counsel to glance over a document like the association rules and by-laws for a condominium he wants to purchase. Counsel's response to such a request must be left to his judgment, but the best recommendation is to do as little personal legal work for any corporate employees as possible.

The best advice to implement this first key to practicing law by finding solutions is to focus on the main principle: Be a team player, but remain a professional. But remember that is only a starting point. Each attorney will have to set and maintain his own personal style, tone, and stage for his practice of law in the corporation. Will he become known as an attorney who does not return telephone calls? Or one who will give in on any argument if the layman shouts long enough and loud enough?

Counsel should not fool himself by thinking that clients do not notice these things or that they are not important to his ability to practice effective corporate law. This key establishes the groundwork from which he can proceed toward finding solutions. It is a critical extension of the foundation laid in Part A. Counsel simply will not be able to maximize his ability to find solutions to the problems that will confront him as a corporate counsel unless his practice of law is first attuned to corporation, its operating style, its goals and strategies, and the people in it.

Now, before going to KEY TWO, examine the following brief case study about a corporate counsel who deliberately focused his practice of law toward one corporate executive in the corporation, and decide whether you would have done likewise in the same circumstances.

Case Study Number Six: PINNING YOUR STAR TO ONE EXECUTIVE

The Situation

A senior vice president in charge of sales for a large corporation took a liking to the legal skills and style of one of the associate-level attorneys in a seven-man law department. Part of the sales function in this corporation involved the negotiation of complex, lengthy contracts, with the assistance of a corporate attorney. As time progressed, the vice president of sales always requested this attorney to accompany him on a trip that involved contract negotiations. Seeing this, other salesmen in his group also began requesting this attorney to accompany them on such trips.

The attorney, similarly enamored of the vice president of sales, began to accommodate his work load and schedule to that of the vice president or his staff whenever possible. It was not long before the attorney was doing little but negotiating sales contracts, usually ones for the senior vice president or his staff. As a result, other legal work arising in the corporation was increasingly handled by other members of the law department. This attorney knew he was "pinning his star" to one executive and becoming known as the "sales vice president's attorney."

The Question

Based upon these meager facts, what would you have done if you were this attorney? How would you evaluate his stage for practicing preventive corporate law? Was the situation that this corporate attorney found himself in good or bad? With respect to himself as a professional? With respect to the corporation as a whole? And the law department?

What Actually Happened

This is what happened. The situation progressed to the point that the corporate attorney found himself traveling with the senior vice president of sales not just to negotiate contracts but also to assist in making sales calls. They made an effective team, and the attorney enjoyed the sales aspect of these trips as much as, if not more than, the legal aspect. Not long afterward, the senior vice president was promoted to president of the corporation and when putting his new management team together, suggested to this attorney that he take him out of the law department and make him director of the purchasing department. That was done, and although this attorney performed well in that nonlegal position, a person with more pertinent experience may have done better.

When the senior vice president he had "pinned his star to" was again promoted, this time to vice-chairman, the new president of the corporation appointed a different person director of purchasing. The vice chairman, still looking out for "his attorney," quickly arranged for a transfer to another nonlegal position that eventually did not work out, and finally the attorney returned to the law deparment.

Author's Comments

As you can well imiagine, this story could have had many different endings. More than one attorney has successfully moved from the legal area to a nonlegal area. Other attorneys have ended up on a casualty list when a certain executive with whom they were identified was removed from the mainstream of the corporate management. I think this attorney ended up somewhat perplexed by his misadventure, but he probably did not regret the opportunity and excitement that it provided.

This example was not given to tell you whether the attorney did the right thing or not. That is a personal judgment and decision each attorney will have to make. It placed an obvious burden on other members of the law department, but those things can be handled by proper administration. The corporation may will have benefited from utilization of the attorney in this manner. This example is given instead to illustrate a situation that you may encounter during your career of practicing corporate law. If you find yourself in such a situation, you will have to make your own judgment about the proper course to take. I hope this example will at least prepare you to make such a decision should it confront you. And I hope I have convinced you that a corporate attorney does not need to "pin his star" to one executive or group in order to succeed within a corporation.

Key Two: Find the Real Problem

Introduction

There may be one problem or several. There may be no problem at all. Or the problem could be a business question rather than a legal question. The point is that counsel must find the real problem if he is going to find the real solution.

Some attorneys are skillful at finding issues, even to the point of manufacturing them if they do not immediately see any and then in finding answers to the issues they have manufactured. But little is accomplished in the practice of preventive law by setting up "straw horses" and then knocking them down with an answer based upon an impressive grasp of legal theory. It seems only too natural for an attorney who is a specialist to be alert to problems in his or her area of specialty. Recall the example in Step Four in which the attorney became a member of the patent bar and thereafter devoted a substantial amount of his attention to that subject, even though the need for those services was minimal. That is an example of something to be avoided.

Counsel wants instead to find the real problem in the set of facts and circumstances confronting him. Then he can find the real solution. A solution, however impressive, to a manufactured or unimportant issue is not really a solution at all. Counsel may not always know whether he has actually found the real problem, but he should at least think he did. Because the real problem confronting counsel is not always immediately apparent or easily found, it is worthwhile to consider techniques or principles that will assist him in determining those issues of most consequence.

These are the principles to be discussed in this Key, that is, the ones that will help to find the real problem. The dictionary defines a problem as a question raised for inquiry, consideration, or solution. Logically, counsel must first learn what that question is, many times by listening to a person try to describe a set of facts to him. If he fails to listen, he may never find the real question. With some laymen, counsel must be patient. An example of a corporate counsel who could have practiced more effective preventive law had he been a better listener and more patient will be examined.

Being a good listener will also greatly assist counsel in marshalling the facts, a second important principle. Counsel simply must marshall the facts, or as many as he can in the time available to him, if he wants to pinpoint the real problem. Then, as is characteristic in a corporate preventive law practice (as opposed to an "after-the-fact" adversary practice), the business and law issues are frequently comingled, so it will be critical to distinguish and separate them. And it is important not to forget to look for law/business issues. Finally, having applied these principles to the circumstances confronting him, counsel will be ready to use his legal judgment within the business context to weigh and evaluate the issues and determine those having real and practical merit. By implementation of the principles in this Key, counsel will develop the process of analysis and judgment so crucial to finding the real problems.

Being a Good Listener Is Crucial

Imagine an officer or employee of a corporation coming into counsel's office with only an uneasy, undefined feeling of what the problem is. He may not even know what questions to ask. How will counsel find out what the real problem is unless he is a good listener and gives that person a chance to express himself and perhaps determine for himself what the problem is? Sometimes it is necessary to let people just ramble on and on. Although it may seem time-consuming at the moment, if in so doing, counsel finds the real problem that he might not have otherwise found, then how time-consuming is it really?

Be a Good Sounding Board

During his career of practicing preventive corporate law, counsel will find, if he has not already done so, that he will frequently be used as a "sounding board," that is, a manager or officer of the corporation will think he already knows the answer to a problem, but he just wants to bounce it off counsel. He just wants to check it with him to see if there are any legal problems. Or maybe he really hasn't completely defined the real problem yet, but after talking with counsel, he decides for himself what the problem is or that there really is no problem at all. Does that sound familiar? If it doesn't, then counsel may want to stop for a minute and reflect upon whether he is a good listener.

One of the most valuable functions a corporate attorney can serve is acting as a sounding board. His skills as an attorney enable him to think objectively about a situation and arrive logically at the proper analysis of the various problems and alternative solutions. It is these skills that encourage others to bounce their ideas and problems off counsel. And while they use him as a sounding board, he is given a remarkable opportunity to practice very effective preventive law. He is usually participating at a very early stage in the development of an idea or a problem. Through this early participation the opportunity to detect or prevent potential legal problems is greatly enhanced.

But if counsel fails to be a good listener, the probability of his being used as a "sounding board" by other persons within the corporation is significantly diminished. How can someone sound out their idea or problem with counsel, when he will not allow them to get it out in the first place, or in their own way and time? If after some meetings, counsel feels that he accomplished very little—just listened and offered a comment, question, or nod of agreement here and there, with the other person doing most of the talking and then obviously being satisfied in his own mind at the end of the meeting—then he can probably safely conclude that he acted as a effective sounding board. Put another way, he was able to perform effectively as a sounding board because he was a good listener.

Look at the following example, of a young corporate counsel and ask yourself how good a listener she was and whether a layman would be inclined to use her as a sounding board.

> A young attorney recently graduated from law school was by nature very talkative, quick-thinking, and often witty. She was still exhuberant from her successes in law school, and now after obtaining her first major job as a corporate attorney, these characteristics seemed to be magnified. Although it was often entertaining to talk with her, it was also sometimes difficult and frustrating. She would continually interrupt you to either complete the thought you were expressing—presumably to show you how quick and perceptive she was—or, with the confidence of having guessed what you were going to say, she would interrupt, offering her own opinion. She was often correct when anticipating what another person was going to say, so perhaps it was frustrating for her to sit there and wait for the other person to finish. People sometimes tired of her interruptions and did not bother to correct her when she did put the wrong words into their mouths or did not bother to finish their revealing recitation of a set of facts. It was sometimes easier to agree with her than to try to explain a finer point of distinction in an opinion, issue, or set of facts.

Was this counsel a good sounding board? Do you think she would be able to find the real problem to a set of facts confronting her? Maybe. What if the facts and circumstances were not clearly given to her? What if the person she was talking to was not sure himself what the problem was? Or if the person she was talking to had difficulty expressing what he was trying to say? This attorney probably missed the real issue more than once, at least at first blush, became she was not a very good listener.

Have you ever noticed how some people seem to do most of the listening in a conversation, while others do most of the talking? Countless reasons can be offered why one person appears to be a better listener then another, but it is usually the case that attorneys who have practiced law for several years are more consistently better listeners than many younger attorneys.

The ability to be a good listener is a trait found in most successful attorneys, and almost always in corporate attorneys who are practicing effective preventive law.

Be Patient

Being patient is a common characteristic of a good listener that is wise to develop. Remember, some layman are a little bit afraid of attorneys. They may know very little about the legal profession and associate it only with crimes and the police. They may be a little bit in awe of an attorney, or they may be suspicious that an attorney will trap them into saying something that they do not want to say. Whatever the case, it is wise to be sensitive to their demeanor and respond accordingly. If instead counsel belittles them or acts superior or aloof, it is unlikely that he will obtain all the facts he needs to find the real problem. Counsel should be glad they came to him and encourage them to talk while he listens.

The following example is a vivid experience on point.

> One morning several employees of the company were scheduled to be deposed by opposing counsel in the company's headquarters building. One employee whose deposition was to be taken was located in another state and flew in late the night before. Early the next morning, the corporate counsel and outside counsel held a meeting and briefly explained to these employees the facts of the litigation. The outside counsel discussed some of the questions that might be asked by opposing counsel during deposition and reviewed what some of their testimony might be.
>
> Having learned from prior experience, the corporate counsel was careful to explain the purpose and the procedures involved in a deposition in as plain English as possible. Counsel asked the employees whether they had any questions and tried to answer them as well as he could. Under the unavoidably rushed circumstances counsel felt he had prepared the employees for the depositions as adequately as possible, and since it was time to begin, they walked

> down the hall to the room set aside for them to use. Introductions were made, and the depositions began.
>
> During a break in the first deposition, the company employee who had flown in from out of town the night before pulled counsel aside and rather sheepishly and in halting English wondered whether he could ask a question. Counsel said, "Of course." From talking earlier with others in the company, counsel know this employee to be a hard-working, stable individual, well-suited to his trade but without much formal education or exposure to large corporations. Since he seemed somewhat ill-at-ease and reticent, counsel had made an extra effort in the meeting earlier in the morning to be sure that he understood what would be happening when his deposition was taken.
>
> What was his question? "Was the attorney (outside counsel) in the meeting with us this morning on our side or the other side?" Can you imagine what might have happened if counsel had not gotten that straight prior to his deposition? What if he had thought the attorney asking him the questions was on his company's side?

Reflecting upon that incident, counsel realized that the meeting just before the depositions was a hurried one. They were short of time, it was early in the morning, and at least with regard to this individual, he was not as patient as he should have been. The employee obviously had questions to ask and did not understand what was happening, but counsel was unable to draw him out. In point of fact, counsel probably just did not pay enough attention to him and actually take the time to listen to the very few comments that he did make. He was the type of person with whom counsel should have used more patience.

Marshall the Facts

Being a good listener and being patient will assist counsel in discovering the real question or problem. It will also assist him in his effort to marshall all the facts. Without knowing the correct facts or enough of the facts, counsel is unlikely to find the real problem.

A lot of effort can be wasted on counsel's part when he has not marshalled all the facts or when he has incorrectly evaluated the facts he has learned. There is nothing more discouraging then having spent hours of legal work on a particular set of facts and problem only to find out later that it was the wrong issue, that is, not the real problem.

Communicate

Another technique to use in marshalling all the facts to find the real problem is simply to communicate with the people in your corporation. If a department manager or salesman sends a memo asking counsel to review a customer's purchase order form, it is often prudent to quickly call him, before beginning work on it, to see if there are any additional, changed, or other pertinent facts counsel should know. On many occasions, this simple communication will save an otherwise wasted effort. The following incident experienced by a corporate counsel is not uncommon.

> The manager of the purchasing department sent a memo to corporate counsel requesting him to review the language in a contract form of a supplier who was to furnish a major component part for a unit manufactured and distributed by their corporation.
>
> After a brief review, this corporate counsel saw several problems with the proposed contract, primarily in the warranty area. The supplier agreed to warrant their component part against only certain, specified defects, and then for a period of only 90 days following delivery. Having pinpointed this problem area, counsel spent a good deal of time drafting alternative language that he hoped would solve the problem. Since his corporation warranted their manufactured unit against major defects for one year following the date of purchase, he drafted language that was consistent with that. In addition, he drafted two other warranty paragraphs that, although less desirable, would be acceptable if they were needed by the purchasing manager during negotiations. One

of these warranties contained detailed language providing for a proration of cost between their corporation and the supplier company based upon the primary cause of the defect causing the warranty problem.

Corporate counsel also made several other changes in the contract language, including changing the time of delivery notice period to be consistent with their production scheduling requirements. She was justifiably pleased with her analysis of the contract and her efforts in redrafting it.

After sending these comments to the purchasing manager, she received a telephone call from him. He thanked her and asked if she could come up and talk with him about the language concerning the delivery time of the components. The purchasing manger said that the supplier needed either five weeks notice before delivery or any shorter request for components must be limited to a certain maximum quantity. He wanted counsel to work up some language to satisfy these requirements. Counsel said, "What about the warranty section?" He said, "Oh, he agreed to our standard warranty a long time ago." Thanks for telling me, counsel thought to herself.

This is not an uncommon situation likely to confront counsel in his practice of corporate law. A person requesting legal services often does not adequately explain what he is looking for or provide all the facts. Most of the time it is unintentional; but it makes no difference who might be at fault.

Counsel is the one who must be sure he knows the facts before he attempts to work on a task and determine what the real problem is. If he fails to do so, as in the example, he will risk wasting a good deal of his time. In addition, what must the client think of counsel when counsel has spent most of his time on the wrong issue? In the example more then three fourths of the memorandum dealt with warranty language. Do you think the purchasing manager felt contrite because he failed to mention that the supplier had already agreed to the warranty language? It is unlikely that the thought even occurred to him. A few might have even thought to themselves, "Those attorneys are in their little own world and really don't know what's happening. He should have known we wouldn't agree to warranty language like that."

The point is—communicate, communicate, communicate! Counsel is working in a corporate environment, where things are done as a team, in meetings, and by working closely together. Laymen expect that sort of communication from the law department, and assume counsel will ask questions if he needs additional facts. A simple phone call can save time and frustration and can greatly assist counsel in marshalling the facts so that he can find the real problem.

Ask Questions

Closely allied with the technique of learning all the facts by communicating is asking questions. Some people become irritated when many questions are asked, but counsel must nonetheless continue on. It is impossible find the real problem without knowing all the facts, and asking questions is sometimes the only way to uncover them. Some people, for reasons of their own, will not want to provide all the facts.

For example, in one such instance a manager of a small subsidiary called counsel to say that he had received an labor (EEOC) complaint filed by a secretary whom he had fired two weeks earlier. The secretary charged that the subsidiary manager did not have good cause to discharge her and that he had tried to badger her into quitting several times by treating her badly. The subsidiary manager said the main reason he fired her was because she was carrying on a relationship with the warehousing manager and spent so much time at the warehouse that she was not properly performing her duties in the main office as secretary. After questioning the subsidiary manager at length, counsel felt fairly comfortable that he could defend the EEOC charges. However, he wisely decided to question the warehouse manager to see whether he might supply any additional facts. After talking briefly with him, the complexion of the case changed dramatically. He said that the reason the subsidiary manager fired the secretary was because he was jealous. He said the subsidiary manager was constantly asking her to go out, but she always refused. Naturally, counsel had to determine which set of facts was true by asking everyone many more questions.

Here the subsidiary manager told some of the facts, but not all of them. What he said was true but incomplete. Only by further questioning did counsel later learn all the facts. The real problem in this case quickly changed from one of gathering and presenting the facts to the EEOC of improper job performance to one of defending against possible sexual harassment. Imagine how counsel would have felt had he walked into the EEOC hearing unprepared on that set of facts.

By asking questions, counsel is also encouraging the other person to talk. Then he can apply his skills of listening to find out what the real problem is. In this same vein, counsel might say, "I'm sorry, I don't understand. Will you repeat that?" Sometimes a person will shed a different light on what he just said when he is asked to repeat it. The fact that counsel may appear to be uncomprehending by asking a person to repeat an answer should be of no concern to him at all. He is trying to uncover the real facts and real problem.

Being a good listener, being patient, and marshalling all the facts through communicating and asking questions, are essentials for finding the real problems, without which the effectiveness of the practice of preventive law will be significantly diminished.

Distinguish Between Law and Business Issues

Suppose at this point counsel has not found the real problem, or at least does not think he has. What should he do then? He should continue his analysis by trying to identify and separate the law issues, on the one hand, from the business issues, on the other. This technique will often clarify otherwise ambiguous-appearing issues and problems. Law and business issues are frequently comingled in the corporate environment. Counsel will sometimes be able to identify the "real problem" as being a business decision rather than a legal one. Remember, the objective in this Key is to find the real problem and recognize it for what it really is—regardless of whether it is a business decision or legal issue.

If the real problem is indeed a business decision, whether it is a marketing, purchasing, a finance question, or whatever, but not primarily a legal issue, then counsel should identify that issue to the business managers and leave it for them to decide. On the other hand, counsel will not be practicing effective corporate law if he is applying the principles of his legal training and knowledge to arrive at what he mistakenly thinks is a legal decision when it is really a business decision to which the principles of profit and loss should be applied. He will also become frustrated for not being able to find a very good solution. The following example demonstrates this. Read it carefully; discussion of it will continue into the next section.

> Counsel is a corporate attorney for a company that manufactures and distributes consumer products. Typically, a product division in the corporation will develop or acquire the prototype of a new product and then test-market it on a limited basis before selling it to the public at large. During this initial testing stage, the company usually does not offer a warranty on the product. In fact, corporate counsel usually writes disclaimers of warranty. However, on this occasion the competitors of the corporation already had a nearly identical product on the market, and time was crucial.
>
> The marketing director of the corporation walks into counsel's office and says, "Do you think we should offer a warranty on our new product . . . like our competitors are doing?"

How would you answer the marketing director's question? Think about it for a minute before continuing.

Without more, most lawyers should agree that the decision whether to offer (or disclaim) a warranty on a product that the company manufactures is a business decision to be made by the marketing department, production department, sales department, or perhaps by the president of the company. It is not a legal decision. The particular language constituting the warranty is, of course, correctly a legal matter upon which counsel would advise the marketing director, but not the limited decision of whether to extend the warranty. So you were correct if you identified the real question or problem in this example as being primarily a business issue for the business managers to decide and answered the marketing director's question accordingly.

What might have happened in this instance if the corporate attorney had not distinguished between that business issue and legal issues? The following is one variation that could have occurred.

> Corporate counsel might have thought to herself, "Sure, I know all about warranties, I'll handle this for him". So counsel says, "If our competitors can offer a warranty, why can't we? Tell you what. Give me a copy of their warranty, and I'll write you one that looks just as good but really doesn't offer anything. That way you won't have to worry if your new product isn't any good." The marketing director says, "Great!" And she writes a warranty that contains a lot of legal sounding language and looks impressive to some people but, in fact, does not say much. At least she thought it did not—until her company ended up in court over the language.

What has the corporate counsel accomplished by this approach? She may have created more problems then they had otherwise. She, in effect, made a business decision for the marketing director by applying her legal knowledge unwisely. Clearly, she did not distinguish between the business issues and the legal issues. The real problem that needed to be identified and answered was not the one she assumed. She assumed they wanted (or needed) to extend a warranty on their product but that it should not really offer anything because they had not finished test-marketing the product. Had she reflected for a minute and tried to isolate the business objectives from the legal issues, she would have determined that the real problem to be decided first was the business decision of whether to offer a warranty.

Now, does anything seem to be missing in the analysis and technique used so far to handle the marketing director's question in this example? The decision to extend the warranty is a business matter, while the language of the warranty to accomplish that business objective is clearly a legal matter. But the marketing director is sitting in counsel's office for a reason.

Do Not Forget Law/Business Issues

If counsel thought the marketing director in the product warranty example was sitting in her office for a reason and that the purpose for his being there was not completely satisfied by her analysis and advice, then she was correct.

Although some corporate laymen will simply want to use counsel as a sounding board or occasionally try to use him to make a business decision for them, thinking that it will take them off the hook if something goes wrong later, the more likely case is that the corporate manager wanted some practical advice to his problem—in short, a solution. So even though an analysis of a set of facts by corporte counsel that clearly defines the business issues from the legal issues is often extremely helpful to corporate managers and is prerequisite in the process toward finding the real problems (and, in turn, the real solutions), analysis of the problem should not always end at this point.

Most notably, when the business and legal issues seem to be inextricably intertwined, by going one stage further and looking for law/business issues, counsel will usually find a clearer and more realistic definition of the real problems. Remember, a legitimate and desirable function in corporate law department today is to advise on law/business issues, that gray area somewhere between the pure law question and the pure business question. And because law/business issues are increasingly confronting today's corporate counsel, some of his greatest contributions to the corporation and most effective preventive corporate law can be practiced by advising on law/business issues.

The missing or incomplete step in the analysis of the product warranty example was the failure to determine whether there were any law/business issues that should have been addressed (after segregation of the business and legal issues).

Examine the product warranty example again. The question asked to corporate counsel by the director of marketing was whether she thought a warranty should be offered on the new product being tested by the corporation. The legal issue and the business question have already been identified. Is there also a law/business issue, and if so, what is it? Remember, the marketing director is sitting in counsel's office for a reason. Think about it for a minute, and then examine this approach by corporate counsel.

> Corporate counsel replied to the marketing director's question by saying, "Whether or not to extend a warranty on this new product is a business decision I can't make, but I can tell you some of the issues and risks that warranties typically address, and why.
>
> "For example," she continued to say, "how would you answer these issues: What particular components of our product do you want to warrant? How reliable are those parts? How much would it cost to repair or replace those parts? How many complaints from customers have we received during the current testing program about defective parts? Do we have the existing facilities and capabilities to repair defective parts? How much money is our company willing to allocate to a warranty program? To what extent do you think the sales of our product would be hurt by not offering a warranty, or one as extensive as our competitors are? What does our competitor's warranty say; and what about it do you like or not like?"
>
> After having discussed these questions and some of the answers to them, she told the marketing director that typical product warranties extend for a limited time period, from 30 days to perhaps a year or two. She also stated that although some warranties guarantee "complete satisfaction", the more common warranty covers only specified defects. In addition, warranties will usually cover only the cost of new parts required to repair the product, not the cost of labor or shipping and handling. She said that regardless of what kind of warranty, if any, was finally extended, from a legal standpoint certain disclaimers of implied warranties would probably be advisable, depending upon applicable state laws.
>
> She suggested if he would find out the answers to these issues and some of the specific business objectives the company would have in mind when ex-

tending (or not) the warranty, then she could draft the legal language to meet those objectives. She also said she could attend any meetings he might have on this subject and offer suggestions or comments from a legal viewpoint.

Now, what did counsel accomplish with this approach? First, she correctly segregated the business issues from the legal issues. Then she went on to identify and discuss law/business issues of what risks are frequently addressed in warranties and some reasons why; she offered further assistance on these law/business issues; and she said she could handle the legal issue of drafting the warranty.

Most importantly, she did not decide the business issues, but by addressing the related law/business issues, she may have saved herself a great deal of time by avoiding the drafting warranty after warranty, each one a little different, as the business managers making the decisions progressed in their decision-making process about the warranty objectives. By participating in the development stages of the product warranty, she may well have discovered legal problems before they surfaced, giving herself an opportunity to practice effective preventive law. And she offered some practical advice and useful suggestions to the marketing director about alternative approaches to the problem confronting him. (Query: solutions? The handling of law/business questions and weighing alternative answers will be discussed in detail in KEY FIVE: EXAMINE THE ALTERNATIVES.)

But for now, with regard to the techniques for finding the real problem, what has this example of counsel addressing the law/business issues demonstated? Was the real problem in this example the business decision of whether to extend a warranty; was it the law/business issues of what risks should be addressed; or was it the legal issue of what language should be in the warranty? Does it have to be one or the other? Not necessarily. Remember, a situation can have several real problems or none at all. In this case the business issue and the law/business issues are both real problems, which counsel's analysis should have found and which counsel would have properly addressed. Counsel would not have ignored the real problem of the law/business issues by saying to the marketing director, for example, "When you decide what you want in the warranty—let me know—and I'll write it for you.

At the stage of development of the warranty issue in this example, the legal language by itself was not yet the real problem nor an issue with which counsel would want to have mistakenly treated as the most important question or real problem. On the other hand, it could have been a real problem had the marketing director walked into counsel's office and asked for a warranty that included the words "guaranteed to full satisfaction" but nonetheless had language so that the company would have no liability.

To summarize, counsel must implement this principle of segregating the issues into his own practice of corporate law if he is to clarify the frequently commingled and ambiguous factual issues that will confront him. Counsel's handling of the issues in the product warranty example showed that distinguishing among the legal, law/business, and business issues helps to identify the real problems, a prerequisite to finding solutions. Another technique for determining which issues represent the real problem is discussed in the next and final principle of this Key.

Weigh the Issues in a Business Context

What is a simple and meaningful way to paraphrase this last but crucial principle in our search for the real problem?

DON'T MANUFACTURE PROBLEMS THAT DON'T EXIST!

Weigh and evaluate all the issues, use a little judgment, and refrain from manufacturing any of those issues into problems that really do not exist. Failure to apply this important principle has prevented more than one very fine corporate attorney from becoming the truly capable and effective corporate counsel he could otherwise have become. Indeed, some corporate counsel fail to apply this principle not because they are unable to do so, but because the thought never occurs to them. They are so involved in their own world of legal issues, the thought to step back a minute and consider the importance of the legal issues in terms of the overall business objectives and purposes does not occur to them.

Remember? Something very similar has been discussed before. In the introduction to this Part B, a solution was defined as those alternative courses of action or decisions that accomplish the business purposes . . . to the extent possible, while still maintaining high quality legal compliance within determined levels of legal risk, exposure, and cost to the corporation. It is no different here. Counsel will not consistently find the best solutions to the questions and circumstances confronting him unless he first identifies those issues (the real problems) that are of most consequence or merit as viewed from within the business context and corporate environment in which they have arisen or will later exist. Put another way, the real merit of a particular issue is not found in a conclusion manufactured by counsel from within a vacuum or limited perspective but instead consists of a considered judgment arrived at by weighing the issues from both a legal and business standpoint, to the extent possible.

Does this principle in any way diminish the importance of first finding all the possible legal issues that might exist or later arise in a problem counsel is handling? Certainly not! Implicit within the discussions throughout this Key is counsel's need always to search for all the legal issues. That has not been necessary to discuss because attorneys know to do so. In fact, the necessity to identify all the legal issues is one of those things that law professors keep saying that truly do carry through in importance to the practice of law.

After counsel has identified all the possible legal issues, does this principle in any way diminish the importance of researching the applicable points of law and evaluating the merits of each legal issue on its own, apart from any business considerations? No! The merits of some legal issues will be of such critical importance that any possible business considerations will be vitiated. To effectively weigh the legal issues in a business context, counsel must first proceed from a solid base and firm knowledge of the merits of each legal issue.

What this principle means is that after counsel has identified all the legal issues (and law/business issues) and determined their merits from a legal standpoint, he should use some common sense and judgment and ask himself whether all these issues are really pertinent. Do they represent a real problem in the matter at hand, or are they of relatively minor importance? Try to evaluate their relative importance in part by weighing them against any business issues previously segregated and perhaps determined to be real problems. Counsel need not be a business manager, or know as much about the business as one, to make this comparison. A detailed and definitive comparison is not necessary, only a general judgment about their respective merits. After this kind of comparison and weighing, if counsel decides that a legal or law/business issue could represent a real problem in the matter, then that judgment justifies his continued critical attention and investigation into the issue, perhaps ultimately resulting in finding the real problem, and later the real solution. On the other hand, if this comparison indicates that a particular legal issue is not of major importance compared to other issues that, in fact, represent the real problems, then while still handling the legal issue with "... high quality legal compliance within determined levels of legal risk ...," counsel should be mindful of its relative minor importance and treat it accordingly.

A hypothetical based upon an actual incident illustrates this crucial process of weighing the issues in the business context.

> Two attorneys and several laymen spent the better part of two days negotiating the contractual terms of documents that would represent the agreement between the parties, by which a medium-sized industrial manufacturing facility would be engineered and constructed in the United States for a Canadian company. In-house corporate counsel with five years' experience represented the engineering/construction firm, while the Canadian company was represented by an outside counsel with ten years' experience in private practice, who was also the counsel who represented the bank that had issued a letter of committment to fund the project.
>
> The documents assembled for discussion were numerous and varied, but they consisted primarily of a lengthly standard form contract supplied by the engineering/construction firm, along with several appendices and attachments supplied by both parties. Greatly simplified, the following were the primary concepts covered by these documents: what was to

be engineered and constructed, for what price, the procedures by which the project would be developed, built, and paid for, the required level of quality and functionability, and the allocation of responsibility and liability for known and unknown risks.

During the course of negotiations over the two-day period, most of one of those days was spent discussing, negotiating, and redrafting the sections of the documents that pertained to the procedures by which the engineering / contraction firm would be able to draw monies for reimbursement of their services. These final redrafted sections were very clear and precise with respect to procedural forms to be used, the necessary approvals, inspections, and so on, required before a draw would be issued. In fact, this section became the most extensive section in the contractual documents. Despite this, although a great deal had been changed procedurally in this section, very little was changed substantively from the original drafts. In effect, the engineer / contractor had the capability to draw the same amount of money based upon the same percentage of completion, but with several new documentary requirements.

On the other hand, relatively little discussion and few questions were asked about the several other primary concepts set forth in the documents. By and large, the limited negotiation on the other points worked to the advantage of the engineering / construction firm, which had supplied its standard form contract containing language slanted in its favor, and to the disadvantage of the owner, the industrial Canadian company.

Now, given these limited facts, how well did the outside counsel represent his client, the Canadian manufacturing company? Did he weigh and evaluate the issues within the business context of his client to determine which issues were of most consequence or merit? Did he find the real problems?

Most lawyers would agree the contract language requiring the owner to reimburse the engineer / contractor for services performed was a primary issue and would have represented a real problem to the Canadian company had it not been properly set forth. But what about the other major concepts? What about the quality and functionability of the finished product? Did the language adequately provide that the completed facility would perform as intended? Is not what his client would end up with at least as important as the procedures by which it would be paid for? And what about the allocation of liability for unknown risks?

It is safe to conclude that the outside counsel in this example either did not first analyze and segregate all the issues into law, law / business, and business issues in order to identify the real problems, or having done so, he did not then step back a minute and weigh their relative merit in the business context of his client. Perhaps his expertise in banking matters and procedures (recall that he was outside counsel for the bank issuing the commitment letter) inadvertently caused him to focus his knowledge and skills on that area of the contract documents to the neglect of several other important sections. Whatever the reasons, did he focus on all of the real problems? Did he not, in fact, manufacture a problem that did not exist? Over 50 per cent of the meetings were spent discussing and redrafting the financial reimbursement contract sections, even though the resulting changes were more procedural than substantive.

One last observation on this example: It is not as easy as it looks, as many lawyers know. Even finding all of the issues and real problems in the complex, entangled factual mazes often encountered in the corporate world can be a significant achievement, let alone then being able to stand back from the often intense, fast-paced circumstances to realistically and effectively weigh the relative merits of each of the issues. Nonetheless, that is corporate counsel's job, or should be, and it is unquestionably a way in which to practice preventive corporate law most effectively. Some of the judgment necessary to properly weigh the issues in the business context will only come from experience, but a continual effort to implement the principle discussed in this section will make counsel that much more skilled and effective in ultimately finding the real problems. Remember, any lawyer with a little imagination can dream up a laundry list of issues, but it is the more uncommon lawyer who can then take those issues and properly identify which ones are of the most consequence and merit to his client.

To recap, the objective in this Key has been to examine techniques of analysis that will help corporate counsel find the real problems in the situations confronting him as he practices corporate preventive law. By first finding the real problems, he is then half way down the road toward finding the real solutions, his ultimate objective. He will also be effectively applying his skills and knowledge as an attorney to the business environment in which he is practicing law. Counsel should be a good listener and sounding board, be patient and marshall all of the facts, before then looking for the issues, not just the legal ones but the law/business and business issues as well. And by all means, he should always use a little judgment and weigh the relative merit of each issue in its business context, as well as from the legal standpoint.

Read carefully the factual situation and note the comments made by the corporate department managers and officers during the meeting recounted in the following case study. It is an excellent illustration to see whether you can pick out the same real problems the corporate counsel in the case study did and whether you see others he may have missed.

Case Study Number Seven: IS THE DEALER GOING UNDER?

The Situation

Counsel is a corporate attorney in an agricultural products company that earns approximately 60 per cent of its revenue through the manufacture and distribution of agricultural fertilizers wholesaled to farmers in local areas through a system of independent dealers. Because of the recessionary economy and record-setting crop yields driving down commodity prices, the agricultural industry and the company's fertilizer business has been experiencing a severe downturn during the past two years. Many economists are predicting a turnaround in the next year.

About this time counsel attends a meeting in a conference room in the company headquarters with several people. Among them are the corporate vice president of marketing and sales, the manager of a subsidiary that distributes the company's fertilizers in a certain geographical region, the corporate financial officer, the credit manager, and the corporate operations manager overseeing all subsidiaries. The purpose of the meeting is to decide what to do about a large independent dealer through which a subsidiary of the company has been distributing fertilizers in a local area for several years.

The problems with this dealer and a few background facts follow. The corporation (in this case through its wholly owned subsidiary), in effect, consigns most of its fertilizer products (in a bulk, fungible form or in a labeled bag) to dealers at the beginning of the spring season when demand is greatest, and then in smaller increments until late fall. The dealers make minimum payments on the product throughout the season until "settlement day" at the end of the fall season, when inventory is taken, all accounts are rectified, and commissions to the dealers are paid. The subsidiary manager and the operations manager are currently in "settlement day" negotiations with a large dealer and report much difficulty and problems. The dealer argues that he has lost money this year and last year because the wholesale prices the company is charging for its fertilizer are excessive in view of the recession, that his figures prove a greater amount of commission is owed to him, and that the company's inventory figures are incorrect. He is generally being uncooperative and delaying settlement. By the subsidiary manager's calculations, the dealer owes the company $20,000 from the year before and in excess of $60,000 for this year. The dealer does not agree with these figures and says that he does not have the money to pay the account anyway; yet he wants an agreement from the company to furnish him with inventory on consignment next spring so that he can continue in business. He says that next year will be a good year and that he will then pay all accounts in full.

Here are some of the comments made in the meeting. The credit manager has had it with this dealer and wants the past due accounts cleaned up. He is of the opinion, as is his supervisor, the corporate financial officer, that this dealer is basically insolvent and close to bankruptcy. They think the company should take him to court to get the money owed, regardless of whether the company plans to do business with him in the future. The subsidiary manager thinks the company should hang in with the dealer through the next year, which promises to be a better one. He says this dealer is a well-known respected distributor in his region of operations and that his sales alone account for more than 15 per cent of the annual revenues of the subsidiary. He states that even if they could find another dealer to replace him, it would take a minimum of two years to get a new dealer established in that area and operating at a profit. The corporate marketing and sales vice president, to whom subsidiary operations report, agrees that this dealer represents a significant foothold in a geographical region into which they have expanded during the past several years and is reluctant to discontinue operations with the dealer. He, too, thinks the market will change next year, but he also says that he does not want to throw good money after bad, and if they have to cut our losses and run, they will.

The Question

Here are some of the questions they ask counsel during the meeting: What do you think we should do with this dealer? Do you think we should continue doing business with him? Can we file a lawsuit against him for the money he owes us?

What happens to our inventory he has now if we file a lawsuit? Do you think he will go bankrupt? If we continue to do business with him, can we make him pay us before any of his other creditors?

If you were sitting in the meeting how would you analyze this situation? What are the real problems? Are there any legal decisions to be made? What are the most pertinent legal issues? Are there any law / business issues? Does counsel have all the facts? Has he listened to what everyone has said?

What Actually Happened

The corporate attorney begins by saying, "I can't tell you whether or not you should continue doing business with this dealer—that's a business decision you'll have to make. I can tell you this, however. If for whatever reason this dealer goes into bankruptcy, your chances of collecting much of the past due accounts is not very great. Typically, in a bankruptcy action, whether it's a Chapter 11 reorganization or a liquidation, you will be lucky to collect even 20 cents on the dollar two years after the action is filed."

He further states that he thinks a lawsuit could be filed now on the past due accounts, but that he would need to go over this and last year's accounts in detail with the subsidiary and credit managers to verify their accuracy and compliance with the agreements between the parties. He says he could check real estate records, credit agencies, and other sources to determine whether the dealer would have any assets available to pay a judgment, assuming the company could obtain one. In addition, he suggests requesting the dealer to furnish an audited financial statement or allowing our auditors to investigate his financial records, which might show whether a lawsuit would force him into bankruptcy.

Having made these comments, he then pauses a minute and makes these observations, "I think the real problem here is whether continuing to do business with this dealer is worth the risk? In other words, how much control do we have? If we continue to do business with this dealer and supply him with a large amount of inventory, what controls do we have on that inventory? Can it be segregated in his warehouse and identified as our product so that in the event of bankruptcy we can reclaim it? Do we have any control over the proceeds he will receive when he sells the inventory? Can we earmark those funds for payment to us? Can we obtain the right to inspect his inventory and audit his books on a weekly or monthly basis? Would it be feasible for us to place an operating manager at his location to keep track of our inventory and his business?"

In summary, he expresses the opinion that because of the apparent financial condition of this dealer and the amount of money he currently owes the company, if the company decides to continue doing business with him, it should be done only if adequate controls and procedures can be agreed upon to minimize the company's risk. He suggests that some type of accord and satisfaction agreement regarding all present and past due accounts, including repayment procedures and schedules, and secured with collateral if possible, plus other written agreements specifying the arrangements for any future business, including the filing of financing statements on inventory, provisions for auditing, and other legal protective devices, might bring the potential risk within an acceptable range.

Many of his comments and others are discussed in this and subsequent meetings. The company does continue doing business with this dealer the next season but under very strict operating agreements, resulting in a paydown during the following year of some of the total debt owed to the company.

Author's Comments

What do you think? Did this corporate attorney identify the real problems? I think he came close to them. He correctly identified the overall problem of whether or not they should continue doing business with this dealer. He also correctly identified that issue as a business decision.

He then identified two pertinent legal problems. The first was whether the past due accounts were accurate and verifiable for use as evidence in litigation and were, in fact, consistent with the agreements between the parties (since the dealer was disputing this). Second, assuming a lawsuit could be filed, he questioned whether there would be any assets that could be attached to pay a judgment and whether such litigation would force him into a petition for bankruptcy, either voluntarily or otherwise.

Next, the corporate attorney identified another very real problem, the law/business issue of whether they had adequate controls to minimize the risk if they continued doing business with the dealer.

Did he listen? Yes. To everyone's point of view as indicated by his comments directed toward the concerns of both the credit manager and the subsidiary manager. Did he marshall all the facts? No. And he knew he could not in this meeting, which was the reason for his saying that he would need to review the accounts and agreements in detail prior to determining whether or not a lawsuit could and should be brought.

Did he pinpoint all the legal issues? Not precisely in this first meeting. But he would identify more legal issues as the facts came out. Did he identify the pertinent legal issues and the real problems? Did he weigh and evaluate the issues within the business context, using some judgment? I think so. What do you think? I do not believe he manufactured issues that did not exist. That is to his credit.

Did this case study frustrate you a little bit? Did you feel as though you did not have enough facts to pinpoint the legal issues, and perhaps the real problems? If it did, I share your frustration. This is a typical example of many situations that will confront a corporate attorney. It will seem that you will never have enough facts. That is why you must marshall as many facts as possible. It will also seem that the issues are rarely black and white. Often they are in that gray area containing the law/business issues previously discussed. Frequently, people will want answers and legal advice on the spot. You will want to say, "Wait a minute. Let me take some time, get some more facts, do some research, find out what the issues really are, and then I'll tell you how to do it from the legal standpoint." That would be nice. Unfortunately, that is not the way it usually works (see Key Three: Apply the Law).

Key Three: Apply the Law

Introduction

The next logical step to find an answer or solutions to the questions and real problems presented is to apply the law.

The classic and unquestionably best method to apply the law to a problem is the one counsel is already very familiar with from law school and later as a practicing attorney. After being presented a set of facts or circumstances, counsel must interpret and analyze the facts, research the applicable statutory, regulatory, and case law on point, and apply the correct principles of law to the key issues through a disciplined and rigorous process of logical thinking. Being able to think logically is one of the greatest assets and abilities counsel can possess when practicing effective corporate law.

But what is unrealistic about this classic method of applying the law? The circumstances in which counsel must apply the law. The circumstances confronting counsel in his practice of corporate law can sometimes at best be described as "imperfect." As was vividly demonstrated in the case study at the end of the last Key about the independent dealer that was on the verge of bankruptcy, sometimes counsel will be confronted with situations in which he does not know all the facts, will not know which facts are reliable, or even know what the real problems are. And in those circumstances, he is asked to apply the law and give an answer. Situations like those are difficult at best, and for that reason they are the main subject of discussion in this Key Three. There is no doubt that counsel will know how to effectively use the classic method of applying the law when the opportunities permit or the situations demand, so it is not necessary to discuss that process.

But what must be discussed is what corporate counsel should do when he is asked to apply the law in an "imperfect" situation. Should he take a stab in the dark or "shoot from the hip"? Is that approach likely to result in the correct answer to the problem? After that difficult topic is examined, some circumstances in which it may be appropriate for counsel to give a "partial answer" to a question confronting him will be discussed and why it is sometimes important, regardless of the circumstances, to say, "I don't know the answer," and use the classic method of applying the law.

Before going any further, one critical observation and caveat is necessary. These techniques of applying law in imperfect circumstances are not necessarily advocated nor recommended as a style of practicing law, particularly when there is another choice. Little can harm an attorney's credibility and effectiveness more than being perceived as too lazy to analyze a problem in depth and thoroughly research the law before giving an answer.

But because of the derogatory connotations often associated with these approaches to applying the law, they are infrequently mentioned and, for that reason alone, are worthy of counsel's attention. Then, if presented with an imperfect circumstance in which counsel has no other alternative, at least he will be more prepared to handle the situation in the most effective manner possible at the time. Always keep in mind, however, that the classic approach to applying the law by thoroughly investigating the facts and researching the law before carefully reasoning out the correct answer to a problem is invariably the most desired and most commonly used method of applying the law in the practice of corporate law.

Should One Shoot from the Hip?

Should counsel be the fastest dispenser of law in the law profession? No! Does counsel nonetheless have to "shoot from the hip" in some limited circumstances when practicing preventive corporate law? Yes. In fact, in a few instances, shooting law from the hip can be the most effective method of preventing more serious legal problems from occurring soon thereafter. Counsel, however, should quickly qualify this "Yes" by saying that a legal answer so dispensed is only an "educated guess." And notwithstanding the circumstances, counsel will sometimes want to refuse to give his "best guess" and simply say that he does not know the answer but will look it up.

What exactly is "shooting from the hip"? One of the reasons that corporations establish in-house law departments is so that the officers and managers of the corporation will have immediate access to legal advice. Occasionally, a legal problem in the real world of business demands an immediate decision. Recall the example about the OSHA inspector sitting in the plant manager's office while the chief executive officer in the headquarters building is trying to get hold of a partner in the outside law firm to find out whether they should allow the inspector to walk through the plant without a warrant. That is an instance in which counsel would probably not have enough time to undertake a detailed analysis and research of the applicable law on point. He will have to give his "best guess."

The following is a more detailed example of what is meant by "shooting from the hip." Here, two publicly owned companies are engaged in merger discussions, and counsel is in-house corporate counsel for the corporation that is the target acquisition candidate.

> Two publicly owned corporations have been engaged in merger discussions for a period of about three weeks. The discussions are still very preliminary and tentative; in fact, the acquisition or selling price of the proposed transaction has not even been mentioned.
>
> Counsel is in-house counsel for the company that may be acquired. Although the law is imprecise in this area, he has concluded that public disclosure of these preliminary discussions is not required—at least not in the present stage, and perhaps not until a definitive agreement or letter of intent has been agreed upon.
>
> In the late morning on the Friday during the third week, the company president receives a telephone

call from an official of the stock exchange on which the shares of common stock of the company are registered. The official states that value of the company's stock has risen 4 points since the exchange opened this morning (a rise of over 50 per cent) and the trading volume has been unusually heavy. He says that they are considering suspending trading activity in the company's stock; and he wants to know whether the company president can account for this activity and whether he intends to make a public announcement about an event which may explain the reason for this activity. The company president asks the stock exchange official if he can put him on hold for a minute, does so, and has his secretary run to counsel's office to get him. The company president quickly explains the situation and asks counsel's advice about the necessity of making an announcement about the merger discussions.

Counsel thinks quickly. He knows generally that the Security and Exchange Commission regulations require disclosure of an event or facts which a member of the investing public would want to know if they were considering buying or selling the company's stock. He concluded earlier that the merger discussions were at such a preliminary stage that disclosure under this principle was not required. Circumstances, however, have changed. Because of the run-up in price of the company's stock, it seems likely that some traders, arbitrators, or insiders have learned about the merger discussions and are buying stock in anticipation of a final acquisition price higher than the current market level. Under these circumstances counsel reasons that an investor in the company's stock would want to know the reason for the significant increase in the value and trading volume.

Therefore, counsel tells the company president, in view of the new developments and his understanding of the law, the company should now make a public disclosure of the merger negotiations by telephoning and telexing a press release to the wire services and local media, by notifying the potential acquiring company in the merger discussions so they can coordinate their own release, and by so informing the stock exchange official still holding on the telephone line.

The company president informs the official, and counsel goes back to his office to quickly write a short press release.

Was the corporate counsel in this example "shooting from the hip"? Definitely. The attorney in this case quickly analyzed the facts, applied the general principles of law as he knew them, and arrived at a well-reasoned, logical decision. It was a type of situation that required a rapid and correct decision.

Although the company president in this example may have been able to delay the decision by telling the stock exchange official that he would call him back within 30 to 60 minutes, he certainly did not have the luxury of pondering the decision over the weekend and deciding whether or not to make an announcement after the stock exchange opened on Monday morning.

Should the corporate counsel in this case have said to the company president, "Let me research the case law on this point and get back to you as soon as I can"? Probably not. It is doubtful whether he would have been able to find case law on point within the time necessary to make a decision. What he did instead was to apply the law as he knew it to the set of facts presented before him. He utilized his skills and judgment as an attorney in the situations at hand, with the result that he correctly and effectively practiced preventive corporate law. He may have prevented a far more serious legal problem from occurring by failing to make a timely disclosure to the investing public.

There is a proper place and need in practicing preventive corporate law to exercise the ability as a corporate attorney to think logically with the facts and law as he knows them at the time and to issue an immediate and accurate legal decision. This aspect or technique of applying the law is what is meant by "shooting from the hip." Admittedly, it's dangerous because it can also become a trademark of the lazy attorney, whether in corporate or other areas of the legal profession. Simply because counsel may be required to shoot from the hip at certain times does not mean that on other occasions investigation and research should be dispensed with. Nonetheless, counsel is well advised to prepare himself for those situations that demand he "shoot from the hip."

Prepare Yourself

Counsel should consider some practical and prudent ways to improve his ability to dispense law quickly and accurately. They can be summarized in two words: Prepare yourself.

In the previous example corporate counsel had done some prior research on when a public disclosure of merger discussions was required. Obviously, counsel's ability to make a quick and accurate legal decision when the circumstances demand will depend, to a great extent, upon his prior preparation by knowing the legal issues and law most often affecting his company and industry. There is no better way for counsel to enhance his ability to handle situations that demand immediate legal decisions than to become an expert in the law affecting his industry most often and by knowing the industry problems likely to confront him. Here, the good foundation established (in Part A) will be of significant value.

Another excellent method that is helpful in making immediate legal judgments is trying to anticipate future problems that might arise. For example, if counsel has heard that some company officers have been talking with the managers of another company about a joint venture project, then he might want to review the fundamentals, advantages, and disadvantages of joint venture agreements against other forms of business combinations. So, too, if counsel knows that the company is considering closing one or two production plants and laying off the work force, it would be prudent to review the personnel policies and labor regulations that would apply to seniority, discrimination, and so on, as well as the company's policy on severance and vacation pay if that applies.

Because counsel is practicing *preventive* corporate law, his objective is to prevent legal problems from occurring. How can he address these legal issues before they arise if he does not try to anticipate them? Sometimes questions will be brought to counsel at an early stage, and he will easily be able to anticipate what legal problems could arise. But that is not always the case. He may need only reflect for five or ten minutes upon the potential problem and the general principles of law; other times he will want to do some in-depth research; or if he lacks the time, he can use outside specialists. This kind of anticipation is an extremely valuable technique for counsel to prepare for those situations in which he must shoot from the hip. In fact, it actually diminishes his need to shoot from the hip because he already knows the law pertinent to the problem. While at that moment it may seem to consume valuable time, if a legal problem is thereafter prevented, no doubt far more time was actually saved.

Should Partial Answers Be Given?

Another less dramatic "imperfect" situation that will be encountered far more often as corporate counsel is one in which counsel will be asked to apply the law before having investigated the facts thoroughly or researched the law on point in depth when the circumstances do not require an immediate answer. The difference between the "imperfect" circumstances here and those discussed in the preceding section is one of immediacy.

The extent to which one situation may require a more immediate answer than another is sometimes a most difficult question and will largely be a matter of judgment. Just be sure the judgment remains counsel's. Avoid being hoodwinked into thinking a situation is more immediate than it really is. Laymen managers will commonly say that they need an answer right now or the business deal will fall through or for whatever other reasons. Counsel will learn, however, that this is usually not the case, if he is not already so aware. Remember, counsel is a professional who is responsible to exercise high standards of legal analysis and compliance and must take the time necessary to do so.

So what should counsel do about the "imperfect circumstance" in which he is asked to apply the law when the situation is not one of immediacy? He may want to give a partial answer, qualified as such and followed up by a thorough investigation, in-depth research, and rigorous logical thinking (the classic approach) with the end result of giving either a confirming answer or a modified answer. On the other hand, he may want to simply say that he cannot give an answer now (see the next section).

One of the distinguishing characteristics of a preventive corporate law practice is the opportunity to participate in the early stages of an idea or problem. Counsel can use his skills as an attorney and knowledge of the law to lend focus and direction to the development of ideas and problems in the corporation. He can do so by giving partial answers to the questions asked about the law during these early stages. For that reason it is sometimes appropriate and desirable for counsel to consider giving a partial statement of the law (when so qualified) and then follow up with the classic approach of investigation and research.

The following example illustrates this type of developing situation and the giving of a partial answer in response in more detail.

> Counsel is sitting in his office when his secretary says the company president would like to see him for a minute.
>
> Upon reaching the company president's office, it becomes apparent that the president has been engaged in a meeting for some time with the executive vice president, the vice president of operations, and a field plant manager. As counsel stands just inside the door saying hello to everyone, the president says, "We've been talking about adding a new automated production line to our manufacturing plant in Arizona. Would we have to get Board approval before going ahead with it?"
>
> What should counsel say? Should he say, "I don't know, I'll check on it." He certainly should not be afraid to say that. But if in his capacity as corporate attorney he has acted as Secretary to the Board and has had occasion to review the Articles of Incorporation, By-laws, and various minutes of the Board of Directors' Meetings, he would probably be prepared, as this counsel was, to ask such questions as "How much money are you talking about? Will it involve the construction of an addition to the facility, or will it simply be a modification to an existing production

> line?" Finding out that it will involve approximately 7 million dollars, he asks, "What is the value of the facility?" Upon learning that the market value is 25 million dollars, he quickly calculates the cost of the expansion to be in excess of 25 per cent of the market value of the facility. Counsel already knows that the company owns two other comparable manufacturing facilities, which are the majority of fixed assets held by the company.
>
> Counsel recalls a Board resolution enacted several years ago requiring that all capital expenditures of a significant or unusual amount receive Board approval before commitment. He is not sure of the exact language, nor has he reviewed the Board minutes since then to determine how this resolution has been implemented by the subsequent practices of the officers and directors of the corporation.
>
> So what is counsel's answer? Should he say, "I'll have to go back and review the original Board resolution on capital expenditures, plus any similar approvals in subsequent Board meeting minutes before giving you an answer?" Probably not. The better answer in this case would be a "partial answer." The next Board meeting is several weeks away, and he will have time to do the required investigation and research. Counsel can give focus and direction to their ideas and meeting at this stage with a logically reasoned answer. He answers, "I would say 7 million dollars is probably a significant enough capital expenditure, since it is almost 25 per cent of the value of one of our primary facilities, to require Board approval before commiting to that expenditure. I'll have to check the original Board resolution and the subsequent Board minutes to confirm that, but I think that it would be considered a significant capital expenditure." The president says, "Thank you. Please check it, if you will, and let us know what you find out."

The attorney here has given a partial answer to the legal question. With his general knowledge of corporate law and prior familarity with the corporate Articles, By-laws, and the original capital expenditure resolution, he was able to apply his skills as an attorney and make a logical, well-reasoned judgment. He researched the point later, confirmed his earlier judgment, and informed the president of the company accordingly. The president then told him that because they had agreed with this judgment and for other reasons, they had decided to delay further consideration of this project until the beginning of the next fiscal year.

Should counsel have given this partial answer? Would it have been better for him to simply say he did not know and would get back to them? In this instance he gave the best response. He gave the president and others a direction and focus to their discussion. They were able to establish a priority, that is, the advisability of additional capital expenditures at that time and, in so doing, arrived at a timely decision without further delay. His advice may have prevented them from going ahead and making the capital expenditure without the necessary Board approval. Importantly, counsel realized he did not have all the facts and knowledge and qualified his answer by stating that. He did not simply say, "It sounds O.K. to me. Seven million dollars isn't that much, and, after all, you are president of the company." And if he had not been familiar with the Articles, By-laws and so on, the best response would have been to say that he did not know the answer rather than to guess or take a stab in the dark.

Situations like these are judgment calls. If counsel thinks he has enough facts and knows enough law on point to make a well-reasoned, logical answer to a question presented during the developing, early stages of a situation then he should not be afraid to do so in a judicious manner, particularly if counsel has only been practicing corporate law for a year or two. He probably knows more law then he thinks he does. If he is like many other attorneys, both inexperienced and experienced, he will often have the feeling that he never knows enough law and never has enough time to properly research the issues. He should remember that he is not alone in that feeling and try to forge ahead when appropriate. Often, the application of general principles of law, for example, "Was there a breach of contract?" or "Was negligence involved?" when combined with his specialized knowledge of the industry law will enable counsel to confidentally handle the "imperfect" circumstances that will confront him.

In contrast to the imperfect circumstances that demand an immediate answer, here counsel has an option. He can and should respond with partial answers to developing circumstances when he can correctly focus and direct, from a legal standpoint, the discussions at hand. Use of his skills as an attorney this way in the corporate environment will tend to prevent legal problems from arising later and will assist others in arriving at more timely and appropriate answers to problems. Counsel must not, however, neglect to follow-up his partial answers with the more thorough classic approach of legal analysis. And under some circumstances counsel's best response will be to say that he doesn't know the answer but will find it.

Know When To Say You Do Not Know

Counsel should never be afraid to say that he does not know an answer. Is that not the direct opposite of the prior principle that it is acceptable to give partial answers? No! In those situations counsel knew enough of the facts and enough of the law to give a qualified answer and a direction and focus to developing circumstances. Here, he does not know enough law on a particular issue or enough facts to make even a qualified response. What should he do? Guess? Of course not. He simply says that he does not know and that he will have to check. If someone asks how many days the company has to file a response to a complaint or motion for judgment and counsel does not know what the applicable rules in that state, should he say, "Probably 20 days"? He could, but the better response is to say that he does not know but will look it up. Unless a useful purpose is served by giving a partial answer and counsel is equipped to give one, he should simply say that he does not know the answer.

Is this such an obvious point that it need not be discussed? The answer might be surprising. More than one attorney who has been caught offguard by a sudden question or by trying to impress someone with his knowledge of law answered before thinking, when he should have said simply, "I don't know, but I'll check it for you." Place yourself in the shoes of the corporate counsel in the following example and decide how you would have handled the question put to her.

> Counsel is corporate attorney with three years' experience in a privately held, power utility company. Her responsibilities to date have been to advise upon and handle the legal work arising within the purchasing department. As a result of a recent promotion, she now handles all of the legal work for a large operating division within the company. She reports with a dotted line to the president of this division, who is an aggressive, hard-charging, ambitious executive.
>
> After she has been in this new position for a few months, she discovers to her dismay that this executive is the type of layman who does not believe in "gray" areas of the law and thinks that when he asks a legal question, the answer should be "in black and white." On a few occasions counsel has tried to explain to him that she cannot give him a black-and-white answer because it depends upon the facts uncovered during discovery and the trial and upon the opinions of the judge or jury. She thinks he believes that she simply does not know the law; and that, combined with her exposure to unfamiliar issues of law in this new position, has left her in a somewhat distraught state of mind.
>
> One morning he calls her to his office, and acting as if there was a crisis (his usual style of operating), he tells her that he is going to fire an employee (a salaried worker) for insubordination and tell him to clean out his office and leave this afternoon. He wants to know how much notice and severance pay, if any, he's required to give the individual.
>
> Although having previously dealt with only a few personnel matters, counsel thinks she knows the answer to these rather simple issues, and not wanting to appear completely stupid, she takes a stab at it. She knows as a general principle of law that a person without an employment contract can be terminated at will by the employer and that termination for

> insubordination is not a discriminatory issue under the Civil Rights Act. Furthermore, she knows that it is customary within the company and industry to give salaried workers termination notice equal to their pay period, in this instance, two weeks. She recalls the company policy states that days of vacation must be taken during the year or otherwise forfeited without pay.
>
> Therefore, she correctly reasons that a severance check for two weeks pay is required because of the lack of notice and so informs the executive. But she incorrectly reasons that in view of the company vacation policy, any days of vacation earned but not taken by this employee would be forfeited (without pay) upon termination. She does not mention this point to the executive. She hopes that he appreciates her definitive statement on the law.
>
> When she gets back to her office, she thinks that she should look again at the company policy statement regarding vacation days. She finds that she remembered it correctly. But still uncertain, she decides to check some law reference books. She finds some cases which hold that regardless of a company policy statement, an employee who is terminated is entitled to be paid for earned but untaken vacation days for the current year. Having arrived at this conclusion (some two hours later), she now finds that she must call the executive and tell him if this employee has any currently earned but untaken vacation days, he must be paid for them also. She finds that he has already terminated this employee and given him a final check. Imagine what this executive says to her!

How should counsel have handled the situation in this example? Counsel should have known she was not sure about the law on point and should have declined to give an answer on the spot. Although the executive acted as though it were a crisis situation, it really was not. He was planning to terminate the employee later in the day, but it probably could have been delayed. Therefore, shooting from the hip was not required. Was this a developing circumstance of a problem or idea in its early stages in which a partial but qualified answer would have given focus to the discussion? No. Here the action was already decided upon; the only issue was the correct law on point. Even though counsel had some background in the applicable law, she should have known she was not adequately informed, and the circumstances did not require a qualified answer or her best guess but rather an exact and correct answer.

The correct approach in this case, and in the majority of situations that will confront corporate counsel, is to use the classic method of taking (and insisting upon) the time necessary to research the law on point. She should have remained a professional responsible for high standards of legal analysis and compliance. Because of the close client relationship in corporate law, it is not always easy to refuse to give counsel's best educated guess, but he must do so unless the circumstances truly demand otherwise or the situation is an early developing stage.

If counsel knows that he does not know the law on point or thinks that he does not, then he should not give an answer. A wrong answer in law is worse then no answer at all. And incorrect answers will eventually catch up with counsel. Some people will know when he is bluffing, and a surprising number of layman are well-versed on particular details and nuances of certain regulations or law. Besides, most laymen do not expect counsel to immediately know all the answers.

By way of comparison, consider that most attorneys in private practice will rarely give an answer on the spot. Although there are several reasons for this, one is that they want to be exactly sure of the facts and the law on point before giving an answer because they may lose a client or a lawsuit otherwise. As a corporate attorney counsel will not always have the luxury of being able to investigate all the facts and do in-depth research before giving answers; nevertheless, if he has the opportunity, he should take it. And importantly, if he needs that opportunity because he does not know the law on a particular issue, then he must say, "I don't know. I'll find out."

The principles of "shooting from the hip" and "giving partial answers" are denied legitimacy by some, but their existence is a fact of reality in the world of preventive corporate law (and to a lesser degree in other segments of the law profession). When properly employed in limited circumstances, these principles can result in accurate and effective answers and sometimes in solutions to the problems under consideration, whereas, as a practical matter, the same is unattainable following the classic approach. Therefore, counsel is well-advised to think about, and reflect upon, these principles of applying the law, even if he now disagrees with them. Read the following case study, which illustrates a practical application of one of the principles.

Case Study Number Eight: RIGHT OF FIRST REFUSAL

The Situation

Counsel is a corporate counsel for a diversified corporation that conducts business operations involving the transportation of oil and gas by pipelines throughout the southwestern portion of the United States. Having recently joined the company, she is not familar with the typical terms and provisions found in the many ownership, joint venture, and leasing agreements through which the company uses various pipelines.

One morning the vice president of materials and supplies asks counsel to come to his office. When she arrives, the vice president is on the telephone but upon seeing her, asks the party he is talking to if he can put him on hold for a minute, which he does. He quickly tells her the following:

> This is our joint venture partner on the pipeline we own with him in Oklahoma. He says he's got an offer from somebody to buy his half interest in the pipeline and wants to know if we want to buy it instead. We've got rights of first refusal. We don't want to buy it, but we don't want him selling out to one of our competitors either—and he won't tell us who the buyer is that's made the offer. He says he wants an answer right now! What do you think we should do?

Counsel asks the vice president a couple of quick questions and finds out that there is a joint venture contract in the files which he thinks has language regarding the right of first refusal. She further learns the joint venture partner is simply an investment speculator who helped fund the development and construction of the pipeline in return for a share of the revenues and tax write-offs and probably would now like to get rid of his 50 per cent equity interest. She asks him how much the offer is for, and he says they have not finished negotiating a final price, but it will probably be around 3.5 million dollars, or slightly above the book value of a one-half interest in the pipeline.

The Question

What advice should be given to the vice president? Does this situation demand an immediate decision? Should counsel shoot from the hip and say, "Rights of first refusal are usually upheld by the courts, and we'd better tell him we'll match the offer if you think it's being sold to a competitor of ours"? Or is this a situation that does not require an immediate response and that requires some investigation and research first? If so, counsel should reply, "I don't know what the answer is. I'll have to read the joint venture agreement and do some research first. Tell him we'll call him back tommorrow morning." How should counsel answer if she had enough of a background to give him a partial answer?

What Actually Happened

In this case corporate counsel replied:

> I'll have to pull out the joint venture agreement and see what it says regarding right of first refusal, but usually you have a time period within which to respond of not less then 24 or 48 hours and often longer—after a firm offer has been received. Why don't you ask him if he knows how much time we have to respond according to the terms of the agreement, and also ask him when he thinks he will receive a firm offer from the potential buyer?

The joint venture partner says he does not know how much time is allowed to respond but thinks it is required immediately. He also says he should have a firm offer from the buyer by late today or early tomorrow. Still talking on the telephone, the vice president scribbles these answers on a piece of paper for counsel to see. Counsel then mouths the words to him, "Call after firm price," as he shakes his head in understanding and agreement. The vice president tells the joint venture partner that the company may be interested in exercising their right of first refusal and to get back to him as soon as he has a firm offer from the potential buyer.

Counsel goes back to her office and pulls the joint venture agreement from the company files. It does, in fact, in an addenum to the agreement, have a detailed first right of refusal governing the sale of an ownership interest in the pipeline. She studies all of the joint venture agreement (including the project development documents) as well as the right of first refusal and concludes they are valid documents. She researches the applicable law, including a check of the pertinent real estate and commercial law provisions under the Oklahoma state statutes, and determines that those provisions have been complied with. She then advices the vice president late that afternoon that the right-of-first-refusal agreement requires the joint venture partner desiring to sell his interest to furnish to the other partner an affidavit stating he has received a bona fide offer for his interest and the price. Following receipt of the affidavit, the other partner has 15 working days within which to exercise his right to purchase the interest, and another time period within which to close the transaction.

The vice president says he has not heard from the joint venture partner. Counsel suggests that a letter be sent to the partner acknowledging his telephone call and requesting that when he receives a firm offer, he put it in the form of an affidavit required by the right-of-first-refusal agreement and send it to us so that the company could make a decision within the time period set forth in that agreement. The vice president agrees with this approach, asks her to draft such a letter, which she does and which is subsequently sent. Nothing more is heard from the joint venture partner. After a passage of time the vice president and counsel conclude the joint venture partner really did not have much of an offer, if he had one at all, and was simply trying to persuade the company to purchase his equity interest.

Author's Comments

Was the approach taken by the attorney in this case correct? As it turned out, her approach did result in a solution to the problem, which is the ultimate objective, but let's analyze this counsel's approach in more detail.

She took the approach of "giving a partial answer." Having dealt with rights of first refusal before, she knew that a specific time period within which the right could be exercised was usually agreed upon between the parties. She logically and correctly reasoned that since a firm price, and therefore a firm offer, had not yet been received by the joint venture partner, that although the matter may be a pressing one, it was not so immediate that she had to "shoot from the hip." But because the situation was an early stage of a developing problem to which she could lend focus, she advised the vice president accordingly with a partial answer and allowed herself time within which to follow up with the proper investigation and research (the classic approach). Had this attorney not been familiar with rights of first refusal, then the third approach of saying, "I don't know, I'll have to check. . . ," would have been the proper response to this situation. Under the facts presented, it would have been a mistake for this counsel to have taken the shotgun approach and stated a conclusion about the right of first refusal, either one way or the other.

Corporate counsel was presented here with an imperfect circumstance not unlike those that counsel will encounter many times during his career as corporate counsel. She was faced with an incomplete set of facts and incomplete knowledge of the law on point and yet was asked to give her immediate legal analysis and decision. To her credit this attorney took a proper approach within those limits and effected a solution.

But more than that, this case illustrates the unique opportunities corporate counsel will have to apply the law in a preventive and effective fashion. Consider, for example, whether this vice president could have involved outside counsel during that telephone conversation, even if he had chosen to do so at such an early stage. More typically, outside counsel would not have become involved until they were trying to undo a mistaken action already taken. Also, although the classic approach to applying the law probably would have worked (depending upon the vice president's actions) under this set of facts, in other situations it would not have resulted in the most effective application of a lawyer's skills and knowledge to the business environment nor in the best solution.

Key Four: Know When To Go Outside

Introduction

An essential part of effectively applying the law to the real problems corporate counsel has found is to know whether he needs to draw upon the services of a private law firm or upon the expertise of an attorney specializing in the practice of a certain area of the law.

A basic premise underlying the principles in this Key is the objective of the corporate law function to "... maintain high quality legal practices ..."—also a part of our definition of a solution. Here, that objective simply means that before counsel can find the best answer or solution to an issue, he must first have a comprehensive knowledge and understanding of the pertinent law on point. If he does not, then he must use the resources available to acquire it. This may require the use of outside counsel for either manpower or expertise or the addition of an attorney to the corporate staff in the long run. Whatever the case, as a professional, counsel will need to develop the judgment to know when to utilize the services of private law firms or legal specialists and when to rely upon his own knowledge and understanding of the law on a particular issue (or upon his ability to acquire it). In this Key some practical guidelines to assist counsel in that determination will be examined.

Issues Beyond Counsel's Ability

Whether an issue involves an area of law that is beyond counsel's present capability to handle can be a difficult assessment and judgment to make, particularly for the less experienced and less confident attorney. Nonetheless, in order to maintain a high quality level of legal practice and find the best solutions to the problems confronting him as corporate counsel, counsel must make a thoughtful and considered decision. The areas in which counsel and the typical law department would most frequently decide to use the services of outside counsel will be discussed and some of the reasons for this decision examined.

Beyond the Law Department's Scope

This will be the most common area in which either counsel or his superior in the law department will decide to use the services of a private law firm. Most corporate counsel and corporate law departments have predetermined areas of the law that will not be handled in-house, either for budgeting or other reasons. Typically, the more general and routine matters and frequently occurring issues unique within the industry will be effectively handled in-house by a relatively stable number of staff counsel, while the more specialized and unusual cases requiring a narrow expertise or an inordinate amount of time to handle will be researched, investigated, or litigated by outside counsel.

For example, despite the recent trend in corporate law departments to handle increasingly more specialized areas of the law in-house, most corporate counsel still consider it more cost effective to utilize outside counsel for the occasionally occurring case of major litigation requiring substantial discovery and trial work. Similarly, in small- and medium-sized companies in a service-oriented industry, for example, corporate counsel may have little occasion to deal with matters in the antitrust area, therefore making it prudent and cost-effective to rely upon the expertise of an attorney in private practice specializing in that area.

Some corporate law departments will have a defined policy enumerating the legal areas in which the services of outside counsel will be engaged, and others will use a more informal, case-by-case determination. Indeed, depending upon the level and responsibility of counsel's position and the style of administration in the law department, he may have little occasion to actually make the decision of whether outside counsel should become involved in a particular issue. Notwithstanding this, there will be several matters he will handle during his career as corporate counsel in which he will need to either recommend or decide whether outside counsel should be engaged. Therefore, it will always be prudent for counsel to question whether a problem (or some issue therein) he is handling is within the scope of capability of his position or the law department's, and if it is, whether there is any other substantive reason to engage outside counsel, such as the lack of available time or resources.

Lack of Time or Other Resources

There is another common instance in which outside counsel will be used. Few attorneys will say that they have the necessary time always to perform their very best possible legal work on every legal matter they handle. Sometimes the bottom line (the realistic fee chargeable to other corporate departments, projects, or divisions if applicable in your corporation) or, more often, simply the number of hours in a day affects the quality of a counsel's legal work, although ideally it should not. At the same time, however, most of these attorneys would correctly say they consistently perform high quality legal work.

This standard of consistent high quality legal work is the desirable and realistic objective that should be maintained in the practice of preventive corporate law. Sometimes good judgment must come into play. If counsel or other members of the corporate law department who may be able to assist him do not have the available hours in the day to handle an issue effectively and comprehensively because of other more pressing matters, then the assistance of outside attorneys should be recommended and used. Unfortunately, the ultimate determination will sometimes be made administratively, for example, in terms of whether sufficient funds remain in the legal budget. But the primary principle to observe if counsel makes such a determination should be what is the appropriate resource for high quality legal work on a particular matter, not whether inside or outside counsel handled the issue or whether the law department has exceeded its projected expenditures that year.

Similarly, when other resources to perform high quality legal services like comprehensive updated legal reporting publication are not adequately available in-house, then the assistance of outside counsel with those resources should be engaged. The following example illustrates the decision by a small corporate law department to engage the services of several private law firms because they lacked both adequate manpower and adequate published resource material.

> Because of inflation and substantial increases in the cost of money during the late '70's and early '80's, many companies found the interest rates they had been charging on credit balances allowed to their customers were below the market rates and their own cost of borrowed money. In effect, these companies found themselves in the position of subsidizing their credit sales.
>
> As a result, one company decided to increase the interest rate charged on credit balances to their customers to the maximum amount allowed by statute in each state in which they operated. Because this company operated in 23 states, each having a different set of consumer laws regulating the maximum permissible interest rates, exemptions, notice requirements, and so on, the chief corporate counsel for this company determined it was beyond the level of manpower and resources available within his department to retrieve and competently interpret each such body of regulations. This determination was made in part after research within the department was unable to locate an accurate compilation and reproduction of the various state regulations on point.
>
> Therefore, the chief counsel allocated the research of the regulations in the few states contiguous to their principal offices to staff members, while the services of appropriate outside local counsel were engaged in the remaining states.

Another frequent area in which corporate law departments will utilize the services of outside counsel is in specialty areas of the law.

Specialty of Law Beyond Counsel's Expertise

In the specialties of law with which the corporate law department has little occasion become involved, the use of attorneys in private practice specializing in that area can be significantly more cost-effective and result in a higher quality legal product than if the same function was staffed in-house. The most common specialty today not staffed in-house is that of the trial litigator, partly because of the unpredictable need for such services. Depending upon the size of the law department and the diversity of the company's operations, there may be issues in other specialty areas of the law that, purposely, are referred to outside counsel. For many small companies and law departments, complex security and tax matters are referred to outside specialists, although as a company becomes larger, these specialities are often among the first to be brought in-house.

From the standpoint of counsel's personal practice of preventive corporate law, whether to refer an issue that is involved in a specialty area of law to outside specialists should hinge upon the complexity of the issue as well as his concern for a quality legal product. Throughout his career, corporate counsel will develop a degree of expertise in one field or another, whether by choice or necessity. Simply because an issue is within a specialty usually referred to outside counsel does not mean that given the adequate time, resources, background, and opportunity, counsel could not handle an issue in that specialty himself. Again, it is a matter for well-reasoned judgment whether an issue is beyond counsel's ability.

The following is an example of a clear-cut specialty found within the legal profession today that few corporate law departments deem necessary or cost-effective to staff in-house.

> A large consumer product-oriented company determined that the future profitability and maybe survival of its principal operations depended upon finding new ways to acquire the primary raw material which they upgraded in their manufacturing process in sufficient quantity and at below market cost. Known worldwide reserves of this raw material were concentrated within a few developing third world countries, which had recently agreed among

> themselves to limit production and exports in an attempt to increase world demand and prices. As a result, this company's continued source of supply at low prices was doubtful.
>
> The corporate executive group determined that their best, if not only, opportunity to stabilize the effects of these conditions upon their operations was to acquire or merge with one of the few large domestic wholesale firms which bought, traded, and sold this raw material worldwide. Having dealt with these firms in the past, the company knew that any such effort on their part would undoubably be rejected in favor of continued independent ownership; consequently, a plan to launch a hostile tender offer for control of the company deemed most susceptible was formulated.
>
> The chief counsel for this consumer product-oriented company discussed the matter with his in-house staff attorney who handled the security and exchange commission work and other issues involving their publicly traded stock and debt financings. They concluded a major acquisition of this type, particularly if vigorously defended against, would be beyond their resources and real expertise. They anticipated a two-tier, cash-and-stock tender offer, with accompanying registrations, proxy solicitation statements, and other security filings all drafted and filed within a matter of weeks or at most a month, along with several probable court pleadings in several states and jurisdictions. They immediately and confidentially contacted a prominent law firm that specialized in, and did little work other than involving, major acquisitions, frequently hostile. From this firm they obtained a proposed legal action plan and an idea of the costs, which the chief counsel then included in the corporate strategic plans under consideration.

This illustration is a clear example of a relatively narrow specialty application of the law usually requiring the assistance of the appropriate outside counsel, not only for expertise but for manpower. Note, however, that had the proposed acquisition involved the cash purchase of a small privately held company, the chief counsel and his staff attorney would no doubt have handled the transaction in-house.

Some common situations then in which a typical corporate law department would use the assistance of a private law firm or specialist are those that are outside the predetermined scope of the department functions or are caused by the lack of available time, resources, or expertise. In doing so, counsel and the law department will have made the proper determination to result in a high quality legal practice and product, which, in turn, will point the way to the best answers and solutions to the problems confronting them.

For a Second Opinion or Local Representation

Some circumstances will justify a second opinion. The law is not so well-defined nor a single individual's knowledge of the law so broad or deep that a lawyer is always fully confident with his own judgment. Obtaining a second opinion from another attorney may be as simple as asking another member of the law department staff what he thinks. In fact, that is often the best way of checking the legal analysis of an issue. At other times counsel will want to obtain a second opinion from a specialist practicing in a certain area of the law. Corporate counsel of publicly owned companies will sometimes draft the routine security and exchange commission filings in-house and then give the entire document to outside counsel specializing in that area for a final examination to determine whether anything has been inadvertently overlooked. Such a procedure has obvious merit. If counsel has been working several weeks on a complex transaction with much documentation and detail, asking another attorney, whether in-house or outside counsel, to briefly review the transaction from his own objective and detached viewpoint also has obvious merit.

Counsel may find it necessary to obtain a second opinion in order to bolster the credibility or significance of his legal decision. Although that purpose is not the most desired reason for obtaining a second opinion, consider the following example.

An attorney became senior counsel for a company during a period of time when it was disputing with another company over a joint venture development project. A short three-page preliminary joint venture agreement had been signed by the two companies about 18 months ago. This agreement was in the nature of a letter of intent, describing the important conceptual aspects of the relationship, the funding obligations, the rights of each party, and so on.

It was not long before the company management asked this senior counsel whether they could withdraw from the joint venture and, if so, what problems might result and whether any of their costs would be recoverable. Counsel spent several days reviewing the preliminary joint venture agreement and other documentation accumulated since then; discussed the project with the several corporate managers and the outside counsel who had drafted most of the preliminary agreement; and reviewed contract, agency, and partnership principles and other law governing joint venture agreements, as well as pertinent state statutes. He then wrote a definitive memorandum concluding that the company had the right to withdraw from the development joint venture at any time but could probably not avoid its share of funding through the end of the first development phase and could not recover the funds invested to date.

When he discussed these salient points with the president of the company, it became obvious that the president was not pleased with the bad news. During the course of the conversation the president said, "Do you think it would be of any value to have the outside attorney who helped us write this agreement take a look at it?" The senior counsel replied, "I've talked briefly with him, and I think he agrees with my analysis, but since he's the one that wrote the agreement, a second opinion wouldn't hurt." They then requested the opinion of this outside counsel, which was substantially similar to the analysis written by the senior counsel.

Did it make good sense to get the second opinion requested in this example? Probably. Not only because the second opinion came from the attorney who had participated in drafting the original agreement but also because it was a critical issue involving substantial money and obligations. Also note in this illustration there was an overtone of credibility, or the lack thereof, which was resolved by obtaining a second opinion. Counsel should never be afraid to get a second opinion when he thinks it necessary.

Another situation in which the assistance of outside counsel should be considered is when local or special representation would be of value. The most frequent example would be in connection with litigation proceedings or in other proceedings before governmental bodies or quasi-public agencies, in which a knowledge of the local procedures and practices can be of unique importance. A special knowledge of the people and procedures within the myriad federal agencies, for instance, may be instrumental in receiving expedited review of a claim, proposal, or request. Counsel who specializes in practicing before a certain agency would possess a great amount of special information difficult to obtain in any other way. Similarly, when a case is argued before state agencies, such as tax and revenue commissions, in which the hearing or court results may not be published or widely distributed, representation by local counsel experienced before that regional commission would have obvious merit.

The following is a less obvious example of an instance in which the special knowledge of local counsel provided useful bargaining leverage during a meeting over a contract dispute.

> A manufacturer of process industrial equipment supplied several large stand-alone process units to a chemical plant being built by an industrial chemical company in a semirural area located in a state substantially distant from their corporate headquarters. Because of a dramatic decrease in the market demand for the product to be produced at this plant, the chemical company delayed completion of the plant and finally suspended its start-up and subsequent operation. Concurrently, the company slowed or stopped payment on equipment and other costs

> incurred in development of the plant, causing the process equipment supplier to file a supplier's (mechanic's) lien in the local court to force final payment on the units they furnished.
>
> The corporate counsel for the equipment supplier engaged local counsel to file the mechanic's lien and prepare a complaint for formal litigation. The day before she was scheduled to meet with the chemical company at the plant site to discuss the payment in arrears, she met with the local counsel. She learned from him that the development of the chemical process plant had provoked considerable opposition from the local population and community leaders and was still viewed with disfavor. They felt the highly automated plant would only be a source of pollution and would result in the depletion of their natural resources, which would be marketed out-of-state, without an equal benefit accruing locally. Corporate counsel correctly concluded this information might provide a useful bargaining leverage in the meeting the following day.
>
> During the meeting with the chemical company, this local counsel described the past and current local community attitude about development of the chemical plant and further opined there would be substantial adverse publicity both on a local and state level if formal litigation was required to resolve this dispute, adding that, of course, a jury trial would be requested. Due in large part to these assertions, the equipment supplier was able to obtain a favorable settlement without further legal process.

This situation is a good example of the special local knowledge that outside counsel can often provide. And in court proceedings, knowledge of a local court's past decisions or unwritten rules of the court can be of crucial significance. Similarly, counsel will occasionally be confronted with a local attorney representing a party who will attempt to persuade or intimidate counsel by saying something like, "We don't do things that way here." In such an instance counsel's most prudent posture is to at least obtain the advice, if not representation, of counsel from the same locality.

Of equal, if not greater, importance in knowing when to use outside counsel to help counsel achieve a high quality legal product is knowing when not to use them.

Know When Not To Go Outside

A few inexperienced corporate counsel automatically assume that any matter handled by outside counsel will result in a higher quality legal product than if it were handled in-house. In fact, this view is self-servingly shared by some attorneys in private practice who have not had the occasion or taken the time to recognize the greatly increased sophistication and capability of many corporate law departments during the past decade or two. Corporate law departments are no longer mere conduits or traffic control centers to the outside private law firms, if indeed they ever were. However, since little useful purpose will be served by debating the merits of those viewpoints, the important principle of this section will be examined from the more positive approach of what are the advantages to handling a legal matter in-house.

Probably the greatest single advantage in having in-house corporate staff attorneys handle a legal matter is the enhanced opportunity to apply a preventive law approach and find a solution to a problem rather than being limited to the more traditional dispensing law or adversary approaches. In-house corporate counsel are in a unique position within the law profession to have the opportunity to learn about their client(s) in-depth, about the business, the people, and the industry laws and regulations that have the most significant impact upon their company. This knowledge is prerequisite to practicing effective preventive corporate law and to finding the best answers and solutions to problems in the corporation. Therefore, it is axiomatic that any definition of a high quality legal practice of corporate law must include this ability to practice effective preventive corporate law.

On the one hand, in-house corporate attorneys will consistently have the opportunity to practice effective preventive law but at times must request the assistance of outside counsel when resources or capabilities are limited; on the other hand, outside counsel will rarely have the opportunity to acquire the background necessary with any one client to practice truly effective preventive corporate law but will frequently, in the case of medium- to large-sized firms, have access to greater manpower and areas of expertise. This means that in determining whether a legal matter should be handled in-house, counsel should give substantial weight to the distinct advantage and value in his ability to practice effective preventive corporate law. He should also consider the value in applying that capability to monitor, control, and use the information provided by outside counsel to find the best answer and solution.

There are several other advantages to handling legal matters in-house, which are really part of the preventive law capability. Often in-house counsel will be experts in a body of law, not only substantively but also practically and realistically in applying it to the matters at hand. Although an outside specialist may be able to recite case citations supporting the preferred construction of a law or regulation, that will be of only limited value unless he also has the experience and background in the industry to visualize the effective implementation of that legal principle to the facts of the real problem. And, as is so often the case, when the assistance of business laymen is needed to help investigate and sort out a complex factual situation to find the real problem and issues in the first place, the in-house corporate counsel has the invaluable client relationship that enables him to draw quickly upon the resources and expertise of the corporation. Other advantages in using in-house corporate counsel have been previously discussed in other contexts; namely, the ability to talk in the same industry sublanguage, to draft useable documents, to "read between the lines", to understand the business objectives, to know the cross-over effect of legal decisions, and so on.

Counsel should not short-change himself or the rapidly evolving, extremely effective new discipline of the preventive corporate law practice. He is a far more competent and expert practitioner of the law than some believe. As the resources and capabilities within in-house corporate law departments continue to expand and become more sophisticated, as they surely will, the need for reliance upon the manpower or expertise of outside counsel will undoubtably diminish proportionately, as it should.

The following is an example of a corporate counsel who did not entirely share this viewpoint and some of the apparent reasons why. Read the somewhat slanted facts and decide whether this corporate counsel was correct in her judgment and perception.

> A large corporation had a small law department consisting of three attorneys. The department was unstructured, and after several years one of the attorneys, in effect, became the de facto or self-appointed head of the law department. Perhaps because this corporate counsel had never been exposed to another company or firm or perhaps because she had always been and still was under the doubting and questioning superior to whom the law department formally reported (a senior administrative vice president with a law degree but no practice experience), this attorney developed the following philosophy of law practice within the corporation. She considered the bodies of law that affected their corporation to be so vast and complex that no one person or law department could manage them adequately. She also believed this to be the primary reason for the desirable trend in the law profession toward specialization. As the apparent result of these two suppositions, she eventually came to view the majority of matters coming before the law department to be in one specialty area of the law or another. Although she might perform some preliminary legal work on a matter with which she had some familarity, she would invariably go to a large, private, local law firm to obtain the services of, or at least concurring opinion of, an attorney she deemed to be a specialist. On other occasions she would go to out-of-state and request the assistance of nationally recognized law firms specializing in a certain area of the law. In this manner she felt confident in achieving a high quality legal product (and in having irrefutable answers to her superior's questions).

> The situation progressed to the point that often when the laymen in the corporation asked this corporate counsel a legal question, her response would be, "I understand the problem. Let me contact a specialist in this area, and I'll get back to you". In effect, this corporate counsel became a mere conduit to the outside law firms except for limited and routine matters of law.

Was this corporate counsel correct in her philosophy or style of in-house corporate law practice? Partially correct? She may have been partially correct because of the department's lack of resources and capabilities. Her philosophy, however, was certainly not appropriate for an effective preventive law practice, nor is it appropriate for the vast majority of corporate law departments today. Comments by the laymen in the corporation for which she was corporate counsel might be surprising. They would often complain that it took them forever to get an answer from the law department and said they did not know whether the law department actually knew anything or did anything, since they always seemed to go to outside counsel.

Most corporate managers and employees prefer to have their legal problems and questions handled by an in-house corporate counsel who they know understands the problems and business of the corporation, rather than an outside counsel whom they rarely see and almost always have to educate before asking questions or giving answers. This opinion of corporate managers has merit. Counsel will become a specialist in those legal matters affecting his company most often, usually more of an expert than outside counsel. The corporate counsel who thinks that any associate or partner in a private law firm is automatically an expert is kidding himself. The quality of work can vary substantially between law firms and within one firm itself.

The one exception justifying the type of corporate law practice embodied by counsel in the previous example is when a deliberate decision has been made to have only a limited number of corporate counsel in-house, primarily to coordinate and implement legal matters, while relying primarily upon the services of outside counsel.

To recap, if counsel is in a position as a corporate counsel to decide whether to engage the services of outside counsel, he should use good judgment. The objective is to provide high quality legal service to the corporation for which counsel works, both in terms of practicing preventive law and in terms of practicing the more traditional adversary law and dispensing law. Whether those services can be provided by the resources within the corporate law department or will require the assistance of outside counsel is the decision to be made.

The following case study illustrates several principles of this Key in a very practical and realistic situation confronted by one in-house corporate counsel.

Case Study Number Nine: THE MINING PARTNERSHIP

The Situation

Four corporations have formed a consortium to mine and upgrade a mineral ore contained in a large tract of land owned by one of corporations. A benefication plants is to be constructed at the mining site to process the mineral ore into a finished product, which will then be allocated among the corporations and sold by each in wholesale and retail markets. Because of the large quantity of estimated mineral reserves, the project duration is estimated to be 25 to 30 years. The corporation owning the land and mineral reserves is the dominant partner in the joint venture and has attempted to establish policies and conditions favorable to itself by drafting the initial project and joint venture documents submitted to the other partners for consideration. These documents are voluminous and complex.

Counsel is in-house corporate counsel representing one of the other partner corporations. He has more than ten years' experience practicing corporate law and has handled several large joint venture projects similar to this one, although in a different industry. He has reviewed these documents in detail and researched several points of law and engaged the services of a tax specialist in a local law firm to review certain sections of the documents. During the next 14 months his company and the other joint venture partners have participated in a very cumbersome and extended negotiation of the concepts and language in these documents. Because counsel is still dissatisfied with several major concepts (as are some of the other partners), he recently asked one of the senior partners in a private law firm, whose judgment he respects, to review the documents with him and give his opinion. He does so and confirms counsel's judgment on most points.

Negotiations have now reached the stage at which counsel's company is apparently faced with some insurmountable obstacles. The primary points in dispute are the allocation of voting shares in the committee directing the joint venture activities; the extent of control over the operating expenses authorized by the partner who will manage the mining and upgrading operation (the dominant partner), especially regarding their home office charges; the proper proration and valuation of capital funding, including the dominant partner's contributed mineral value; the establishment of production levels based upon the partners different desires and needs; and the distribution of assets and liabilities in the event of liquidation or indefinite suspension of operations. These points have been argued repeatedly and forcefully by counsel, his company management, and the other partners with their counsel, to little avail.

In an effort to resolve the apparent stumbling block in the negotiations, counsel is considering whether to search for an attorney or law firm that specializes in the development of mineral mining ventures of this type and to ask their opinion about the major points in dispute.

The Question

Based upon these facts, what should counsel do? Would obtaining an additional opinion of outside counsel in this case be helpful? Would the advice of a "specialist," that is, an attorney more accustomed to dealing with mining ventures, of this type assist the company? Or would such an opinion be an unnecessary expenditure of fees and time?

What Actually Happened

In this case the corporate counsel requested the opinion of outside counsel. He did because he wanted to reduce the frustration that he and his company's management felt at this stage of the negotiations and because he thought that the opinion of a "specialist" might confirm or enhance the equity of their negotiation positions and, perhaps, their bargaining leverage. An attorney who had dealt with mining venture projects for several years was located and asked to review and write a memorandum as a third-party observer about the fairness of, and any unusual aspects of, these joint venture agreement and project documents.

After several months a lengthy memorandum was finally obtained from this outside "specialist" that, for the most part, confirmed their previous negotiation positions and assumptions. The fee for this memorandum and several lengthy phone calls spent discussing it were significant, although not so large in comparison to expenses so far incurred by the company on this project. The presentation of this memorandum to the dominant mineral-owning partner during a following meeting failed to impress him or produce any significant modified results. Looking back, counsel decided that engagement of this outside specialist was unnecessary. But counsel consoled himself with the fact that this was hindsight, and had the facts been different, the outside counsel's assistance may have been of greater value.

Author's Comments

Should this corporate counsel have engaged the outside counsel "specialist" to review the documents? Was a specialty area of the law really involved in this situation, or was it merely a matter of basic contract and joint venture principles? These are difficult questions, and under another set of facts or with another "specialist", the decision by this corporate counsel may have proved effective. This case has been presented to demonstrate a practical and real situation not unlike ones that will confront corporate attorneys when deciding whether the assistance of outside counsel or a specialist is appropriate. As previously discussed, if an area of law is beyond the expertise in the law department, it is usually prudent to engage a specialist, and second opinions can also be useful, sometimes for bargaining leverage in negotiations. In this case the area of law and industry was probably not sufficiently obtuse or complex, if indeed it was even a specialty, to be beyond the capabilities and background of this experienced corporate counsel. That, however, is simply one judgment, and if you have a different opinion, you may be correct.

Key Five: Examine the Alternatives

Introduction

This is the final Step and Key in the quest for the solution. Here corporate counsel will take the final step beyond the traditional practice of the law—and truly apply his or her skills and knowledge as an attorney to the corporate environment.

Several of the principles in this Key will follow naturally and logically from those learned earlier. First, counsel must ask, "How can it be done?" And not "Can we do it?" The distinction between these two questions illustrates the different approaches between truly searching for an alternative and solution to a problem, on the one hand, and simply dispensing a statement of law, on the other. Next, all the possible alternatives to the problem or question must be uncovered. Here the principles learned by segregating problems into law, law/business, and business issues, and those issues found by searching for the real problem will be of great value.

Then a complex but practical hypothetical based upon an actual situation confronting a corporate counsel in a computer company will be examined and solved by first finding the issues, then uncovering all possible alternative courses of action, and, finally, determining which of those alternatives is the solution and why. Finally, some practical pointers for finding solutions will be briefly discussed; for example, whether there is "another business purpose" and whether this is the "simplest alternative."

Application of this Key will demonstrate the real value of the principles of practicing preventive corporate law learned to this point. Here counsel can bring everything together and apply it so that the most effective preventive corporate law is practiced and counsel can make his greatest contributions to the corporation.

Counsel will always be well-advised to apply the principles of this Key even though he may think he has already found the solution to a problem (by taking the adversary approach, for example). Searching for all of the possible alternative answers to solve a problem, followed then by a judicious weighing of each in the business and legal contexts, is an arena in which corporate counsel can greatly excell, and one that should not be neglected through failure to apply the principles in this important Key. Now, first ask: "How can it be done?"

Ask How Can It Be Done

The correct question is not "*Can* we do it?" but "*How* can we do it?" The difference is one of approach or attitude toward the legal question and problem. If a counsel is content to think he has completed his job after advising a layman that the proposed action or idea will not be in compliance with a particular rule of law or a regulation, then counsel has failed to take the more important step of examining whether there are any other alternatives that might still satisfy the business objectives but also comply with the law.

Remember, when most people ask counsel the question "Can we do this?" what they really mean to say is "How can we do it?" They are interested not so much in what the law says about a particular point as in what alternatives exist to accomplish their business objective in view of what the law says. They want counsel's recommendation of the best alternative. If one simply says, "No, that can't be done legally," or "No, that's too great a risk from a legal standpoint," then what has been accomplished other than to announce a rule of law?

Similarly, if counsel responds to a layman's question by simply saying, "Yes, the Articles of Incorporation of our company authorize us to engage in the type of business activity you are proposing," without going further and saying (when he knows the proposed business activity is a high risk with significant potential liability), "although because of the high risk of your proposed business activity, we may want to consider forming a subsidiary corporation," then although counsel may have answered the limited legal question, he did not take the additional step of searching for alternative approaches that might minimize future legal problems to the corporation. In other words, counsel did not give the layman a solution, or as previously defined, ". . . the best alternative . . . that will accomplish . . . the business purpose . . . within determined levels of minimum legal risk. . .".

Using another example, if counsel is notified of a contract dispute or complaint in litigation and he simply says, "Let's sue them" or "We'll file a counterclaim against them," he may get a gold star for taking the adversary approach. But what about the alternatives? What about conducting a thorough investigation of the facts and then objectively determining which party is most at fault, before deciding to "Sue them"? Greater legal risk, exposure, and cost to the corporation may well be avoided through a negotiated settlement or compromise; and it might also be more consistent with the business objective of maintaining good customer relations.

Regardless of the way the question, problem, or idea is presented by a layman, counsel must always ask himself the question how can it best be accomplished, from both the business and legal standpoint? Counsel should find the solution to the problem, not just one of the answers to one of the limited legal issues.

The following is a simple factual situation about a proposed warehouse lease agreement that contains language inconsistent with the corporate law department policy. Corporate counsel in the law department must respond to the layman corporate manager, who has requested him to review the lease. Keeping in mind the principle just discussed, decide how counsel should respond.

> Counsel is an attorney in the law department for a company that wholesales and distributes high-cost, perishable commodities to retailers. The company owns several warehouse/distribution centers throughout the United States used to briefly store and then ship the commodities. Because of the high unit cost and perishable nature of the inventory, the

law department with concurrence of corporate management has established a policy that all such warehouse buildings, including any stored inventory, will be fully protected with "All Risk" insurance coverage with a specified minimum deductible.

One day a regional distribution manager of the corporation comes to counsel's office, saying that he has found the ideal location for such a storage and distribution center. He says that it is strategically located for the planned expansion of his territory and market but because his current budget does not include sufficient capital to build a warehouse at this location, he has obtained the appropriate corporate approvals to lease an existing building nearby. He says he just finished negotiating a "great lease" with the owner of this warehouse building and asks counsel to "just glance at this lease agreement to see if you see anything unusual. We want to sign it and start delivering our inventory there tomorrow."

Note the manager here was only indirectly saying, "Can we do it?" He was really saying that he was going to do it, wasn't he? That should clearly lead the corporate attorney in this example to the approach of "How can we do it?" Recognize, however, that although that approach is correct, counsel does not reach it because of what this distribution manager says or the way he says it but because counsel is an attorney practicing preventive law who wants to find a solution, if possible.

Corporate counsel reads the lease agreement and finds that the owner of the warehouse provides fire and extended coverage insurance on the building but specifically excludes coverage on any contents stored therein.

What should counsel do? Should he immediately reply, in accordance with law department policy, that the lease is unacceptable because there is no provision for insurance coverage on the inventory? Certainly that is a correct decision based upon good legal judgment of the risks involved and is consistent with the existing policies of the department.

Should he say anything else? Some attorneys would not. But an attorney practicing preventive law should know better. Are there any alternative ways to protect against the risk of loss of the inventory? Could the company provide the insurance coverage necessary on the commodities even though they are stored in a warehouse owned by someone else? Yes, at a cost. Could the company also pay the additional cost of insurance to the owner of the building if he agreed to add a rider to his policy to protect your inventory? Yes, at a cost. Could the company make the decision to store only limited quantities of the commodities at this location and self-insure (no coverage) the risk? Maybe.

> After thinking about some of these alternatives, counsel telephones the distribution manager and tells him that the lease is not acceptable because of the uninsured risk on inventory. He states, however, that if the company provides the insurance coverage for our inventory and the warehouse owner agrees to reimburse us for that premium cost or perhaps if we pay him the extra cost necessary to obtain a rider on his insurance policy to cover the inventory, then the lease might be acceptable. The distribution manager asks how much that would cost, and counsel replies that he does not know but can find out. He says to counsel's surprise, "I might be able to work something out like that because under the monthly lease we've discussed payments are significantly lower then the market rate in that area."
>
> As it turns out, the manager agreed with the owner of the building to increase the monthly lease payments by an amount equal to one half of the increased premium cost for a rider to the owner's policy. After doing so, the lease payments were still a little below market rates, and, more favorably, any losses suffered by fire or other occurrences would be against the owner's loss experience record rather than the company's. Counsel redrafts the lease agreement upon that basis, and it is signed by the parties.

Here the acceptable alternative course of action was easily arrived at by counsel. In the next section a much more complex example will be examined. Nevertheless, this example illustrates the principle one should implement in the practice of preventive law. Take one more step and look for a solution. Do not wait until the business manager complains, "Well, how can we do it then?" Ask that question yourself!

Then after doing so, think beyond the pure legal issue and consider the law/business and even business issues, as the corporate counsel did in this example. The pure legal issue here was whether the lease agreement provided adequate protection against risk of loss to their product. It did not, but answering that legal issue alone would not have solved the real problem, which was the need for a warehousing/distribution center at that location. So while asking how it can be done is an essential, initial approach to finding a solution, one must then follow through by thinking beyond the pure law issue—and search for all the possible alternative answers to the question, idea, or problem.

Search for All the Alternatives

This is an area in which a corporate counsel can excell. The skills of an attorney to question, investigate, and think logically and deductively, combined with his knowledge of the law as well as the corporation, uniquely qualifies a corporate counsel among those in the corporate world to ferret out all possible alternative courses of action to resolve a problem or go forward with planned objective. His ability to apply a preventive law approach and deal with issues involving a commingling of legal problems and business problems (law/business issues) distinguishes him from corporate layman management, who frequently lack the ability to effectively deal with such issues.

Being able to search for and find all the possible alternative answers to corporate law/business issues is perhaps the most effective and productive application of an attorney's skills and knowledge within the corporate environment and one that all are well-advised to concentrate upon and refine as their career progresses.

Some helpful and practical techniques to use when searching for all possible alternative answers to the issues and problems confronting corporate counsel follow.

Use Imagination

Be a little creative. Let the mind wander, if that helps. Even daydream a little. It might be useful to scan or make up a checklist of common issues occurring in the body of laws or regulations confronting counsel. Or perhaps diagraming the central issue by putting it in a circle and then jotting down all the possible alternative answers to the problem, as the spokes of a bicycle wheel fit into the hub of the wheel, would be helpful. Whatever the approach or technique one finds most useful, the object at this point is not to find the best alternative (that comes later), but to search for all the possible alternative courses of action, however fanciful, that might even remotely resolve the problem confronting counsel and the corporation. Then one can most easily see where each of them leads and pick the best from among them.

This approach of using one's imagination is not unlike searching for all the legal issues in a factual situation or problem. The difference is far fewer attorneys take the time to fully employ this approach, usually because they are only concerned with the pure legal issues and their answers—not the real solutions to the real problems. Other times, attorneys are so pushed or overloaded with work that it appears easier and quicker to go with the first, workable legal alternative they think of. But if a corporate counsel wants to practice his most effective preventive law in the corporation, he must first exert some effort and take the time necessary to search for all the alternative answers to a problem. Usually in the long run, more time is saved by counsel's using this approach. Whatever technique is most useful to prompt a person to sit back and use a little imagination when thinking about the various possible alternative ways to answer a problem should be used. This is not yet the stage to be limited within the confines of a rigorous and disciplined thought process. Think of all the alternatives first, and then reconsider them later to find the best ones.

Use Issue Analysis as a Format

The technique of analyzing a factual situation or problem by first identifying the law, law / business, and business issues provides a superior format to then search for alternative answers. In that manner, counsel can be sure of covering a large portion of the spectrum.

Again using the simple facts about the warehouse lease agreement in the last section, recall one of the legal issues was whether the language provided for adequate insurance coverage of the inventory, and one alternative approach to that issue was that it did not but it might be modified so that it would. One of the law/business issues was how the insurance coverage could be provided and still have a lease agreement acceptable between the parties. An alternative answer to that law/business issue was to have one party furnish the insurance and adjust the expense accordingly. One of the business problems (or objectives) was to have a warehouse/distribution center at that location. One alternative answer was to obtain corporate management approval to self-insure (assume) the risk of loss and sign the lease agreement as is. Another alternative might have been to look for a different building in the same general area. And there could have been many more issues and alternatives in that example, particularly if the parties had not agreed upon the appropriate cost adjustments to provide the insurance coverage.

Although the issues in a problem cannot always be clearly characterized as pure law or pure business, neither can the alternative approaches to solve the problem be seen as always clearly emanating from the catagories of law, law/business, or business issues.

Nevertheless, this issue analysis format is a very effective, logical way to help uncover all of the possible alternatives and a superior technique for corporate counsel to implement in his personal preventive law practice. It enables one to grasp the problem objectively from all perspectives, to see the total picture, and importantly, to see all the possible alternatives, not just those that answer one or two limited issues.

Obtain a Second or Expert Opinion

Another person's perspective, background, or expertise can sometimes assist counsel in finding alternative answers that he would not have otherwise found. On occasion, a person will become so immersed a complex factual situation that simply discussing it with another attorney in the law department or an outside law firm will give a fresh perspective and suggest other alternative answers.

A review of the warehouse lease agreement in the last section with the corporate insurance manager or an outside insurance broker may have helped counsel to determine whether or not the risk of loss to the inventory standing alone was insurable and, if so, whether it was commercially feasible, what amount of deductible was advisable, and so on. They might have been able to suggest even better alternatives. Similarly, if a corporate counsel is handling the dissolution of a subsidiary corporation, the expertise of persons within the corporate finance and tax departments can greatly assist in finding alternatives that have the least impact upon the company's current operating statement, for example. Obtaining perspective of another person, regardless of whether his expertise lays in the business area or a legal specialty, can often suggest new and different alternative answers to a problem.

There are other approaches a corporate counsel may use to search for all the alternative answers to a problem. Three primary techniques have been discussed here, in addition to simply asking how it can be done. But the important thing to remember in one's practice of corporate law is to *do* it! Search, and then keep searching, for all of the possible alternative ways to handle a problem.

Because this principle is so crucially important in the effective practice of preventive corporate by finding solutions, the next two sections will present a complex but not uncommon example of a situation many corporate counsel will encounter during their careers and how, in detail, to apply this principle and others in a practical way to first find, and then decide upon, the best alternatives.

A Complex and Practical Example

Examine the following complex multi-issue example, which is not unlike situations corporate counsel will encounter during his career, and see how many different alternative answers to the problems can be found.

First, read the facts confronting this corporate counsel in a computer industry and place yourself in his or her shoes.

Then think back through all the principles discussed so far in "Part B, Find the Solution," to see whether any of them should be applied before beginning the search for the alternatives. For example, remember to first identify the issues so that issue analysis can be used as an approach to search for all the alternatives. Following the facts, a list of the principal issues appears so that you can compare the issues you found with them.

Then, use the principles discussed in this Key to search for all the alternatives. Ask how it can be done, and use a little imagination. Find as many different alternatives as possible; then compare your results with those presented. Spend some time on this example because it will be used again in the next section to determine which of the alternatives are the best and represent the solution.

The Facts in a Computer Company Case

Counsel is in-house counsel for a corporation in the computer industry. The company manufactures computer/data processing equipment and specializes in designing and furnishing of the total system necessary to meet the business customer's needs, including the mainframe computer, communication components (input and output), other hardware components, terminal stations, and all required software programs.

The typical "Total Systems Package" marketed by your company begins with the consulting phase to determine which mainframe, peripheral hardware, and software is most compatible with the customer's needs and then continues through the phases of system design, installations, and optional employee training or maintenance service programs. The fees and costs for each separate phase of this package are quoted at hourly rates (which include a mark-up for fee), multiplied by the actual time required in each phase, plus the wholesale price for any hardware/software furnished (also including mark-ups); or if the Total Systems Package is purchased, then the hardware/software prices remain the same, but the total accumulation of hourly rates is estimated and then quoted as a fixed percentage fee applied on the aggregate hardware/software cost furnished in the package.

An account executive and salesmen in the company have been negotiating with a potential customer for several months. The negotiations are about to come to a conclusion and will involve the purchase of a Total Systems Package. The company will provide all of the services and products that this customer requires, with one exception. Because of the character of this customer's business, it requires a data memory storage unit beyond the capability of the memory storage unit manufactured by the company. The company and the customer have identified a suitable memory storage unit manufactured by a competing computer company, which, unfortunately, is not compatible with the systems hardware manufactured furnished by your company. However, the competitor has assured your company salesman and engineers that only a limited amount of redesign and modification would make it completely compatible and functionable with your company's systems.

The problem brought to counsel is this: Everyone knows what he wants, but no one is sure how to get it. Your company wants to provide the Total Systems Package, including the competing company's memory storage unit, so that the percentage fee can be applied to its relatively high cost. The customer is happy with that arrangement and is also satisfied with the warranties contained in your standard systems package (and maintenance programs), which include protection against product defects as well as a warranty that the operating system will perform as intended within the specified design limits. Your company management and you, however, are reluctant to include the memory storage unit manufactured by the competitor (and offered with a less extensive warranty) within your own warranty provisions. They are especially concerned that unexpected testing and debugging of the competitor's memory storage unit may be necessary before compatibility is achieved. Counsel is familiar with the contracts and other documentation used by your company to market the Total Systems Packages, having previously been involved with several similar transactions.

Management asks corporate counsel: *"Is there any way we can include our competitor's memory storage unit in our Total Systems Package and yet not be legally responsible for it?"*

Those are the facts. Does it sound as if your corporate management wants to eat their cake and have it, too? Perhaps. In any event, how should counsel answer this question? Should he say, "Are you guys kidding? If you want to furnish something (the memory storage unit) to a customer and charge them a fee for doing it, then you've got to be willing to stand behind what you furnish—or the law will make sure you do. The answer to your question is no—unless, of course, your customer is naive enough to release you from all liability!"

Of course, counsel would not answer in that aloof and superior way. He should also go one step beyond that simple statement of law. He should ask questions, listen, get more facts, identify the issues, and find the real problem. Then, after applying the law (and going outside, if necessary), counsel should ask himself how can it be done and then search for all of the alternative courses of action to answer their question and, importantly, to find the solution to the problem.

As the corporate counsel here confronted with those facts, what are the law, the law/business, and business issues and the real problem(s)? Reread the facts, think about it, and jot down the issues as you see them, before then comparing your analysis with the one that follows.

The Principal Issues

The following are the principal issues and real problem identified by corporate counsel in the computer company case, along with a brief analysis of each. Compare them with the ones you found.

CHART A

Principal Issues in the Computer Company Case.

Identification of		**Brief Analysis**
LAW ISSUE:	*Risk Of Liability*	Potential for liability resulting from defective or inadequate performance of competitor's memory storage unit, whether by express or implied warranty, by contract, or in tort.
BUSINESS ISSUES:	*Fee*	Memory storage unit must be included in Total Systems Package so the fee percentage can be applied to its relatively high cost.
	Customer Relations	The objective to provide good and complete service to the customer, now and during the warranty/maintenance period.
LAW/BUSINESS ISSUE:	*Ability to Control*	Your company's contractual right to control the performance of the competitor (and his product) may (1) enable you to minimize the risk of liability as well as (2) successfully argue that the memory storage unit is within the total package for purposes of charging the fee.
REAL PROBLEM:	*Proper Balance Between Fee versus Liability*	This represents a typical commingling of the law and business issues and may be partially answered by focusing upon the above law/business issue above.

Do you agree with the principal issues and analyses presented? You may have identified more specific law issues, such as the risk represented by the "less extensive warranty" offered by the competitor, or you may have classified the "contractual right" shown in the law/business issue above as a law issue. Those are legitimate concerns and classifications as are several others not included.

The *Risk Of Liability* issue is identified simply as a broad, general law issue, of which several more specific law issues form a part. And while the business issues of *Fee* and *Customer Relations* are important and obvious, as your involvement with the situation progresses, the business managers may tell you that other business considerations are of more importance, thereby changing that analysis.

The *Law/Business* issue, identified as your company's ability to control (by contract) the competitor's performance, is a pivotal issue. On the one hand, it determines whether the memory storage unit can be deemed part of your total systems package justifying application of the percentage fee to its cost (the business issue). On the other hand, it determines whether the company will be able to significantly minimize the risk of any guarantor obligations your company may have to assume through application of the standard Total Systems Package warranty language (the law issue).

You might have also correctly analyzed the guarantor issue by focusing only upon the contractual language obligating your company to warrant the competitor's performance—rather than focusing upon the issue of controls—and perhaps classified it as a law issue; but because it impinges directly upon the fee application argument, it is more accurately defined as a law/business issue.

At this stage in the development of the facts, the *Real Problem* is the proper balance between the business considerations (fee) and the acceptable level of legal liability, but other real problems could easily surface later. Although some business managers may not agree with our analysis that risk of legal liability is a substantial part of the real problem, remember that counsel is a professional and must convince them otherwise—and stand apart in that judgment, if necessary.

Having now identified the principal issues and real problem in the computer company situation, we can apply the law to those issues and go to outside law specialists, if necessary. For example, counsel may discover certain state statutes that restrict the ability of parties to limit their liability for negligence. The next step is to move forward and search for all the possible alternative courses of action to take in the computer company situation, which is the primary principle of this section to be applied in the practice of preventive corporate law.

Using the issues you identified along with the analysis provided, search for all the possible alternative approaches to answer each one, including the law / business and business issues (which incidentally does not constitute making a business decision as will be discussed later). Be expansive and go where your imagination takes you by constantly asking yourself how it can be done. Also focus on practical ways to solve the issues as opposed to theoretical arguments or approaches. Then compare those alternatives you find with those presented next.

The Alternatives

How many alternative courses of action (answers) to the issues in the computer company case did you uncover? You should have found quite a few (27 appear below). If you did not find that many, you may want to go back and try again. Think of more variations and more specific alternatives to the ones already found.

In contrast to finding the principal issues in a problem, in which the main intent was to correctly analyze the problem and provide a framework for handling it, here we want to find as many different approaches and alternative answers as we can, however slightly different each may be from the other, so that we will then have the most alternatives to weigh and the solution.

Remember, we are looking for answers to the problems that can be implemented by your corporate management to achieve their objectives, not just yours. A theoretical answer to an issue is really not an alternative for that purpose, until you go one step further and recommend a decision or specific plan of action. So if any of your alternatives tend to take a theoretical approach, you may want to change them now.

Most of the following alternatives are organized in the issue analysis format appearing in the last section. The Principal Alternative to the primary issue(s) is listed first, followed by several Collateral Alternatives, which form a part, supplement, or variation thereof. Read through and compare them with the alternatives you found.

CHART B

Alternative Courses of Action in the Computer Company Case

	To Risk of Liability Issue:
A PRINCIPAL ALTERNATIVE:	1. *Exclude the memory storage unit* from the Total Systems Package.
Commentary:	Let the customer decide whether he wants that capability, and if so, he can solicit quotes himself and contract with any company in whatever manner he chooses.
COLLATERAL ALTERNATIVES:	2. Handle memory storage unit with customer under a different contract (outside of the Total Systems Package) with a separately negotiated fee and warranty limitations.
	3. Go back to the separate phase (limited scope) method of providing services and charging fees.
	4. Consider alternative ways to provide for customer's data storage needs: such as time sharing or tie-in with another company's existing but under-utilized memory storage system.
	5. In conjunction with customer, hire outside consultant to reexamine the actual data storage needs of his business.
	6. Provide your company's limited memory storage unit at cost (with mark-up but no fee or warranty), and let owner determine whether he wants to upgrade it later with another company's product.
A PRINCIPAL ALTERNATIVE:	7. *Recommend to customer that they contract direct with competitor* for the purchase, installation, and service of the memory storage unit.

To Risk of Liability Issue: (cont.)

Commentary: This has the advantage of a clear pass-through of liability for defects and performance of the memory storage unit (except for reliance on your company's prior recommendations of the unit) but does not allow your company the ability to control the performance of the competitor (which may unavoidably affect your company's ability to perform) or charge a fee on its value.

COLLATERAL ALTERNATIVES:

8. Manage this third-party contract for customer on an hours-incurred fee basis but with no assumption of liability.
9. Manage and enforce this contract for customer for lump-sum fee and a cap on your liability.

To Fee and Customer Relations Issues:

A PRINCIPAL ALTERNATIVE:

10. *Include the memory storage unit* in the Total Systems Package by having your company subcontract that portion of the work to the competitor.

Commentary: This provides maximum customer service and allows application of the fee in accordance with the Total Systems Package standard provisions but also requires your warranties to cover product defects and his performance, including any gaps between his less comprehensive warranty.

COLLATERAL ALTERNATIVES:

11. Increase the subcontract price to competitor (whether the difference is reimbursable by customer or not) in exchange for his upgrading his warranty to be consistent with your company's.
12. Obtain a performance bond on competitor's work.
13. Find another company that can provide a comparable memory storage unit but with more extensive warranties.

To Fee and Customer Relations Issues: (cont.)

14. Demand that liquidated damages be paid by the competitor if late delivery is caused by delays in achieving compatibility with your company's systems.

To Ability to Control Issue:

A PRINCIPAL ALTERNATIVE:

15. *Subcontract but with a limited warranty assumption* by your company.

Commentary:

This approach allows direct control over the competitor's performance and also permits a negotiable fee posture.

COLLATERAL ALTERNATIVES:

16. Subcontract memory storage unit but expressly assume no liability for warranty (or maintenance) performance, and have the warranty assigned directly from the competitor to the customer.

17. Have your company guarantee the competitor's warranty provisions but only to the extent thereof and then, only on a reimbursable time and material basis.

18. Warrant and assume maintenance on memory storage unit (and apply fee) but only after a six-month compatibility period achieved.

19. Warrant only against major product defects, and exclude performance warranty.

20. Modify the warranty language in your Total Systems Contract regarding the memory storage unit.

21. Assume liability but only in the amount that your fee is applied to the memory storage unit.

22. Subcontract but with no fee and no liability for your company.

Other Alternatives Suggested by Imagination

23. Acquire license from competitor or another company to market and use their memory storage unit (as modified to be compatible with your company's hardware / software).
24. Joint venture with competitor for the redesign of his memory storage unit for compatibility with your company's products and for future manufacture and marketing.
25. Have your company engineers modify the competitor's memory storage unit, if no patent infringement.
26. Provide free use of your company's existing memory storage unit to the customer, in exchange for his payment now (negotiated) for an upgraded product to be developed by your company engineers during the next year.
27. Determine whether any other hardware and/or software manufactured by your company can be modified to allow increased memory storage capacity by multiple hook-ups of existing storage units, for example.

Are your alternatives similar to those just presented? Some of yours may be more creative or superior, for example, if you applied the law in your jurisdiction and determined that a complete waiver of liability is not permitted under a specific statute. It should not concern you if you classified some as answers to law issues rather than law/business issues as here, or vice versa. The important principle to learn is the technique to search out all the alternatives, not whether they are labeled correctly.

Some of your alternatives may be broader and represent a composite of those suggested, which is not wrong, so long as you recognize their components. For example, if you proposed "modify the warranty language" and nothing more, you should understand that alternative is not specific enough to implement as is, and it has value only as a concept or idea.

The alternatives we are searching are specific and practical courses of action or decisions that can be implemented to resolve the problem. Remember, our definition of a solution reads: "... those alternative courses of *action* or *decision*...," not "those alternative concepts or ideas."

Most of the alternatives presented are specific and practical enough to be readily implemented. Do they cover everything? They cover the issues we identified earlier and a few others that originated from the imagination. The collateral alternatives proceed logically from the principal alternatives like the spokes from the hub of a bicycle wheel. In short, haven't we correctly asked ourselves how it can be done and then used our issue analysis format, plus our imagination to find all the possible alternatives? This is a good, practical illustration of the correct implementation of the principles we've discussed so far in this Key and of some discussed earlier.

It is also a good example of how you, the corporate counsel, can most effectively apply your skills and knowledge to the corporate environment. You are not simply confining your abilities to answering the limited legal issues but instead are searching for alternatives to all the issues, including the frequently commingled law/business and business issues. You are making some of your greatest contributions to the corporation this way because you are better qualified than most laymen to sort out these commingled issues and find the appropriate alternatives. You are practicing that kind of law focused to prevent future legal problems by finding alternatives (and solutions) to the real problems, not just answers to the limited legal questions of the moment.

When viewed in the total picture, the time spent in searching for alternatives is probably the most productive time spent when dealing with a problem. It is well worth the extra effort to spend an additional hour or even an extra day to look at the problem from a fresh prospective if doing so leads to the best alternative solution to the problem. Unfortunately, far too often the case is one in which a corporate counsel is too pushed for time or otherwise not inclined to search out all the possible alternatives and, as a result, ends up giving a short-term or limited answer to the problem.

Having now searched out all of the possible alternatives to resolve the issues and real problem, counsel will find it easier to find the solution. We can now choose the best alternatives from among them, refine them as the circumstances may require, and ultimately choose the correct solution.

Which Alternative Is the Solution?

Have you decided which alternatives are best?

Remember the question your corporate management asked you: *"Is there some way we can include our competitor's memory storage unit in our Total Systems Package, and yet not be legally responsible for it?"*

Does the answer to that question represent the best alternatives or solution? No. The solution is the answer to the Real Problem, which, in this case, is the proper balance between the issues of fee and liability.

Also, consider our definition of a solution again: ". . . those alternative courses of action or decisions which accomplish the business purposes and objectives of the corporation to the extent possible, while still maintaining high quality legal practices within determined levels of minimum legal risk, exposure and cost to the corporation."

Now, which alternatives would you describe as the best? Look at your alternatives again and at those presented in the preceding section, and decide for yourself before continuing on to see whether you agree with the following conclusions that were reached by the corporate counsel in the computer company case. It may assist your evaluation to proceed as the following discussion does, by first deciding which alternatives are best from the legal standpoint, then from a business viewpoint, and finally, from the law / business perspective. Following that analysis, we can then most easily determine which of those best alternatives represents the solution(s) and why. You should find several alternatives that can be considered in the best category.

The Best Alternatives in the Computer Company Case

From the Legal Standpoint

Frcm a purely legal standpoint, most lawyers would agree that the first Principal Alternative identified addressing the Risk of Liability law issue is the best:

> Principal Alternatives #1: Exclude the memory storage unit from the Total Systems Package.

Thus the customer is completely responsible to determine what memory storage unit he wants, to pick the companies that he invites to bid on its supply and installation, and to supervise its installation. The customer must look directly and exclusively to that company for any product defects or warranty problems. This method of exclusion clearly puts the entire burden for the memory storage unit on the customer and effectively insulates your computer company from liability.

Ironically, however, from a purely business standpoint, this alternative is probably the worst (and would therefore not constitute a solution). It provides the customer with the least amount of assistance (actually none) regarding memory storage unit. In addition, no fee can be charged on the unit, and no control can be exercised by your company to assure its timely delivery and installation, which, in turn, may affect your company's ability to perform.

For the most part, the same is true regarding the Collateral Alternatives (#2 through #6), although reexamining the customer's real data storage needs (#5) and seeking other ways to fulfill such needs, for example, by tie-in to third-party computers (#4), would be slightly better from the business standpoint because more service is provided to the customer but still not enough to justify charging a fee.

The second Principal Alternative (#7) approach to the Risk of Liability issue:

> Principal Alternative #7: Recommend to customer that they contract direct with competitor for the purchase, installation and service of the memory storage unit,

is still acceptable from a legal standpoint despite the potential risk of liability resulting from your recommendation of the competitor's product, and it is a little more desirable from a business standpoint because it provides great customer advice and service.

The variations to this approach in Collateral Alternatives #8 and #9 are substantially better from a business standpoint because they provide more administration and control over the work (also a favorable legal consideration), permit a partial fee to be charged, and retain a (negotiated) limit of liability. In fact, these two collateral alternatives are similar to the law/business issue alternatives (#15 through #22) except that the contract is executed directly between the customer and the competitor. They could well constitute the "solution(s)." At this stage, however, they should probably be considered only in a category of second-best alternatives because the contracting posture significantly diminishes the bargaining leverage to justify application of a fee to the work.

From the Business Standpoint

From a business standpoint,

> Principal Alternative #10: Include the memory storage unit in the Total Systems Package by having your company subcontract that portion of the work to the competitor,

excellently resolves the business issues of Fee and Customer Relations. But just as clearly, this alternative is the least desirable from the legal standpoint because it requires your company's standard warranties to apply to the product and performance of another company. And although the Collateral Alternatives #11 through #14 retain the desirable business aspects of fee and customer relations and ameliorate the potential for liability somewhat through various protective devices like liquidated damages and performance bonds, they still remain unsatisfactory from the legal standpoint because your company's standard warranties apply to the work.

Note: Do not be too concerned here about your lack of formal business training (if that is the case) when trying to determine the best alternatives to the business issues. Knowing the business of your company is usually sufficient for you to grasp the primary business objectives, and if not, most laymen will be more than happy to explain the business concerns as they view them.

From the Law/Business Standpoint

Turning now to the alternatives addressing the law/business issue of Ability to Control, we begin to see more of a balance between the business considerations, on the one hand, and the law issues, on the other. This means that the alternatives in this category are more likely to resolve the instant real problem: Proper Balance Between Fee and Liability.

The approach taken by the Principal Alternative:

> Principal Alternative #15: Subcontract but with a limited warranty assumption,

correctly assumes that by subcontracting the work, your company will be in a sufficiently strong negotiating position to justify application of the fee despite the fact that your company's standard warranty provisions will not cover the competitor's product and performance. Several arguments can be asserted to support these apparently contradictory positions, for example, although your company is responsible to administer and manage the subcontract work (justifying the fee), it is not reasonable to require that the full extent of your company's comprehensive warranties apply to the intended performance and promise of product compatibility by another company whose product is not yet fully developed and tested or that the standard warranty language contained in your Total Systems Package was intended to cover only those products actually manufactured by your company.

By examining the Collateral Alternatives #16 through #22, we see several specific examples of this approach, some representing a compromise between full application of the fee and the full limitation of liability. For example, alternative #21 proposes that your company's warranties and percentage fee apply to the competitor's product and performance but that any resulting liability be limited to the actual dollar amount of fee received. This alternative appears to be an eminently "fair bargain" between the reasonable expectations of the parties (the customer and your company), but as events progress, the bargaining leverage of one of the parties might change, decreasing the feasibility of this alternative accordingly.

From your company's perspective, Collateral Alternatives #16 and #17 are probably the best alternatives to the law/business issue because they allow the full application of fee and limit the nonreimbursable assumption of liability the most. The customer, however, would undoubtedly consider alternative #21 to be a better bargain for him. Does the customer's opinion make a difference to us? It certainly does. Earlier in this Key we were searching for all the possible alternatives and were not concerned with what the customer might think. But here we are trying to determine which alternative is the solution, and in order to be a solution, the alternative must work and must be agreed upon by all the parties.

To recapitulate, having eliminated the probability of a solution appearing from among those alternatives addressing only the law and business issues because they fail to achieve the proper balance between those issues, as required by our definition of a solution (and by the "real problem"), you must evaluate the "best alternatives" in this last, remaining law/business category. Would you consider any of them to constitute a solution to the problem confronted by the corporate counsel in the computer company situation, and if so, which ones?

The Solution In the Computer Company Case

In this case, corporate counsel concluded that the law/business issue, Collateral Alternatives #16 and #17 in that order, represented the solution to the Real Problem and most effectively satisfied the definition and principles of a solution.

Knowing, however, that the customer might object to these proposals, he suggested to corporate management that, if necessary, Collateral Alternative #21 would be an acceptable compromise (or solution) from the legal standpoint, as would the remaining, though increasingly less desirable, group of law/business Collateral Alternatives #18, 19, 20, and 22. (Two or three recommended solutions to management are more than adequate in most cases. If more alternatives are recommended, they should be assigned a relative value or otherwise distinguished. See the Key Six.)

In addition to proposing these alternatives courses of action to management as solutions, he suggested that other possible approaches might include a licensing or joint venture arrangement with the competitor company. Counsel succinctly set forth these alternatives in descending order of preference in a memo along with brief explanations.

Do you agree with this counsel's judgment about the solution in the computer company case? You may have found other alternatives you consider to be the solution, which is all right as long as you arrived at your conclusions by using a similar analysis.

For example, as we briefly mentioned earlier, Collateral Alternatives #8 and #9 that respond to the Risk of Liability issue may have been correctly chosen as solutions by you if in your judgment the potential for liability arising from the memory storage unit work was greater than this corporate counsel concluded. And even if not, having the contract for that work run directly between the customer and the competitor provides for some excellent legal safeguards as well as retaining some justification for fee application. So either Collateral Alternatives #8 or #9 could have been correctly recommended to management as the solution, perhaps then followed by Collateral Alternatives Nos. 16, 17, and 21.

On the other hand, if you selected one of the Alternatives #1 through 6 (Principal Alternative #1: Exclude memory storage unit) or Alternatives #10 through 14 (to the Fee and Customer Relations issues) as the solution(s), then under the given set of facts, you probably placed an unnecessary amount of emphasis on the legal issue or the business issue, respectively. The alternatives suggested by the imagination, Alternatives #23 through 27, could have been recommended as solutions by you (as this corporate counsel did), but because of their indirect approach to the real problem, they should be included only in conjunction with other recommended solutions.

Although you may find it unnecessary in your personal practice of preventive corporate law to be so comprehensive and deliberate as this corporate counsel was by first determining the best alternatives within each categories of issues, when one or the other category would obviously not solve the real problem or represent the solution, this type of analyses is very thorough, logical, and has great merit, especially when the problem is a complex one with many competing objectives. It is an approach you would do well to consider implementing in your own practice.

General Principles To Implement

Use Judgment

The most important single principle for a corporate counsel to implement in his personal practice of preventive corporate law to determine which alternative is the solution is to USE JUDGMENT. Not just legal judgment—but the *best legal judgment after consideration of the business objectives.*

This principle has been illustrated in several different ways throughout Part B and is integral to the definition of what constitutes a solution. The best alternatives and solutions to the legal problems in the corporation simply cannot be consistently found by concentrating solely upon the law issues or solely upon the traditional law approaches because they fail to adequately consider the often inextricably intertwined law/business and business issues, which frequently are of equal, or even greater, importance when trying to resolve the real problem. By using all of his judgment focused toward all the issues, counsel will be most likely to find the solution to the real problems and least likely to end up practicing law in a vacuum without regard to the corporate environment.

Evaluate All Alternatives

The primary reason to implement the issue and alternative analysis approach used by corporate counsel to find the solution in the computer company case in the last section is that by doing so, counsel is sure to have properly evaluated all of the possible alternatives.

By examining the alternatives in each issue category to determine the best ones from the standpoint of the law, and then from the business and law/business perspectives, counsel is most likely to apply all his judgment to all the issues, objectively and comprehensively. Then the process of weighing the best alternatives against each other to determine which resolves the real problem (the solution) is most accurately and easily accomplished. Since the majority of problems confronting a corporate counsel during his career will contain law/business and business considerations, not just legal ones, this approach most consistently assures the proper handling of a problem from all aspects and from all points of view. In effect, counsel will have effectively weighed and balanced the legal considerations in light of business considerations and will have applied his skills and knowledge as an attorney most productively to the real problems presented in the corporation setting.

Using the issue and alternative analysis approach is also helpful when counsel is not sure of the real problem or has determined that more than one real problem exists. By necessity in these cases, all possible issues and alternative answers must be evaluated until the facts become more clearly defined. Thus the systematic and thorough evaluation of all alternatives provided by this approach is prerequisite to the effective handling of these problems.

Remember That Solutions Are Fluid

Solutions should not be deemed to be etched in stone but instead regarded as fluid and subject to reevaluation as circumstances unfold. Business strategies change, a party's attitude can fluctuate, facts giving rise to the problem in the first place can evolve into an entirely different situation, all during the time within which counsel is searching for the solutions to the problem at hand.

So while one must still make a determination and recommend a solution to corporate management, counsel is well-advised to keep an eye on the problem he is handling, to see whether any changed circumstances warrant a different alternative solution. By using the issue and alternative analysis implemented by counsel in the Computer Company Case, one is best prepared to effectively handle changed circumstances because he is not confined within the singular viewpoint of a limited issue of law, having already covered the spectrum of alternatives from several different perspectives.

Make a Decision

What should counsel do if after having diligently implemented the principles of this Key, he is nonetheless unable to find a solution to the problem?

That is possible. Sometimes a solution will appear to be no solution at all, but rather just the "least bad" alternative of several undesirable courses of action. If counsel is unable to determine which alternatives should be considered the solution, then he must simply present to corporate management those alternatives deemed most favorable, with the comment that from a legal standpoint, none of these alternative courses of action are desirable. In a limited number of cases counsel will be unable to obtain sufficient facts or reliable information to make even that determination. For example, if the law is vague on a particular point or if counsel does not have the resources available to research the issue in-depth, then he will only be able to say to management that he does not know the answer (solution) but will continue searching for it. Those situations, however, will generally be few. More typically, a corporate counsel has not found a solution because of failure to adequately analyze the problem and all of the possible alternative answers or because counsel is afraid or reluctant to make a decision about which alternative is the solution.

Never be afraid to use judgment and make a decision. If counsel has been unable to find a solution, it should be because the law is vague or for a similar reason, not because he was too timid or afraid to commit to a decision. Remember that with the skills and knowledge of an attorney, counsel is more qualified than most in the corporation, to handle the law and law-related problems confronting it.

So when examining the alternative courses of action to solve a problem, remember to implement the best legal judgment after consideration of the business objectives; be sure to evaluate all of the possible alternatives; consider the solutions found to be subject to change as the circumstances dictate; and above all, do not be afraid to make a decision about which alternative is the solution.

A few practical pointers that are sometimes helpful when searching for a solution will be discussed in the next section.

Some Practical Pointers

Here are some practical pointers that may help in finding the best alternative or the solution to the problem being handled by corporate counsel. Although they may not always be pertinent to the issues at hand, when they are, they are eminently useful. When reading through this section, do not be surprised if one point or another reminds counsel of an occasion when he used a similar technique to find a solution, or could have done so.

Is There Another Business Purpose?

Sometimes knowing the "other business purpose" will affect the search for alternatives and, ultimately, the solution. Although the business purpose of the corporation is to make a profit, occasionally there are short-term business objectives indirectly related to making a profit. Other business purposes of this type can result from the corporate political motivations of a rising, aggressive layman manager out to make his mark (or hide his mistake). And they can arise for other reasons as varied as the people who make up a corporation.

When confronted with a problem or situation in which there may be "another business purpose," the best posture is to try to find out what it is. This is because it is extremely difficult for an attorney to correctly handle a problem unless he knows all the facts and all the objectives behind the question, business plan, idea, or problem presented. It is analogous to finding the real problem; counsel must find the real business purposes before he can find the real solutions.

Probing for other business purposes by intensive, cross-examination, questioning, and skepticism may cause resentment among the corporate laymen, who feel that this is "none of counsel's business" and that counsel should "stick to the law." But the fact is that counsel is "sticking to the law" when he tries to uncover other business purposes because they usually dramatically affect both his analysis and recommended solution to a problem. The following case of a corporate counsel asked to draft the necessary documents to acquire a small, privately held corporation clearly demonstrates this point.

> Corporate counsel for the acquiring company is asked to draft the preliminary documents to purchase a small privately held corporation, including a three-year employment agreement intended to assure retention of the founder, major stockholder, and president of the company to be acquired.
>
> Counsel drafts a stock acquisition agreement reciting the cash price (which he has been told) for the

purchase of all stock of this closely held corporation, along with several appendices, which list the assets to be transferred, accounts receivable outstanding, the inventory, the liabilities to be assumed or excluded, and so on.

Counsel also drafts the employment contract to be executed with the owner/president of the company to be acquired. As requested, it covers a three-year period at a stipulated salary (at which point counsel thinks he should get into business rather than being an attorney). Counsel also includes several standard clauses, such as a covenant against working for a competitor within a limited geographical area and time and a paragraph giving the company the right to terminate the agreement without liability for good cause, like misconduct and similar reasons.

Counsel gives these documents to the layman manager whose division is responsible for the acquisition. He reviews them and comes to counsel's office saying that the paragraph giving the company the right to terminate the employment agreement for misconduct and other reasons is not acceptable and must be removed. Counsel is surprised and asks why?

He replies that the owner of the company will not agree to sell his business without an ironclad three-year employment agreement. Counsel points out that the best alternative is to have at least some language regarding termination because circumstances can change greatly over a period of three years and because a court may not allow termination without penalty unless expressly provided for between the parties. He responds that this acquisition is very important, that this point is not negotiable, and that in any event they are willing to forfeit the amount of money which would be paid under the employment contract, if necessary, to conclude this deal.

Therefore, counsel considers this instance to be one in which the stated business purpose outweighs the legal considerations and redrafts the employment agreement accordingly by removing all provisions regarding termination.

About 18 months later, again to counsel's surprise, the same manager comes to him and asks if there is any way to get out of that employment agreement. Counsel says, "You're kidding? What's the matter?" He says that the former owner is no longer performing his job and that it has simply gotten to the point where he would rather not have him around than have him at work doing nothing.

Counsel reminds the manager that he was told to make the employment agreement ironclad, so that there was no way we could get out of it because that was all the owner would agree to. The manager says, "I know that. But isn't there some way we can still get out of it?" Counsel responds, "I doubt it. At least probably not without ending up in court, and I'm not sure I would want to take the case." Counsel suggests that the best alternative might be to agree upon some kind of settlement representing a partial payment on the remaining term of the employment contract.

After talking some more, the manager finally admits to counsel that the real purpose of having an ironclad employment contract with such a high salary was that it was intended as partial payment for the owner's company. For tax reasons (of dubious validity), the owner did not want to receive the entire purchase in the year of acquisition. Furthermore, the manager liked this arrangement because this way the acquisition price for the company appeared lower to his superiors and was easier to get approved.

If the attorney in this case had known this "other business purpose" from the beginning, would he have come up with another alternative or argued his case differently? He very well might have. He may have argued that paying part of the acquisition price for the company as salary has very questionable tax ramifications and that the excessive portion of the salary could be imputed to be part of the acquisition cost by tax examiners with the result that the company's financial reporting of the acquisition would constitute a misrepresentation. And counsel may have proposed better alternatives, for example, structuring the acquisition payments on an installment basis over the three-year period.

As demonstrated by this case, knowing the real business purpose about situations can dramatically change the alternative approaches counsel has come up with and considers to be the solution. Counsel will not always be able to discover the other business purposes; sometimes the business managers themselves may not have a clear idea of the real purpose. Notwithstanding this, it is wise to exert every effort to uncover the other business purpose behind those factual situations and problem whenever counsel thinks one may exist. And in those situations in which he is certain a business manager is trying to hide the "other business purpose" from him, counsel will know that it is time to raise a red flag.

Is This the Simplest Alternative?

Sometimes the simplest alternative is best. How many times has a layman said, "Don't give it to the attorneys—they'll screw it up!" Although that attitude expressed by some laymen may be wrong and it is unfortunate if it exists in a corporation, it does say something that is worthwhile to think about. If somebody does not want to bring a problem to counsel because he thinks he will "screw it up," then regardless of whether he is right or wrong, counsel has lost an opportunity to practice effective preventive law. Remember, counsel must get the client into his office before he can learn about the problem.

This kind of comment by laymen can be attributed to several causes, but one of them is that some attorneys tend to make things more complicated then they really need to be. One example about excessively long contracts was discussed in Part A, in which it was noted that if counsel learns the business and knows the law in your industry, he will not need to use so many boilerplate provisions in an over-abundance of caution. As with the simplest contract, sometimes the simplest alternative is the best one. It most closely represents the intent and desires of the parties and is an alternative approach with which they can work, understand, and use. It will sometimes eliminate disputes that can arise from excessively complicated alternatives.

Here is a good example of a case in which the simplest alternative turned out to be the best one and the solution.

> Counsel for a corporation in the construction industry has been drafting and negotiating the contract documents to build a multimillion industrial project. For the most part, the construction costs are to be reimbursed in the amount actually incurred, plus a fee based upon the original estimate of such costs.
>
> One area in the contract has become quite complicated compared to its negligible value in the total project. Small hand tools used by the various tradesmen on a construction project of this type are frequently provided by the contractor (your company) with reimbursement by the owner at actual cost or at a fixed percentage of the total project cost. But because one of the negotiators representing the owner is a "tough and crusty" purchasing manager, they are inordinately concerned about the theft and disappearance of small hand tools. As a result, some very detailed language has been developed for that contract section. It includes an appendix in which an attempt has been made to list every type of small hand tool that might be used on the project, including a column showing the price for that item. Then, language was drafted to provide for a small tool office with a badge system in which all small tools are to be checked in and out by the tradesman needing them each day, plus a 24-hour security guard. An inventory is to be taken once a week by the company owner. Missing or damaged inventory will be noted in this report, along with a signed statement by the company giving the reasons therefor. These statements will be used by the owner to determine whether the loss or damage was the result of the negligence of the company or its employees, in which case reimbursement of the replacement cost will be denied.
>
> Counsel and the other negotiators for your company are well aware that these provisions for small hand tools are extremely cumbersome, would require substantial administration time, accounting, and pa-

perwork, and are simply not practical for a project of this magnitude. Because counsel had been unable to so convince the owner, however, counsel has tried to protect the company by inserting language to minimize the legal risks. The latest point of dispute is proposed language that would limit the denial for reimbursement of missing or damaged inventory to cases involving only gross negligence, and then only when a majority of a committee composed of two owner representatives and two contractor representatives is in agreement. Counsel also wants language excluding small hand tools below a unit cost of $50 from these nonreimbursement provisions.

One afternoon during a break in the negotiations, counsel and the other negotiators in your company, who are all obviously exasperated with the small hand tool provisions, try to figure out how to solve the problem. Counsel asks them if it is possible for them to come up with an estimate of the entire cost of providing small hand tools to the project. They say they think so and call the home office to ask a cost accountant run an analysis of the small hand tool costs on similar projects constructed by the company. Counsel and they then decide that since the objective of company is not so much to make a profit on small hand tools but to instead insure that they are adequately provided to the project, they will show these cost estimates to the owner with the proposal that the company provide all small hand tools needed on the project for a lump-sum reimbursement equal to this estimate, plus a small contingency. The company then would provide at its option a small tool office, security, or whatever else it deemed appropriate.

This concept was, in fact, agreed upon by the owner and satisfied his concern about excessive costs resulting from theft and damage. As a result of agreement on this alternative, the language in the contract regarding small hand tools quickly decreased to one short paragraph from several pages earlier. This far simpler alternative actually represented a clearer statement of both partys' intent and was one that

> could be used and understood more easily, with far less probability of conflict and dispute arising later.

This is an example in which the simplest alternative turned out to be the best one. Other examples of this principle will become apparent as counsel practices corporate law, if they have not already. It is a practical pointer well worth remembering. If counsel can find an alternative that will be easier for parties to use and understand, then, at least with regard to those attributes, it is usually better. If counsel can revise a document so that it is only three pages long, rather than seven or ten pages, it is often more intelligible and usable.

When searching for the simplest alternative, also be sure to consider its nonlegal attributes. Sometimes the nonlegal character of an alternative can dramatically affect its acceptability among the parties, even though it is the same as a less desired alternative from a substantive legal viewpoint.

For example, counsel's objective may be to formalize an oral agreement between the parties by committing it to writing. One alternative would be to send a letter to the other party containing the substantive terms of the agreement and request him to initial a copy and return it. The other obvious alternative is to draft a formal contract and have both parties sign it. Both these agreements would be effective from a legal standpoint, with one perhaps being no better than the other. But from a nonlegal, practical standpoint, it might be far easier to memorialize the agreement between the parties with a letter than the formal contract, which might require certain corporate approvals and maybe even formal negotiations. Remember the objective is to find the best alternative or solution to the problem, as here represented by the simplest alternative of the letter agreement, not to impress the parties with legal drafting skills or to enable a larger fee to be charged for a more complex work product, if that applies.

Can the Concept Be Quantified?

Quantifying a concept is often a useful technique to find the solution to a problem—perhaps because so many words and phrases mean different things to different people. Since an attorney is frequently involved with the written language, counsel should remember to implement this practical pointer whenever possible. It simply involves taking an imprecise concept and quantifying it numerically to remove ambiguity or differently perceived interpretations.

This quantifying of concepts and words can be effectively applied in a variety of situations, ranging from a simple clarification of a phrase like "*periodic* reports" to "*monthly* reports" or to more innovative clarifications of complex concepts like "inherent product deficiency" by defining it in terms of costs, for example, ". . . however, in no event shall the term 'inherent product deficiency' be deemed to include costs which in the aggregate, *exceed* ___ *dollars*", or perhaps in the reverse ". . . however, in no event shall the term 'inherent product deficiency' be deemed to include costs which in the aggregate *do not exceed* ___ *dollars*".

The following example demonstrates how quantifying a term or concept can lead to the best alternative and solution.

> The issue is the difference between the terms of simple negligence, unusual negligence, and gross negligence. None of the parties in this negotiation are having much fun. Counsel, in particular, does not like the term "unusual negligence", not knowing exactly how it would be interpreted by a court or jury. It was suggested by the opposing party as a compromise between the terms "simple negligence" and "gross negligence." Counsel knows from law school and experience as a practicing attorney that negligence is an illusive concept to define because it means different things to different people.
>
> In an attempt to resolve the prolonged discussion on these different concepts of negligence, counsel suggests that maybe the language could be clarified by quantifying it. Everyone in the meeting looks at him questioningly.
>
> Counsel points out that everyone is in agreement that the company should not be held responsible for the acts of simple or ordinary negligence by its employees (those being acknowledged as an unavoidable aspect of the operations). He further says that real area of conflict is at what level of negligence the

company should be responsible for the acts of its employees. Should that level of negligence be "unusual negligence," whatever that means, or should it be "gross negligence"? "Let's see if we can define what we mean in terms of dollars and cents instead of words," he says. "Let's say that any act by one of our employees that causes direct damages in an amount exceeding $250, for example, would be called gross negligence or, if you like, unusual negligence, for which our company would be responsible. Any act causing damage in a lesser amount would be considered simple negligence and not the responsibility of our company."

The parties respond to this suggestion by agreeing upon a dollar amount which represents in their minds the difference between simple and gross negligence and further stipulate that this dollar amount will be treated as a deductible so that in incidents in which the damages exceed that figure, the company would only be responsible for the excess amount. The final language in the documents recites only the term "negligence" and defines the agreed upon meaning of that concept in terms of dollars and cents. The ambiguous and confusing terms "unusual negligence" and "gross negligence" are not even used.

This example illustrates how language can be quantified to remove ambiguity and impreciseness. When possible, it is desirable to do so. It is an excellent technique to practice effective preventive law because by quantifying imprecise and ambiguous terms, counsel is removing a very real potential for later legal disputes.

This example makes another point. As evidenced by their rather easy agreement upon a dollar amount, the parties really had a similar opinion about the proper allocation of responsibility for negligence, but they were not aware of it because of their different perceptions of the terms *simple negligence, unusual negligence,* and *gross negligence.* In other words, they actually had "a meeting of the minds," but they did not know it because of the wording and language in dispute. Therefore, counsel should always be sensitive to the particular words being used and be sure that they actually represent what the parties think they mean, by clarifying them through the technique of quantifying when possible.

Is the Timing Correct?

Sometimes the proposed alternative is the best one, but the timing is not correct. It may be better to let a problem sit for a few days until everybody's emotions calm down and they are thinking more clearly. This includes the emotions of corporate management as well as those of the other party to the dispute. Sometimes a problem just has to "season" a bit before all the parties are willing to listen to the logical and rational alternative courses of action counsel has found to resolve it.

And there need not always be a dispute to make the timing of an alternative incorrect, although that is most commonly the case. Occasionally counsel will find himself in the position of being the "devil's advocate" or the "bad guy" bearing the news of sad tidings, for example, that demolish a layman's business plan which he or his group has been working on for several weeks or even months. If that is the case, counsel does no harm by saying instead that he does not believe it will comply with the law but he wants to think about it for a while rather than immediately answering the layman's proposal negatively? Who knows, in so doing, counsel may think of a workable alternative. At the least, counsel may have prepared his client for the bad news and also given the client a chance to think about it before hitting him over the head with the answer.

Whether the timing is correct for the alternative or solution is largely a matter of judgment and the circumstances. When the alternative solution involves precipitous and irrevocable action, it is always prudent to ask whether the timing is correct and whether an intermediate step cannot be employed first. Initiation of litigation is a good example of this principle. The nature of litigation (some proponents of adversary law practice might disagree) forecloses many, if not all, other avenues of resolution of the problem, at least in the short-term. Obviously then, if compromise or some other course of action is even remotely feasible to resolve the problem, little is lost by implementing that alternative first, because the opposite is usually the case when initiating a precipitous and irrevocable action.

Consider the following case in which counsel correctly persuaded her corporate mangement to implement an intermediate alternative prior to taking irrevocable action.

> By the time corporate counsel became aware of the on-going dispute between her company and another, the situation had deteriorated to the point that the parties refused to talk to each other. The situation was critical because the dispute was about the management of a joint venture (a third corporation) that counsel's company and the other had formed two years ago to market and distribute their products and that had yet to show a profit.
>
> The corporate managers of counsel's company are fed up and tell her they want to file a lawsuit against the other company to force them out of business or out of the jointly held company or to do whatever is necessary to get them out of the picture. Upon her learning that neither party has really sat down at a table and talked to each other for over six months, counsel recommends an alternative intermediate approach. She suggests that before taking the irrevocable action of filing a lawsuit, everybody try to sit down and talk. They reply that they doubt whether the other company will attend such a meeting and, in any event, nothing would be accomplished if they did.
>
> Counsel answers by stating the other company might respond if a formal board of directors or shareholders meeting was called with a specific agenda to be considered, including the areas in dispute. She also points out that this intermediate step may yield useful, if not essential, evidence necessary to support a cause of action in litigation.
>
> The special notice and agenda was sent, and the other company attended with their own proposal resolutions and retained outside counsel. After lengthy and difficult discussions, it was determined that the

best solution for all would be to liquidate the company (and share most liabilities), with each party then free to conduct its own business as it chose in that geographical area. Although neither party was pleased with this solution, the time, expense, and sometimes more frustrating results of litigation were avoided.

The proposal to call a shareholders and board of directors meeting in this case was a good intermediate alternative. The timing was appropriate for that step, but not for the irrevocable alternative of beginning litigation. Since the parties were unwilling to talk with each other prior to this meeting, it is highly unlikely they would have done so following commencement of litigation. Although intermediate alternatives like these are not so dramatic or decisive, they are also not so irrevocable. Irrevocable alternatives can be implemented later, but intermediate alternatives often cannot.

Is Compromise an Alternative?

Should counsel ever consider compromise as an alternative? Yes. Even more so in his position as corporate counsel—as opposed to one in the traditional practice of adversary law. Corporate counsel is in a unique position within today's law profession in which he can confront legal problems in their very early and developing stages, not after-the-fact when little is left but to assume the merits of a client's position and litigate.

When confronting problems in their early stages, counsel has the opportunity to practice very effective preventive law by finding a solution to the problem before it reaches the uncompromisable stage. As most lawyers know, the time, expense, frustration, and results of the litigation process in today's civil courts rarely achieves what the parties originally anticipated or had in mind when they began the process.

Although there are several causes for this, one underlying reason is the failure of the parties "to see both sides of the story." And since there are at least two sides to every dispute, each varying in merit, corporate counsel will wisely initially assume the role of an "arbitrator, mediator, or judge," rather than just that of a gladiator who unquestioningly pursues only the merits of his client's cause. By assuming the position of referee and evaluating the dispute objectively with due regard to all sides of the story, counsel is most likely to recognize when compromise is the most practical, preventive, and best solution to the problem.

As counsel's experience and skills in practicing preventive law become more refined, along with increased observation of the results achieved through the adversary practice of law, he will come to recognize, if he does not already, that compromise of a conflict between parties is almost always an alternative worthwhile considering, especially, but not only, in the early stages of a dispute. It is rarely too early or rarely too late to propose compromise as an alternative. It is not uncommon for parties in litigation to proceed through discovery and go all the way to the courthouse steps before one of them proposes a compromise or settlement of the case. If the lines of communication between the parties had been better and the counsels had used a more preventive law approach, these cases often would have been satisfactorily settled far earlier. This will not always occur, but it will occur enough times that counsel should always keep in mind that compromise is a very real and practical alternative when searching for solutions.

One caveat: Some disputes or conflicts are so critical to the company for reasons of policy, right or wrong, that counsel will want to vigorously pursue them through the adversary process to the ultimate conclusion with little regard to compromise as an alternative. Those cases, however, will usually be immediately apparent and few.

Reflection on Examining the Alternatives

Have you ever heard a corporate counsel complain, "I told them what the law was and they could not have cared less—they went ahead and did what they wanted to anyway"? If you have, it is reasonably certain that either the laymen in his corporation did not hold an appropriate regard for the law or—the more likely case—that corporate counsel did not practice preventive law by finding solutions, particularly by examining the alternatives. If counsel fails to ask how it can be done and search for all of the possible alternative answers and solutions to a problem, then how can a layman be faulted for seeming to "take the bull by the horns" and find his own solution? If counsel has failed to weigh all of the alternative courses of action, then he (and complaining corporate counsel) probably would not have even recognized that the layman was trying to do so himself after already considering counsel's limited legal advice.

To some extent it boils down to perspective. If counsel thinks the laymen in the corporation are not listening to his legal advice, then counsel is probably equally remiss in failing to adequately listen to their business considerations. Implementation of the principles of this key into counsel's own practice of preventive corporate law will serve him well. If he does so, by asking himself how it can be done, by searching for all of the possible alternative courses of action to answer the real problems and constitute the solution, and most of all, by applying all of his judgment to all of the issues and alternatives—not just the pure legal ones—then he will not be likely to complain as the aforesaid counsel did. He will have recognized the business objectives of the corporation and applied his skills and knowledge as an attorney to most effectively help achieve those objectives within the constraints and wisdom of the law.

To see if you can correctly apply these skills and principles to a real life situation in the corporation, read the facts in the following case study and ask yourself what you would do.

Case Study Number Ten: THE UNSATISFACTORY PROJECT

The Situation

You are counsel and Secretary to the Board of Directors of a corporation engaged primarily in the export and import of bulk commodities. Two and one-half years ago your company entered into a business venture with two other corporations to develop a major export/import handling and shipping facility on a 300-acre tract of land then owned by one of the other corporations at a southeastern United States deep-water harbor. The principal commodity to be shipped through the facility will be low-grade coal to the European market by the land-owning partner, but in an effort to minimize equity investment and market risk, that corporation conceived and promoted this project as a multiuse facility to be jointly owned and used by three noncompeting companies in the export/import industry. Your company joined this project because it will greatly enhance your exporting capability and provide some stabilization against the cyclical commodity sector it deals with.

A six-page, largely conceptual project agreement has been signed by the participants, which provides for phased development of the export/import facility. Phase I begins with consultant studies to determine the maximum multiuse potential for the facility, followed by development of schematic, and then construction, drawings of the proposed warehouse/terminal facilities, specifications for the bulk handline equipment, and so on. Phase I also includes obtaining the required zoning, environmental, and operating permits. Phase II will commence with construction, and Phase III starts with commercial operation of the facility. The agreement recites no milestone dates for completion of these phases.

At the end of Phase I and prior to commencing construction in Phase II, the agreement provides for a determination of feasibility of the total project. If it is determined that the project is not commercially feasible, then the partnership will be dissolved, and the development costs contributed to date by each partner will be refunded by the land-owning corporation, who may continue with the project itself or abandon it, as it sees fit. The agreement does not otherwise provide for termination or the withdrawal of a partner other than to state that if a partner withdraws prior to the end of Phase I, all development cost contributions made by them will be forfeited (but by implication such withdrawing partner will apparently still retain the obligation to continue development cost contributions).

Since the inception of this project, market conditions have changed dramatically. A world-wide recession, combined with a strong U.S. dollar value, has severely depressed the export market, and, in particular, the demand for low-grade U.S. coal has reached a new 15-year low. For those reasons and because significant difficulty is encountered in obtaining the required local and environmental permits (still opposed by organized citizen groups, local politicians, and the media), your Board of Directors has become disenchanted with this project. They are beginning to wonder whether Phase I will ever be completed so that a feasibility determination can be made. In the meantime your company is continuing to contribute to the development costs (now paying for the services of two outside law firms, a full-time public relations manager, and an environmental expert). Your company is beginning to think it may be pouring good money after bad.

The Board of Directors asks you what options, if any, it has to withdraw from the project and whether it can recoup the money it has contributed to development costs.

The Question

How would you reply? Based upon these limited facts, what alternative courses of action would you recommend to the Board, if any? What would you recommend as the solution?

What Actually Happened

After counsel prefaced her remarks to the Board by stating that the brief project agreement did not provide a specific mechanism for a partner to withdraw from the project until a determination of nonfeasibility is made at the end of Phase I, counsel enumerated the following possible alternative courses of action:

1. *File a court action for breach of contract* against the landowning partner alleging failure to diligently manage and

direct Phase I (among other things), and plead damages in an amount (at least) equal to your development costs contributed to date.

2. *Demand an immediate determination by the partners of project nonfeasibility* because of excessive Phase I delays and changed market conditions, and failing that, petition a court of appropriate jurisdiction to declare nonfeasibility, dissolution of the partnership, and refund of the development costs.

3. *Sell your interest* in the project to the other partners or to any other qualified buyer in an amount as close to your previously contributed development costs as possible.

4. *Assign your project interest* to a third party, provided that the assignee will assume the obligation for future development cost contributions (plus pay you a percentage of your contributions to date, if possible).

5. *Propose a compromise/settlement with the other partners* ideally providing for your immediate withdrawal without further development cost obligation and with a refund of a negotiated portion of your development costs contributions in exchange for your company's covenant not to sue or release any adverse announcements to the news media.

In discussing the merits of these alternatives to the Board, counsel stated that the case for a court action was not a strong one. She stated there is little direct evidence to support a breach of contract (or of fiduciary duty or promoters liability) because neither the brief project agreement nor subsequent discussions set forth any clear expectations of management responsibility among the parties or any prescribed level of development progress to be achieved. Moreover, although the project might be determined unfeasible today, market conditions could change abruptly making it feasible even next week or at least by the end of Phase I. Therefore, counsel stated that if a buyer can be found, the alternatives of selling or assigning the company's interest are the best alternatives. The Board doubts whether they can find a buyer, at least not until the project is determined to be feasible. In view of those facts, counsel then says that settlement appears to be the best alternative.

During the ensuing discussions by the Board members about these alternatives, counsel learned that if the company must forfeit the development costs contributed to date, the withdrawal would have to be delayed for at least six months so that this extraordinary loss would fall in the next fiscal year accounting period when earnings are expected to rebound from their current record lows. Upon realizing this financial problem, counsel thought of another alternative. She suggested they propose a settlement for immediate withdrawal in which the development costs would not be refunded until the end of Phase I, and then in the full amount if nonfeasibility is declared; but if the project goes forward, then in an amount reduced by their percentage shortfall of contributions to Phase I. In that manner counsel opined, because the loss to the company, if any, would not be ascertainable until the occurrence of events well into the next or following year accounting periods, the current earnings would not be affected.

A variation of this settlement proposal was, in fact, made to the other partners and, after intensive discussions and some changes, was agreed upon.

Author's Comments

What do you think? I would say counsel correctly identified the issues of legal action as well as the law/business and business issues concerning refund and the continuing obligation for the Phase I development costs. The facts do not indicate whether counsel found additional alternatives addressing these issues, but she should have. For example, a proposal for suspension of Phase I pending a favorable change in market and local political conditions might have been a good alternative.

The alternative courses of action proposed by counsel cover most of the available options, and she correctly balanced the law and business considerations by judging that compromise or settlement was the best alternative, after being advised that sale or assignment of their project interest was not probable. Commendably, after learning that the "other business purpose" of shifting the potential loss to a later accounting period was a real problem, counsel modified her previously proposed best alternative to satisfy that objective. In doing so, she found the alternative that constituted the "solution." Without doubt, counsel's previous analysis of the issues and search for all the possible alternatives enabled her to follow the flow of the discussions during the Board meeting and apply her judgment quickly and effectively to ultimately find this solution.

Did counsel practice preventive corporate law? Absolutely. You need only speculate about what events might have occurred had counsel confined her advice to the pure law issues or doggedly pursued the adversary approach instead. This case exemplifies why practicing preventive corporate law by finding solutions is so very productive and can be exciting as well.

Key Six: Issue Your Work Product

Introduction

"What did he say?"

"So what's the answer?"

"It's probably lost on his desk!"

What do these three comments have in common? They are typical complaints made by laymen about attorney's work product! That should not be the case. Given the high-quality educational background, resources, and skills of today's attorneys, one would think that counsel would always convey simple, understandable answers in a timely fashion to their client's questions. Part of the reason for failure to do so is that an attorney has focused exclusively upon the legal issue rather than the client's real problem. Fortunately, that will not be the case if counsel has learned the principles of finding a solution in the previous discussions.

Although it is true in some aspects of law practice that the work product is, by necessity, directed toward required rules of formal pleading and procedure or other specialized needs, corporate counsel will be, by-and-large, dealing and working directly with the laymen. For that reason it is worthwhile to consider whether the typical comments made by laymen about attorney's work product previously mentioned have any merit, since counsel certainly would not want to undo all the good work he has done to this point by failing to issue an effective work product.

Another reason may be because the law on a particular issue is complex and not easily interpreted or explained to the average layman. But is not doing just that part of counsel's job as corporate counsel? Corporate counsel's job is to effectively apply the law and his skills within the business environment of the corporation and industry to achieve the greatest possible overall benefit *for his client.* That must include being sure they understand the issues.

Counsel need not make his work product look unintelligible or obfuscate an issue in order to convince a client of his continuing need for counsel's services. In fact, to do so in the corporation is counterproductive because the objective is to find a solution to prevent a problem from escalating rather than to handle a matter designed, in part, to accomplish such other purposes.

What Did He Say?

A frequent complaint by laymen about an attorney's work product is "What did he say?" There are several reasons for this type of comment. Some laymen are simply baffled by the law and its complexity and would repeat this complaint regardless of how clearly and understandably counsel spoke or wrote his memoranda.

On the other hand, some corporate counsel are at fault because they fail to consider for whom they are writing their memoranda, namely, the layman. Some attorneys think that whatever they write should be a legal document appropriate for filing in court. Not so. In most cases corporate counsel's work product will not be filed in court. Its purpose instead is to advise the client about a legal issue and about how to resolve a problem. Counsel is providing a work product for use by a layman, not a judge. The most understandable language counsel can use when talking to a layman is the type of language the layman uses, not the legal jargon counsel has spent so much time learning. Some legal jargon is necessary, but when possible, it should be kept to a minimum.

Short, simple, understandable memoranda usually are adequate to apprise the layman about a legal problem and its resolution. And they are definitely the most effective work product because beyond the first paragraph or two of any attorney's memorandum, the average layman's interest and attention begins to waver.

By way of analogy, counsel should pick any specialty field about which he knows little, maybe accounting or economics, and try to recall the amount of interest he had in reading one of the latest FASB (Formal Accounting Standards Board) decisions or a treatise espousing the relevancy of M-1, M-2, and M-3 statistical compilations to supply-side monetary controls. Depending upon how the treatise was written, counsel probably did not read very far before his interest and attention started to waver, as would anyone else's without the appropriate background and inclination in those fields.

The same understandably applies with the average layman and the law. Most do not have a background nor inclination for the often ambiguous-appearing legal concepts counsel is trying to convey. This does not mean that counsel's memorandum should read like the first page in a best-selling novel, but it does mean that he should make an effort to write and speak as clearly as possible for the layman reader. Do not expect them to wade through four or five pages of single-spaced typing to find the answer or conclusion. And do not expect them to have a *Black's Law Dictionary* or even a *Webster's Dictionary* available.

If counsel feels compelled to recite detailed legal theory, then he should consider putting it in an appendix or attachment to a shorter explanatory memo, or maybe recite it at the end of the memo. Often the usual final, conclusionary paragraph in an attorney's memo is more effectively put first rather than last. And if most of the work product is in the form of a legal document, then a simple, understandable, explanatory memo to the recipient will go a long way toward enhancing their understanding, appreciation, and ability to actually use the work product. To write memoranda this way may sound unprofessional, but it is not. Remember the function and purpose of corporate counsel and for whom counsel is writing his memorandum.

The following illustrates a fine, intelligent corporate counsel who, unfortunately, not only tended to stop short of finding a solution to a problem but also tended to obscure the solutions she did find.

> An experienced and intelligent corporate counsel had an excellent grasp of legal theory and could usually uncover more legal issues in a problem than could any of the other department attorneys. Despite this

> expertise, or maybe because of it, her work product (whether oral or written), although usually exhibiting a comprehensive and thorough legal analyses, often did not give an answer or workable solution.
>
> This corporate counsel's memoranda to laymen frequently ran four to seven pages in length (single-spaced) with some paragraphs covering almost an entire page. Although an admirable statement of the law, to say they were difficult to read—even for other attorneys—was an understatement. If the memo contained an answer, it was often obscured and not found by the impatient or frustrated reader.

As might be imagined, it was frequently difficult to pin this corporate counsel down to any one answer on a problem. Counsel's legal skills in analyzing the issues were a valuable and enviable asset, but, unfortunately, in the corporate setting those skills were not nearly so effective as they could have been if she had then continued on to find a solution and, most importantly, issue a work product that was understandable and usable by the average layman.

When counsel issues his work product during his career as corporate counsel, he must remember to whom and for what purpose it is directed; and he must be sure that at least the solution and advisory part of it is understandable to the layman, his client—so he will not have to waste time later answering the question "What did he say?"

The next subject is a closely allied complaint by laymen about an attorney's work product—"So what's the answer?"

So What's the Answer?

This complaint by laymen about an attorney's work product is not unlike the one in the last section except that here the attorney's memorandum may be perfectly clear and understandable but fails to give an answer or solution to the problem.

Counsel should not hear this criticism about his work product, having learned and implemented the principles in this book. He will have found the real problem, applied the law, and come up with the alternative courses of action and solutions. In his work product he will then go straight to the point and give those alternatives and solutions. He will not neglect to give an answer to the problem, as counsel in the previous section with her four-to-seven page memoranda might have.

However, even though counsel is not likely to fail to give an answer in his work product, there is another point worthy of attention, namely, will the work product that counsel regards as an answer be similarly regarded as an answer by the layman? Not always.

Several attorneys tend to issue a work product by simply enumerating the possible alternative courses of action and leaving the judgment of which is best from among them up to the business manager. But because counsel is uniquely qualified to evaluate the relative merits of the various alternatives, some laymen correctly expect him to do so in his work product, and consider failure to do so as not providing an answer to them.

Of course, when the determination of the best alternatives in a work product is primarily a business decision, then there is no need for counsel to comment separately about the merits of each. On the other hand, there are many more instances involving primarily law and law/business alternatives in which counsel's work product will be more effective and productive to the corporation if he goes ones step further and evaluates the relative merits of each alternative. This might take the form of ranking them in an order of preference, or it could simply be a discussion of each alternative, provided that counsel reaches some conclusions. Ranking recommended alternatives in terms of preference is often difficult to do, but remember that counsel is more qualified than most laymen to evaluate the relative merits of law and law/business alternative courses of action. And failure to speak to the merits of the alternative answers in a work product will sometimes cause a layman to correctly comment, "So what's the answer?"—just as if counsel had provided no alternatives at all.

The following is a simple and practical example of this problem.

> Corporate counsel is requested to review a 25-page contract his company wants to sign. Counsel finds ten paragraphs containing objectionable language from a legal standpoint. In his work product (memo) he states, "Overall this contract does not vary substantially from industry standards; however, you should make the following important changes. . . ." Then he goes on to reference the objectionable language, indicating which words to delete and what should be inserted in lieu thereof.

Here counsel has correctly found the problem areas in the contract and recommended alternatives to resolve them. He began his work product with the good summary evaluation, "Overall this contract. . . ." But could he have gone one step further with a better result?

> Counsel could have begun his work product (memo) by saying, "Because of the potential legal risk, I recommend you do not sign this contract unless you obtain the following three modifications. . . ." He then continues, "The following changes are important from a legal standpoint, and I recommend you obtain as many of them as you can. . . ."

What is the principal difference between these two work products? From a legal standpoint very little, although the second one is more assertive ("do not sign") regarding three recommended changes. Most attorneys would consider the recommended changes in both work products to be substantially similar. But a layman probably would not. Most laymen would not have the necessary knowledge to evaluate the relative merit and importance of each of the recommended changes. The more extensive evaluation of the alternatives presented in the second work product results in a more constructive and useful analysis for the layman. Because of this the average layman would undoubtably consider the second work product to be more of "an answer" than the first. In fact, even from a legal viewpoint the second work product is probably a better answer because it more clearly defines the three most critical areas of legal risk. Certainly from a preventive law standpoint it is superior for that reason.

A "better answer" or more effective work product could also have been achieved in this example by ranking the recommended contract changes in order of importance or by including a discussion about the relative merits of each. Additionally, brief explanatory discussions in the work product showing the reasons for counsel's recommendations and conclusions is a good idea not only because it assists the layman in trying to determine their relative merit but also because it also leads to a greater understanding and appreciation of the issues on his part. But when doing so, counsel should keep his reasons brief and simple—forget the majority and minority case law unless truly on point. Remember, they are more interested in a solution than the finer points of law.

So again, counsel should remember to whom and for what purpose his work product is directed and that although his work product may contain an answer from his viewpoint and that of other attorneys, it may nevertheless fall short of being the most effective answer counsel can give to his clients, the laymen, causing them to remark, "So what's the answer?" And by all means, counsel should not be afraid to make a decision and give an answer (solution) in his work product; in most cases his ability to do so is greater than he thinks.

One reservation on this point: Counsel need not always be absolutely definitive in his work product. Some layman only want "black and white" answers and become totally frustrated (or indignant) when told that the law is not clear on a particular point. If the law or facts are not clear on a particular issue, then counsel may not be able to arrive at a definitive solution—and should not. All that counsel may be able to do is recommend several alternatives, stating that they appear to be the most feasible in view of the uncertain points of law or facts involved. And in a limited number of cases, the ranking of alternatives in an order of preference can be more harmful than helpful, if by doing so, a layman receives a false sense confidence in his ability to handle the more complex issues by himself without further advice. Instances such as these must be handled case-by-case, as counsel deems appropriate at the time.

It's Probably Lost on His Desk!

This satirical comment by laymen about an attorney's overdue work product is probably more common than the preceding two, though usually less justified. Few laymen appreciate the amount of time required to thoroughly research and analyze a point of law and then arrive at the correct alternatives and solutions, let alone put it all into the form of an effective work product. This is especially true when they bring counsel a problem at the last minute and say they need an answer "yesterday."

What can be done to alleviate the causes of this complaint by laymen? Not much, short of burning the midnight oil or asking for more help. There are a few practical pointers in the following discussions that may help but not much really substantive. The timeliness of, or delay in, issuing a work product seems to be a perennial problem for most attorneys. Issuing work product in a timely manner is a desirable objective, since it encourages clients to use counsel more and will get the problem off his desk and mind so he can concentrate on other matters. But, unfortunately, it is often easier said than done, and except in limited circumstances, the high quality of counsel's legal work should not give way to timeliness.

A few practical ways to increase the timeliness of counsel's work product may be surprising because they have already been discussed. Writing short, simple, and understandable memoranda directed toward his client, the layman, is one of them. This not only decreases drafting time (including revision after revision) but often decreases the likelihood of subsequent time consumed unproductively by having to explain in plain English what counsel was trying to say in the first place. Similarly, if counsel knows the business and sublanguage in his industry and has found the real problem and the solution, his time spent drafting memoranda and getting straight to the point is far reduced. So, too, counsel will be sure to marshall all the facts by making telephone calls, if necessary, before beginning to write his analysis of a problem, because an answer to a wrong issue is not only not a solution but also a wasted and time-consuming work product.

In short, most, if not all, of the principles already discussed about practicing preventive law and finding solutions will significantly enhance counsel's ability to work more effectively and productively and, consequently, result in the more timely delivery of his work product.

Another practical way to more timely issue work products is to find out what the real time requirements are for its issuance and then adjust the schedule accordingly. Make the client give a realistic time schedule for his need of an answer. Sometimes they will say that they need an answer within two days because they are anticipating that counsel will be late and they want to be sure to have it within a week. If that happens, it can almost become a game of who gets what answer first and when, which does not help anyone, including counsel.

If counsel's workload is heavy and he is pushed for time, he will have to use some judgment about which project should have priority. It should not be like a fast food line, where first come is first served. Since there will always be emergencies and fires to put out, knowing the realistic time requirements for delivery of counsel's various work products can be of significant help in trying to adjust his work schedule. If counsel is backed against the wall with two projects due simultaneously, sometimes having the corporate managers decide between themselves which project should come first will resolve the dilemma.

Another practical way to issue work products more timely is to recognize that the same results can sometimes be accomplished with a work product that is less than perfect, one that does the job, although not one to frame and hang on the office wall.

This does not require a compromise of high standards of legal practice or thorough research, analysis, and so on. It means a compromise of only the actual documentation of the recommended solution. For example, the easiest time-saver is simply to telephone the answer to the client and write on his requesting memo "per our conversation/date/your initials" and return it to him. This has the obvious disadvantage of not commemorating to record counsel's analysis and recommendation and, for that reason, is not appropriate for complex and critical problems; but it is useful in several other situations. Marking up a client's requesting memo with comments or doing the same to other documents being reviewed and then returning them can save substantial time in issuing work products. For a client at a location other than the counsel's office, dictating the answer and work product over the telephone to his secretary saves time.

There are other useful and practical methods like these that can be developed to help save time in issuing work product. Using techniques such as these routinely, especially when there are other choices, is not recommended, but they are eminently effective when the circumstances require. One time-saving technique used by a few corporate counsel is not recommended. Having counsel's secretary routinely screen his telephone calls or requiring his clients to have appointments to see him does more harm than good because being easily accessible to his clients is fundamental to a counsel's effective practice of preventive law in the corporation.

By way of collateral comment: These time-saving techniques in issuing a work product are rarely seen in the private practice of law—at least not without a lengthier more comprehensive follow-up for several obvious reasons, which explains, in part, their comparatively longer work product time requirements and their tendency to overload with "attorney manpower" if a specific deadline on the work product is imposed.

Overall, counsel should remember that after he has applied the principles of finding a solution to a problem, he is not finished yet. He needs to follow through to the ultimate conclusion by issuing a work product, whether oral or written, that is simple and understandable to the layman and forthrightly gives an answer rather than obscuring or omitting one and, of course, is as timely as possible. By doing so, counsel's practice of corporate law will be most likely to prevent legal problems—rather than cause them.

Now read the case study and decide whether the work product (memorandum) written by counsel follows the principles discussed in this key.

Case Study Number Eleven: THE MEMORANDUM

The Situation

The following is an excerpt from a memorandum written by a corporate counsel to a corporate manager (layman) about the undesirability of the sentence *(Our) Company shall be liable for the negligent acts or omission of its independent contractors* contained in a proposed contract she was reviewing.

Memorandum Excerpt

At common law, parties were generally held to be liable for the damages or loss caused to another party by their negligent acts. This doctrine has been variously interpretated by the state legislatures and courts, but it is generally held that one party owes a duty of reasonable care to another party to protect against causing him damage, loss, or injury (citation). The modern doctrine also holds that between sophisticated parties, such as business corporations, the responsibility for damage, loss, or injury resulting from an omission of such reasonable care or resulting from an act which exhibits a disregard of the same may, for valuable consideration, be contractually assumed before-the-fact by another party (citations). Some cases hold that this contractual assumption of liability for another party's negligent acts or omission to act will not apply and be void if the case involves an act deemed against public policy. Also in a minority of states, the state legislatures have enacted specific provisions against, or with respect to the extent of, permissable assumption by contract of another party's negligent acts.

Notwithstanding the above, however, I believe it would be generally held in the courts of our state of incorporation and in the state of the other corporation to this agreement that if our corporation knowingly assents to the sentence contained in paragraph ____ on page ______ of this document regarding the assumption of liability for the negligent acts and omission of our independent contractors, then our corporation would probably be liable for the damages and losses resulting therefrom. Therefore, I strongly recommend you either try to delete this sentence from the document or modify it substantially. Of course, our actual liability would depend, to some extent, upon whether our contracts with the independent contracts provide that they will be responsible for their acts and omissions and whether, in the case of same, they are reputable and financially capable enough to pay any damages and losses without the necessity of filing litigation against them, and so forth. In any event, however, I think you should consider the legal risk represented by this sentence and the others I have delineated above.

Please do not hesitate to call me if I can be of further help or if you have any questions, and I apologize for my delay in giving you these comments.

The Question

Did this corporate counsel direct her work product toward the corporate manager? Is this memorandum simple and understandable? After reading it, would a layman be likely to say, "So what's the answer?" If you think it needs revision, how would you rewrite it?

What Actually Happened

The layman corporate manager telephoned counsel, thanked her for the memo, and asked her if he could come to her office and ask her some questions.

Upon doing so, they spent the better part of two hours going over her comments and several recommended changes to the document. Following these discussions, the layman manager had a better idea of what the concerns were from a legal standpoint and some ways to modify the language so that it would be acceptable.

Nevertheless, he was still somewhat frustrated and exasperated with this corporate counsel and the memorandum (and with attorneys and the law in general), and being an aggressive and outspoken person, he said as much to counsel before leaving her office.

Because this corporate counsel was conscientious and thought she had written a fairly good memorandum, she asked one of the other department attorneys to look it over and tell her what he thought. The other attorney scanned it, reread a few parts, and replied that he agreed with the legal objections and analyses she had made regarding the document and that she should not worry about that layman corporate manager because he does not care what the law says anyway—he just wants to get the document signed.

Author's Comments

Was it surprising that this layman corporate manager felt the need to ask corporate counsel some questions about her memorandum? Although another lawyer would have a good idea what this corporate counsel was saying and the relative merit or risk of her points, he has the appropriate background and knowledge to understand her work product; but the layman does not.

Consider, for example, how many laymen would know even what an "independent contractor" is, and although that phrase appeared in the sentence objected to, it was not explained or mentioned. And what about the answer or solution? Could a layman figure out what it really was? For example, just look at these following beginning phrases used by counsel in her memorandum (listed sequentially):

> At common law . . .
> The modern doctrine . . .
> Some cases hold . . .
> Also in a minority . . .
> Notwithstanding the above, . . .
> Therefore I strongly recommend . . .
> Of course, our actual liability . . .
> In any event, however, I think . . .

Although this memorandum might suffice as an answer in a law school examination, it is confusing and unintelligible to most laymen and, consequently, represents an unsatisfactory work product for the practice of preventive law in the corporation. Other corporate managers might have simply disregarded the parts of the memo they did not understand and marched right on into the very legal problems counsel was trying to prevent.

Did you try to revise the memorandum excerpt? Look at the revision shown next. It may not be perfect, but it is certainly superior with respect to the principles discussed in this Key.

Revised Memorandum Excerpt

. . . . I recommend you either delete or modify the sentence *(Our) Company shall be liable for the negligent acts or omission of its independent contractors* contained in paragraph ____ page ____. It would make us responsible for the negligence of the companys we use to help us perform the work.

A good argument in favor of its deletion is that we have no (or little) control over the acts of these third parties. An alternative to deletion would be to modify it so that these companys (and not we) are directly responsible to *(the other party)* for their negligence. For example: "(Our) Company shall include a phrase in our contracts with independent contractors reciting they will be liable to *(the other party)* for their negligent acts or omissions."

If you cannot delete or modify this phrase, then to minimize the legal risk, it will be very important to contract only with companies that will agree to, and are capable of, standing behind their work. They should be financially able to respond to damages resulting from their negligence, and it would be advisable to require them to furnish performance bonds as security for same.

Let me know if you have questions or need alternative language for the recommended changes.

Epilogue Story

Conversation Between the Old Salt Litigator and a Young Corporate Counsel

"You're really not practicing law, are you?" said the old salt litigator to the young corporate counsel as they were chatting in the lobby of the ABA Convention hall waiting for the meeting to resume.

Somewhat taken aback by the brusqueness of the remark and not knowing what else to say, the corporate counsel replied, "What do you mean?"

"I mean you're not practicing *real law,* are you, son? Why, when I was your age, I'd already sharpened my teeth on half of the judge's podiums in town; and you just told me you've never even been in a courtroom as the attorney-of-record."

By this time, the not timid young corporate counsel had collected his wits about him and replied with a half smile on his face, "If what you mean is . . . I'm not generating fees by promoting adversary law, . . . then I suppose you're right."

The old salt just stared at him. If he wasn't such an old pro, his face would have showed surprise. He said, "Maybe I misjudged you, son. I believe you might have the makings to be a pretty good attorney. Too bad you don't have court experience, though. Fees don't have a thing to do with it. What does, however, is that our basic system of justice is founded on the adversary process—it's fundamental to it. Each side is entitled to his day in court and has the right to prove the other party is in the wrong. Without that you might as well forget about the jury and everything else. It's in the courtroom where the real battles are fought and *real law* is practiced. Any attorney worth his salt knows that!"

"No, sir," said the corporate counsel. "It's just attorneys like you who have made it that way. Our system of laws and justice is really based upon our collective notion of civilized conduct—on what we think is right and wrong. The function of the true attorney is to foster that kind of understanding and appreciation in his client in an effort to prevent legal problems from occurring or escalating. Not the reverse, as you might have it, by giving your clients a false sense of security in your shrewdness to get them off the hook through adversary tactics."

The old salt looked briefly at the floor, shaking his head. "Is that what they teach you in law schools nowadays? I can't believe it. Let me tell you, sir, if you had ever been faced with incarceration of your client or the reality of your client being hit with a multimillion dollar judgment, I'd like to see how far your lofty ideals would get you. It's a win-or-lose situation, my friend . . . and you're going to tell your client he should lose because of some notion of civilized conduct? Good luck, sir!" he said as he turned and started to walk back into the meeting room.

"Wait a minute, sir, if I may. Perhaps you're right, but let me give you an example of a case I handled this past week."

The old salt hesitated and raised his bushy eyebrows.

The young corporate counsel continued quickly, "The executive management of our corporation wanted to break a major supply contract we signed several years ago because we're losing money on it. Even though we receive nearly ten million dollars of revenue from it a year, because of recently enacted government price supports, we will, in effect, be losing almost a quarter of a million dollars on it this year alone.

"I spent several weeks studying the contract, researching case law, and talking to the managers in our company who had been involved with this contract. I finally determined that we didn't have a case to break the contract but that we could make a good argument for renegotiation based upon the force majeure conditions of the government price support enactment.

"Last week we just finished some lengthy and very tough negotiations with our customer, and primarily because of this force majeure argument, we were able to get our supply con-

tract prices increased so that at least we will break even for the remainder of the contract term, plus we were able to negotiate a new much more favorable long-term supply agreement with this customer.

"In other words, because I analyzed the situation objectively and found a solution to the problem satisfying all parties, we were all able to avoid the time, expense, and acrimony that would have resulted from using your system of adversary process. In fact, I prevented a far more serious legal problem from occurring than if we had tried to break the contract without justifiable cause."

Looking expectantly at the old salt litigator, the young corporate counsel concluded by saying, "Now wouldn't you call that practicing *real law,* sir?"

"Well, I don't know, counsel; you tell me. You were there; I wasn't," replied the old salt.

"I will say this much, however. I remember a case I had several years ago that you couldn't have given me a plug nickel for; and yet I took it to trial and won a half-million dollar judgment for my client. What do you think of that, son? You see, that's the beauty of our adversary system—you just never know what the result will be until you take it all the way to the end."

"What was the net to your client of that half million dollars?" the corporate counsel questioned.

"What?" said the old salt.

"How much did your client get after subtracting all the court costs, your fees, and the value of their time and frustration by being involved with the case?" he said.

"Well, let's see," the old salt thought, "the case went on for five or six years because we finally had to get it overturned on appeal . . . but the point is, son, we won! Besides, he casually added, smiling, I've got to justify my existence to my client and keep my docket full, don't I?"

"I beg your pardon?" replied the startled young corporate counsel.

"Oh, never mind, counsel; I was just joking—you wouldn't understand anyway," replied the old salt as he put his arm around the young corporate counsel's shoulders and they returned together to the ABA convention meeting room, each now having a growing respect for the other.

Index of Subjects

Adversary law. *See* Law, practice of
Alternatives, examining, 203–250
  see also Solutions, finding
  best alternatives, computer industry example, 223–228
  case study, 246–250
  computer industry example, 211–228
  general principles to implement
    evaluate all alternatives, 229–231
    use judgment, 229
    make a decision, 230
    solutions are fluid, 230
  practical hints
    compromise as alternative, 243–244
    consider nonlegal attributes, 238
    correct timing, 241–243
    know other business purpose, 232–235
    provide simplest alternative, 235–238
    quantify concepts, 238–241
    rank recommendations, 255–257
  steps for
    ask how it can be done, 204–208
    obtain second opinion, 210–211
    practical pointers, 231–244
    search for all possible solutions to problem, 208
    use issue analysis as format, 209–210
Answers, giving of, 254–257
  see also Solutions, finding

Boilerplate. *See* Legal jargon
Business trips, as steps for setting stage for effective practice of corporate law, 123–124
Business/legal issues. *See* Law/Business issues
Business, value of knowing. *See* Corporation, business of

Case studies
  alternatives, examining, 246–250
  applying the law, 180–183
  communicating with other departments, 59–63
  corporate business, learning, 24–28
  industry law, learning, 104–108
  law department function, understanding, 83–86
  outside counsel, when to seek, 200–202
  personnel, getting to know, 41–46
  problems, finding, 160–164
  setting stage, 136–139
  work products, 261–264
Client, determining true, 37–40
Communication
  as technique for finding problems, 145–147
  documents, drafting usable, 13–16, 251–264
  knowledge of corporate business as means to effective, 9–11
  with other corporate departments, 47–63
    case study, 59–63
  questions, asking, to learn facts, 147–148
  terminology, sources for learning, 19–20
  work product, importance in. *See* Work product.
Compromise, as alternative, 243–244
Corporate attorney (counsel)
  see also Corporate law department; Problems, finding; Solutions, finding
  ability of, when issues beyond, 185–186

as arbitrator, 243–244
becoming an expert, 97–100
building foundation as, 3–5
other departments as resources for, 47–63
functions within corporate law department, 4
initial focus of, on most relevant laws, 93–96
legal issues
keeping current on, 100–103
management business objectives, value of understanding, 16–18
personal legal work, avoid performing, 134–135
pinning star to one executive, case study, 136–139
political fights, within corporation, remain aloof from, 131–133
vs. private practice, 8, 127, 128
professionalism, retaining, 127–130
success, steps for, 3–5
Corporate departments
impact of legal decisions on, checking, 51–58
as resources for corporate attorney, 47–63
Corporate law department
advantages of handling legal matters in-house, 195–199
attorney's function, within framework of, 4
avoid working too much for one executive, group, 133–134
case study, 83–86
crossover effects, on other departments, by decisions of, 55–58
framework of, and corporate attorney, 4
functions not part of, 81–82
functions of, understanding, 65–86
giving advice on law/business issues, reasons for importance of, 75–77
outside counsel
when not to seek, 195–199
when to seek, 185–202
preventive functions of, 72–81
reasons for establishing, 66–71
cost justification, 69–70
government regulations, explosion of, 70
immediate access to legal advice, 70–71
lack of law background, 69
traditional functions of, 71–72
vs. preventive law functions, 71–72
working with other attorneys in, 125–126
Corporate management
business objectives, value of understanding, 16–18
preference for in-house counsel over outside counsel, 198
Corporate personnel
case study, 41–46
client, determining true, 37–40
as early warning system, 29–32
as expert resources, 32–34
getting to know, 4, 29–46
knowledge of, and effectiveness, 4
reading between lines, 34–37
Corporate politics, avoid, 131–135
Corporation, business of
see also Law/business issues; Corporate Management
case study, 24–28
communicating effectively through knowledge of, 9–11
how much to know, 8–9
knowledge of, as aid in pinpointing primary legal issues, 11–13
learning, as foundation for effective preventive law, 7–28
methods for learning, 18–23
ask questions, 22
big picture, looking at, 18–19
industry, competitor information, comparing, 21–22
internal, public information, examining, 20–21
terminology of, learning, 19–20
visit operations, 22–23
nonlegal impact of decisions on, 51–55
Counsel. *See* Corporate attorney
Court decisions, affecting industry law, learning about, 91–93
Crossover effect of legal decisions, on other corporate departments, chart depicting, 55–58

Decisions, legal
see also Work product
checking impact of, 51–55
crossover effect of, on corporate departments, 55–58
making of, 230–231, 254–257

Dispensing law. *See* Law, practice of
Documents, drafting useable, 13–16

Early warning system
  corporate departments as, 49
  corporate personnel as, 29–32
  defined, 30

Financial statements, 20–21
Foundation for preventive law practice. *See* Preventive corporate law.

Imagination, using to examine alternatives, 209
Industry law
  categories of, listed, 89
  court decisions affecting, learning about, 91–93
  general knowledge of, 88–93
  laws having impact, become expert in, 97–100
  laws most relevant, initial focus on, 93–96
  learning, to build effective preventive corporate law practice, 87–108
  publishers as sources for, 102
  settlements in, learning about, 91–93
  ways to keep current, 100–101
Issues analysis, as format for examining alternatives, 209–210
Issues, identification of
  business issue, 148–150
  chart, 76
  computer industry example, 211–228
  law issue, 148–150
  law/business issue, 73–81, 151–154. *See also* Law/Business issues

Jargon. *See* Sublanguage; Legal jargon

Law/Business issues
  balancing, 17–18
  case study, 83–86
  chart, 76
  computer industry example, 211–228
  defined, 73–75
  distinguishing between, for finding problems, 148–159
  fine dividing line between, case study, 83–86
  giving advice on
    as preventive law function, 73–81
    reasons for importance of, listed, 75–77
  identification of, 151–154
Law, practice of
  see also Laws, applying; Corporate attorney
  epilogue story, 265–267
  general corporate practice, 88–89
  preventive approach, 1–5, 72–81, 111–116
  specialties, 97–100, 189–195
    case study, 200–202
  traditional approach, 65, 71–72
    adversary, 71–72
    dispensing law, 71–72
Law schools, teaching of preventive law, xi
Laws, affecting industry, categories of, 89–93
Laws, applying
  as step in finding solutions, 165–183
  techniques of
    case study, 180–183
    classic approach, 165–166
    partial solutions, providing, 171–175
    preparation, 170–171
    saying you don't know, 175–179
    shooting from hip, 166–170
      defined, 167
Laws, learning. *See* Corporate attorney; Industry law
Legal/Business decisions. *See* Law/Business issues
Legal decisions. *See* Decisions, legal
Legal fees, increase in, as cost justification for creating law department, 69–70
Legal jargon, avoiding in work products, 252–254
  drafting documents, use of, 13–16
Legal specialists. *See* Outside counsel; Corporate law department; Law, practice of
Legal theory, use in work products, 253
Local representation, outside counsel as, 191–195

Management. *See* Corporate management
Meetings, attending, as technique for setting stage for effective corporate law practice, 121–122
Memoranda. *See* Work products

Outside counsel
case study, 200–202
vs. corporate law department, 189, 195–199
for local representation, 194, 196
for second opinion, 191–195
when not to seek, 195–199
when to seek, 185–202

Patience, as technique for finding real problem, 143–144
People, value of knowing. *See* Corporate personnel
Preventive corporate law
see also Problems, finding; Solutions, finding
vs. adversary approach, 1, 2, 65, 71–72, 112, 195, 243, 265–267
building an effective practice steps for, 2–3
communicate with all departments, 47–63
industry law, learning, 87–108
law department function, understanding, 65–86
learn the business, 7–28
outlined, 2–3
personnel, get to know, 29–46
defined, 1–2
foundation, laying, reasons for, 1–2
functions of, 72–82
giving advice on law/business issues, 73–81
principles of, *see* building an effective practice, steps for, *supra*
purpose of, discussed, 1–2
techniques for
learning the business, 7–28
outlined, 2–5
vs. private practice, 172
Preventive law. *See* Preventive corporate law
Principles of preventive law. *See* Preventive corporate law
Private practice
see also Corporate attorney; Corporate law department; Outside counsel
vs. corporate practice, 127–130
Problems, defined, 140
Problems, finding
case study, 160–164
from corporate departments, 48–51
how to, outlined, 114–116
techniques for
communicating with personnel, 145–148
law/business issues, distinguishing between, 148–159
listening well, 140
marshalling facts, 144–145
being patient, 143–144
sounding board, being a good, 141–143
using analysis, judgment, 115, 139–140

Regulations
government, explosion in, as reason for establishing law department, 70
industry, learning about, 89–91

Second opinions
outside counsel as source for, 191–195
as source of alternative solutions, 210–211
Setting stage, for finding solutions
business trips, go on, 123–124
facilities, visit, 123
meetings, attend, 121–122
other department attorneys, working with, 125–126
social functions, attend, 125
steps for, 117–137
team player, 118–120
Settlements, in industry law, learning about, 91–93
Shareholders, 37
Shooting from hip. *See* Laws, applying
Social functions, corporate, attending, to set stage for practicing preventive corporate law, 125
Solutions, defined, 111–112
Solutions, finding
see also Alternatives, examining
best alternatives as solutions, 223–228
case study, 246–250
computer industry example, 211–228
partial, 175–179
reasons for, 112–114
steps for
applying the law, 115, 165–183
finding real problem, 139–164
setting stage, 117–137
techniques for, 114–116
alternatives, examining, 203–250

use imagination, 209
use issue analysis as format, 209–210
outside counsel, when to seek, 115, 185–202
setting stage, 117–118
being a team player, 118–120
work products, producing understandable, 115, 251–264
Statutes, local, state, federal, learning about, 89–91
Sublanguage, 89, 196
essential to effective communications, 10–11
Traditional law. *See* Law, practice of
Words of art and customs, in industry, learning, 89
Work products
answer, giving of, 254–257
case study, 261–264
issuing in timely manner, 251–264
methods for, 257–260
methods not recommended for, 260
understandable to laymen, 252–254